THE

GERMANIA AND AGRICOLA

OF

CAIUS CORNELIUS TACITUS.

WITH NOTES FOR COLLEGES.

BY W. S. TYLER,

PROFESSOR OF THE GREEK AND LATIN LANGUAGES IN AMHERST COLLEGE.

NEW EDITION

NEW YORK:
D. APPLETON AND COMPANY,
90, 92 & 94 GRAND STREET.
1869.

PREFACE.

This edition of the Germania and Agricola of Tacitus is designed to meet the following wants, which, it is believed, have been generally felt by teachers and pupils in American Colleges.

1. A Latin text, approved and established by the essential concurrence of all the more recent editors. The editions of Tacitus now in use in this country abound in readings purely conjectural, adopted without due regard to the peculiarities of the author, and in direct contravention of the critical canon, that, other things being equal, the more difficult reading is the more likely to be genuine. The recent German editions labor to exhibit and explain, so far as possible, the reading of the best MSS.

2. A more copious illustration of the grammatical constructions, also of the rhetorical and poetical usages peculiar to Tacitus, without translating, however, to such an extent as to supersede the proper exertions of the student. Few books require so much illustration of this kind, as the Germania and Agricola of Tacitus; few have received more in Germany, yet few so little here. In a writer so concise and abrupt as Tacitus, it has been deemed necessary to pay particular regard to the connexion of thought, and to the particles, as the hinges of that connexion.

3. A comparison of the writer and his cotemporaries with authors of the Augustan age, so as to mark concisely the changes which had been already wrought in the language and taste of the Roman people. It is chiefly with a view to aid such a comparison, that it has been thought advisable to prefix a Life

of Tacitus, which is barren indeed of personal incidents, but which it is hoped may serve to exhibit the author in his relation to the history, and especially to the literature, of his age.

4. The department in which less remained to be done than any other, for the elucidation of Tacitus, was that of Geography. History, and Archæology. The copious notes of Gordon and Murphy left little to be desired in this line; and these notes are not only accessible to American scholars in their original forms, but have been incorporated, more or less, into all the college editions. If any peculiar merit attaches to this edition, in this department, it will be found in the frequent references to such classic authors as furnish collateral information, and in the illustration of the private life of the Romans, by the help of such recent works as Becker's Gallus. The editor has also been able to avail himself of Sharon Turner's History of the Anglo Saxons, which sheds not a little light on the manners of the Germans.

5. Many of the ablest commentaries on the Germania and Agricola have appeared within a comparatively recent period, some of them remarkable examples of critical acumen and exegetical tact, and others, models of school and college editions. It has been the endeavor of the editor to bring down the literature pertaining to Tacitus to the present time, and to embody in small compass the most valuable results of the labors of such recent German editors as Grimm, Günther, Gruber, Kiessling, Dronke, Roth, Ruperti, and Walther.

The text is, in the main, that of Walther, though the other editors just named have been consulted; and in such minor differences as exist between them, I have not hesitated to adopt the reading which seemed best to accord with the usage and genius of Tacitus, especially when sanctioned by a decided preponderance of critical suffrage. Other readings have been referred to in the Notes, so far as they are of any considerable importance, or supported by respectable authority. Partly for convenience, but chiefly as a matter of taste, I have ventured to follow the German editions in dispensing entirely with diacritical marks, and in some peculiarities of less importance, which if not viewed with favor, it is hoped, will not be judged with severity. The punctuation is the result of a diligent comparison of the best editions, together with a careful study of the connexion of language and of thought.

The German editions above mentioned, together with several French, English, and American works, have not only been constantly before me, but have been used with great freedom, and credit awarded to them accordingly. Some may think their names should have appeared less frequently; others that they should have received credit to a still greater extent. Suffice it to say, I have never intended to quote the language, or borrow the thoughts of an author, without giving his name; and in matters of fact or opinion, I have cited authorities not only when I have been indebted to them for the suggestion, but whenever, in a case of coincidence of views, I thought the authorities would be of any interest to the student.

I have not considered it needful, with German scrupulosity, to distinguish between my own references and those of others. It may safely be taken for granted, that the major, perhaps the better, part of them have been derived from foreign sources. But no references have been admitted on trust. They have been carefully verified, and it is hoped that numerous as they are, they will be found pertinent and useful, whether illustrative of things, or of mere verbal usage. Some, who use the book, will doubtless find occasion to follow them out either in whole or in part; and those who do not, will gain a general impression as to the sources from which collateral information may be obtained, that will be of no small value.

The frequent references to the Notes of Professor Kingsley, will show the estimation in which I hold them. Perhaps I have used them too freely. My only apology is, that so far as they go, they are just what is wanted; and if I had avoided using them to a considerable extent, I must have substituted something less perfect of my own. Had they been more copious, and extended more to verbal and grammatical illustrations, these Notes never would have appeared.

The editor is convinced, from his experience as a teacher, that the student of Tacitus will not master the difficulties, or appreciate the merits, of so peculiar an author, unless his peculiarities are distinctly pointed out and explained. Indeed, the student, in reading any classic author, needs, not to be carried along on the broad shoulders of an indiscriminate translator, but to be guided at every step in learning his lessons, by a judicious annotator, who will remove his difficulties, and aid his progress; who will point out to him what is worthy of attention, and guard him against the errors to which he is constantly exposed; for first impressions are lively and permanent, and the errors of the study, even though corrected in the recitation, not unfrequently leave an impression on the mind which is never effaced.

Besides the aid derived from books, to which the merit of this edition, if it have any merit, will be chiefly owing, the editor takes this opportunity to acknowledge his many obligations to those professors and other literary gentlemen, who have extended to him assistance and encouragement. To Prof. H. B. Hackett, of Newton Theological Seminary, especially, he is indebted for favors, which, numerous and invaluable in themselves, as the results of a singularly zealous and successful devotion to classical learning, are doubly grateful as the tokens of a personal friendship, which began when we were members of the same class in college. The work was commenced at his suggestion, and has been carried forward with his constant advice and co-operation. His ample private library, and, through his influence, the library of the Seminary, have been placed at my disposal; and the notes passed under his eye and were improved in not a few particulars, at his suggestion, though he is in no way responsible for their remaining imperfections. I have also received counsel and encouragement in all my labors from my esteemed colleague, Prof. N. W. Fiske, whose instructions in the same department which has since been committed to my charge, first taught me to love the Greek and Latin classics. I have only to regret that his ill health and absence from the country have prevented me from deriving still greater advantages from his learning and taste. An unforeseen event has, in like manner, deprived me of the expected co-operation of Prof. Lyman Coleman, now of Nassau Hall College in N. J., in concert with whom this work was planned, and was to have been executed, and on whose ripe scholarship, and familiarity with the German language and literature, I chiefly relied for its successful accomplishment.

I should not do justice to my feelings, were I to omit the expression of my obligations to the printer and publishers for the unwearied patience with which they have labored to perfect the work, under all the disadvantages attending the superintendance of the press, at such a distance. If there should still be found in it inaccuracies and blemishes, it will not be because they have spared any pains to make it a correct and beautiful book.

It is with unfeigned diffidence that I submit to the public this first attempt at literary labor. I am fully sensible of its many imperfections, at the same time I am conscious of an ability to make it better at some future day, should it meet the favorable regard of the classical teachers of our land, to whom it is dedicated as an humble contribution to that cause in which they are now laboring, with such unprecedented zeal. Should it contribute in any measure to a better understanding, or a higher appreciation by our youthful countrymen of a classic author, from whom, beyond almost any other, I have drawn instruction and delight, I shall not have labored in vain.

Amherst College, June 1, 1847.

PREFACE TO THE REVISED EDITION.

THE text of this edition has been carefully revised and compared with those of Döderlein, Halle, 1847, Orelli, Zurich, 1848, and Ritter, Bonn and Cambridge, 1848. The notes also have been re-examined and, to a considerable extent, re-written; partly to correspond with the progress of my own mind, partly in accordance with suggestions derived from the above named editions, and from friendly criticisms either by letter or in the public journals. Among the journals, I am particularly indebted to the Bibliotheca Sacra and the New-Englander; and for communications by letter, I am under especial obligations to Professors Crosby and Sanborn of Dartmouth College, Robbins of Middlebury, and Lincoln of Brown University.

In revising the geography of the Germania, I have consulted, without however entering much into detail, Ukert's invaluable treatise on the Geography of the Greeks and Romans, whose volume on Germany contains a translation and running commentary on almost the entire work of Tacitus. Particular attention has been paid to the ethnology of the tribes and nations, in reference to whose origin and early history Tacitus is among the best authorities. In this department the works of Prichard and Latham have been my chief reliance. Grimm and Zeuss, though often referred to, I regret to say I have been able to consult only at second hand.

In sending out this revised edition of these most delightful treatises of an author, in the study of whose works I never tire, I cannot but express the hope, that it has been not a little improved by these alterations and additions, while it will be found to have lost none of the essential features by which the first edition was commended to so good a measure of public favor

W. S. TYLER.

Amherst, May, 1852.

LIFE OF TACITUS.

It is the office of genius and learning, as of light, to illustrate other things, and not itself. The writers, who, of all others perhaps, have told us most of the world, just as it has been and is, have told us least of themselves. Their character we may infer, with more or less exactness, from their works, but their history is unwritten and must for ever remain so. Homer, though, perhaps, the only one who has been argued out of existence, is by no means the only one whose age and birth-place have been disputed. The native place of Tacitus is mere matter of conjecture. His parentage is not certainly known. The time of his birth and the year of his death are ascertained only by approximation, and very few incidents are recorded in the history of his life; still we know the period in which he lived, the influences under which his character was developed and matured, and the circumstances under which he wrote his immortal works. In short, we know his *times*, though we can scarcely gather up enough to denominate his *life;* and the times in which an author lived, are often an important, not to say, essential means of elucidating his writings.

Caius Cornelius Tacitus was born in the early part of the reign of Nero, and near the middle of the first century in the Christian Era. The probability is, that he was the son of Cornelius Tacitus, a man of equestrian rank, and procurator of Belgic Gaul under Nero; that he was born at Interamna in Umbria, and that he received a part of his education at Massilia (the modern Marseilles), which was then the Athens of the West, a Grecian colony, and a seat of truly Grecian culture and refinement. It is not improbable that he enjoyed also the instructions of Quintilian, who for twenty years taught at Rome that pure and manly eloquence, of which his Institutes furnish at once such perfect rules, and so fine an example. If we admit the Dialogue de Claris Oratoribus to be the work of Tacitus, his beau-idéal of the education proper for an orator was no less comprehensive, no less elevated, no less liberal, than that of Cicero himself; and if his theory of education was, like Cicero's, only a transcript of his own education, he must have been disciplined early in all the arts and sciences—in all the departments of knowledge which were then cultivated at Rome; a conclusion in which we are confirmed also by the accurate and minute acquaintance which he shows, in his other works, with all the affairs, whether civil or military, public or private, literary or religious, both of Greece and Rome.

The boyhood and youth of Tacitus did, indeed, fall on evil times. Monsters in vice and crime had filled the throne, till their morals and manners had infected those of all the people. The state was distracted, and apparently on the eve of dissolution. The public taste, like the general conscience, was perverted. The fountains of education were poisoned. Degenerate Grecian masters were inspiring their Roman pupils with a relish for a false science, a frivolous literature, a vitiated eloquence, an Epicurean creed, and a voluptuous life.

But with sufficient discernment to see the follies and vices of his age, and with sufficient virtue to detest them, Tacitus must have found his love of wisdom and goodness, of liberty and law, strengthened by the very disorders and faults of the times. If the patriot ever loves a well-regulated freedom, it will be in and after the reign of a tyrant, preceded or followed by what is still worse, anarchy. If the pure and the good ever reverence purity and goodness, it will be amid the general prevalence of vice and crime. If the sage ever pants after wisdom, it is when the fountains of knowledge have become corrupted. The reigns of Nero and his immediate successors were probably the very school, of all others, to which we are most indebted for the comprehensive wisdom, the elevated sentiments, and the glowing eloquence of the biographer of Agricola, and the historian of the Roman Empire. His youth saw, and felt, and deplored the disastrous effects of Nero's inhuman despotism, and of the anarchy attending the civil wars of Galba, Otho, and Vitellius. His manhood saw, and felt, and exulted in the contrast furnished by the reigns of Vespasian and Titus, though the sun of the latter too soon went down, in that long night of gloom, and blood, and terror, the tyranny of Domitian. And when, in the reigns of Nerva and Trajan, he enjoyed the rare felicity of thinking what he pleased, and speaking what he thought, he was just fitted in the maturity of his faculties, and the extent of his observation and reflections, "to enroll slowly, year after year, that dreadful reality of crimes and sufferings, which even dramatic horror, in all its license of wild imagination, can scarcely reach, the long unvarying catalogue of tyrants and executioners, and victims that return thanks to the gods and die, and accusers rich with their blood, and more mighty as more widely hated, amid the multitudes of prostrate slaves, still looking whether there may not yet have escaped some lingering virtue which it may be a merit to destroy, and having scarcely leisure to feel even the agonies of remorse in the continued sense of the precariousness of their own gloomy existence."*

* Brown's Philosophy of the Mind

Tacitus was educated for the bar, and continued to plead causes, occasionally at least, and with not a little success, even after he had entered upon the great business of his life, as a writer of history. We find references to his first, and perhaps his last appearance, as an advocate, in the Letters of Pliny, which are highly complimentary. The first was, when Pliny was nineteen, and Tacitus a little older (how much we are not informed), when Tacitus distinguished himself, so as to awaken the emulation and the envy, though not in a bad sense, of Pliny. The last was some twenty years later, when Tacitus and Pliny, the tried friends of a whole life, the brightest ornaments of literature and of the forum, were associated by the choice of the Senate, and pleaded together at the bar of the Senate, and in the presence of the Emperor Trajan, for the execution of justice upon Marius Priscus, who was accused of mal-administration in the proconsulship of Africa. Pliny says, that Tacitus spoke with singular gravity and eloquence, and the Senate passed a unanimous vote of approbation and thanks to both the orators, for the ability and success with which they had managed the prosecution (Plin. Epis. ii. 11).

We have also the comments of Pliny on a panegyrical oration, which Tacitus pronounced, when consul, upon his predecessor in the consular office, Verginius Rufus, perhaps the most remarkable man of his age, distinguished alike as a hero, a statesman, and a scholar, and yet so modest or so wise that he repeatedly refused the offer of the imperial purple. "Fortune," says Pliny, "always faithful to Verginius, reserved for her last favor, such an orator to pronounce a eulogium on such virtues. It was enough to crown the glory of a well spent life" (Plin. Epis. ii. 1).

The speeches in the historical works of Tacitus, though

rather concise and abstract for popular orations, are full of force and fire. Some of them are truly Demosthenic in their impassioned and fiery logic. The speech of Galgácus before the Briton army, when driven into the extremity of Caledonia by the Romans under Agricola, can hardly be surpassed for patriotic sentiments, vigorous reasoning, and burning invective. The address of Germanicus to his mutinous soldiers (in the Annals) is not less remarkable for tender pathos. The sage and yet soldierlike address of the aged Galba to his adopted son Piso, the calm and manly speech of Piso to the body guard, the artful harangue of the demagogue Otho to his troops, the no less crafty address of Mucianus to Vespasian, the headlong rapidity of Antonius' argument for immediate action, the plausible plea of Marcellus Eprius against the honest attack of Helvidius Priscus, and the burning rebukes of the intrepid Vocula to his cowardly and treacherous followers—all these, in the Histories, show no ordinary degree of rhetorical skill and versatility. Indeed, the entire body of his works is animated with the spirit of the orator, as it is tinged also with the coloring of the poet. For this reason, they are doubtless deficient in the noble simplicity of the earlier classical histories; but for the same reason they may be a richer treasure for the professional men at least of modern times.

Of his marriage with the daughter of Agricola, and its influence on his character and prospects, as also of his passing in regular gradation through the series of public honors at Rome, beginning with the quaestorship under Vespasian, and ending with the consulship under Nerva, Tacitus informs us himself (A. 9, His. i. 1), barely alluding to them, however, in the general, and leaving all the details to mere conjecture. We learn to our surprise, that he not only escaped the jealousy of the tyrant Domitian, but was even promoted by him to the office of Quindecimvir and Praetor (Ann. ii. 11). Beyond these vague notices, we know little or nothing of his course of life, except that Pliny says (Epist. iv. 13), he was much esteemed by the learned and the great at Rome, who went in crowds to his levees. Of the time of his death, we can only conjecture, that he died before the Emperor Trajan, but after his friend Pliny—the former, because, had he outlived the Emperor, he would probably have executed his purpose of writing the history of his reign (His. i. 1); the latter, because, if he had not survived his friend, Pliny, who lamented the death of so many others, would not have failed to pay the last tribute to the memory of Tacitus.

It is generally admitted, though without direct testimony, that Tacitus died not without issue. That excellent prince, M. Claudius Tacitus, deduced his pedigree from the historian, and ordered his image to be set up, and a complete collection of his works to be placed in the public archives, with a special direction that twelve copies should be made every year at the public expense. It is greatly to be regretted that such praiseworthy precautions should have failed to preserve for us that treasure entire!

The age of Tacitus is usually styled the silver age of Roman Literature; and it merits no higher title, when compared with the golden age of Augustus. It was the good fortune of Augustus to gain the supremacy at Rome, when society had reached its maximum of refinement, and was just ready to enter upon its stage of corruption and decline. Hence his name is identified with that proud era in literature, in producing which he bore at best only an accidental and secondary part. In the literature of the Augustan age, we admire the substance of learning and philosophy without the show, the cultivation of taste without the parade of criticism, the fascination of poetry without its corruption, and the use of eloquence without its abuse. Grecian refinement was no longer despised; Grecian effeminacy had not yet prevailed. The camp was not now the home of the Romans; neither were the theatres and the schools. They had ceased to be a nation of soldiers, and had not yet become a nation of slaves. At no other period could Rome have had her Cicero, her Livy, and her Virgil.

The silver age produced no men who "attained unto these first three." But there are not wanting other bright names to associate with Tacitus, though most of them lived a little earlier than he. There was Seneca, the Philosopher, whose style, with its perpetual antitheses, is the very worst of the age, but his sentiments, perhaps more or less under the influence of Christianity, approach nearer to the Christian code of morals than those of any other Latin author. There were Martial and Juvenal, whose satires made vice tremble in its high places, and helped to confer on the Romans the honor of originating one species of literary composition, unknown to the Greeks. There were Suetonius and Plutarch; the one natural, simple, and pure in his style, far beyond his age, but without much depth or vigor of thought; the other involved and affected in his manner, but in his matter of surpassing richness and incalculable worth. There was the elder Pliny, a prodigy of learning and industry, whose researches in Natural History cost him his life, in that fatal eruption of Vesuvius which buried Herculaneum and Pompeii. There was also the judicious Quintilian, at once neat and nervous in his language, delicate and correct in his criticisms, a man of genius and a scholar, a teacher and an exemplar of eloquence. Finally, there were the younger Pliny and Tacitus, rival candidates for literary and professional distinction, yet cherishing for each other the most devoted and inviolable attachment, each viewing the other as the ornament of their country, each urging the other to write the history of their age, and each relying chiefly on the genius of the other for his own immortality (Plin. Epis. vii. 33). Their names were together identified by their contemporaries with the literature of the age of Trajan: "I never was touched with a more sensible pleasure," says Pliny, in one of his beautiful Letters* (which rival Cicero's in epistolary ease and elegance), "than by an account which I lately received from Cornelius Tacitus. He informed me, that at the last Circensian Games, he sat next a stranger, who, after much discourse on various topics of learning, asked him whether he was an Italian or a Provincial. Tacitus replied, 'Your acquaintance with literature must have informed you who I am.' 'Aye,' said the man, 'is it then Tacitus or Pliny I am talking with?' I cannot express how highly I am pleased to find, that our names are not so much the proper appellations of individuals, as a designation of learning itself" (Plin. Epis. ix. 23). Critics are not agreed to which of these two literary friends belongs the delicate encomium of Quintilian, when, after enumerating the principal writers of the day, he adds, "There is another ornament of the age, who will deserve the admiration of posterity. I do not mention him at present; his name will be known hereafter." Pliny, Tacitus, and Quintilian, are also rival candidates for the honor of having written the Dialogue de Claris Oratoribus, one of the most valuable productions in ancient criticism.

As a writer, Tacitus was not free from the faults of his age. The native simplicity of Greek and Latin composition had passed away. An affected point and an artificial brilliancy were substituted in their place. The rhetoric and philosophy

* Eleven of these are addressed to Tacitus, and two or three are written expressly for the purpose of furnishing materials for his history.

of the schools had infected all the departments of literature. Simple narrative no longer suited the pampered taste of the readers or the writers of history. It must be highly seasoned with sentimentalism and moralizing, with romance and poetry. Tacitus, certainly, did not escape the infection. In the language of Macaulay, "He carries his love of effect far beyond the limits of moderation. He tells a fine story finely, but he cannot tell a plain story plainly. He stimulates, till stimulants lose their power."* We have taken occasion in the notes to point out not a few examples of rhetorical pomp, and poetical coloring, and even needless multiplication of words, where plainness and precision would have been much better, and which may well surprise us in a writer of so much conciseness. Lord Monboddo, in a very able, though somewhat extravagant critique on Tacitus, has selected numerous instances of what he calls the ornamented dry style, many of which are so concise, so rough, and so broken, that he says, they do not deserve the name of composition, but seem rather like the raw materials of history, than like history itself (Orig. and Prog. of Lang., vol iii. chap. 12).

Still, few readers can fail to pronounce Tacitus, as Macaulay affirms, and even Lord Monboddo admits him to be, the greatest of Latin historians, superior to Thucydides himself in the moral painting of his best narrative scenes, and in the delineation of character without a rival among historians, with scarcely a superior among dramatists and novelists. The common style of his narrative is, indeed, wanting in simplicity, and sometimes in perspicuity. He does not deal enough in the specific and the picturesque, the where, the when and the how. But when his subject comes up to the grandeur of his conceptions,

* See a fine article on history, Ed. Rev., 1828. Also in Macaulay's Miscellanies.

and the strength of his language, his descriptions are graphic and powerful. No battle scenes are more grand and terrific than those of Tacitus. Military men and scholars have also remarked their singular correctness and definiteness. The military evolutions, the fierce encounter, the doubtful struggle, the alternations of victory and defeat, the disastrous rout and hot pursuit, the carnage and blood, are set forth with the warrior's accuracy and the poet's fire; while, at the same time, the conflicting passions and emotions of the combatants are discerned, as it were, by the eye of a seer—their hidden springs of action, and the lowest depths of their hearts laid bare, as if by the wand of a magician. In the painting of large groups, in the moral portraiture of vast bodies of men under high excitement and in strenuous exertion, we think that Tacitus far surpasses all other historians. Whether it be a field of battle or a captured city, a frightened senate or a flattering court, a mutiny or a mob, that he describes, we not only see in a clear and strong light the outward actions, but we look into the hearts of all the mixed multitude, and gaze with wonder on the changing emotions and conflicting passions by which they are agitated.

His delineations of individual character are also marked by the same profound insight into the human soul. Like the old Latin Poet, he might have said,

"Homo sum; nihil *humani* a me alienum puto."

There is scarcely a landscape picture in his whole gallery. It is full of portraits of *men*, in groups and as individuals, every grade of condition, every variety of character, performing all kinds of actions, exhibiting every human passion, the colors laid on with a bold hand, the principal features presented in a strong light, the minuter strokes omitted, the soft and delicate finish despised. We feel, that we have gained not a little insight into the character of those men, who are barely introduced in the extant books of Tacitus, but whose history is given in the books that are lost. Men of inferior rank even, who appear on the stage only for a short time, develope strongly marked characters, which are drawn with dramatic distinctness and power, while yet the thread of history is never broken, the dignity of history never sacrificed. And those Emperors, whose history is preserved entire,—with them we feel acquainted, we know the controlling principles, as well as the leading events of their lives, and we feel sure that we could predict how they would act, under almost any imaginable circumstances.

In a faithful portraiture of the private and public life of the degenerate Romans, there was much to call for the hand of a master in *satire.* And we find in the glowing sketches of our author, all the vigor and point of a Juvenal, without his vulgarity and obscenity; all the burning indignation which the Latin is so peculiarly capable of expressing, with all the vigor and stateliness by which the same language is equally characterized. Tacitus has been sometimes represented as a very Diogenes, for carping and sarcasm—a very Aristophanes, to blacken character with ridicule and reproach. But he is as far removed from the cynic or the buffoon, as from the panegyrist or the flatterer. He is not the indiscriminate admirer that Plutarch was. Nor is he such a universal hater as Sallust. It is the fault of the times that he is obliged to deal so much in censure. If there ever were perfect monsters on earth, such were several of the Roman Emperors. Yet Tacitus describes few, if any, of them without some of the traits of humanity. He gives us in his history neither demons nor gods, but veritable men and women. In this respect, as also in his descriptions of battles,

Tacitus is decidedly superior to Livy. The characters of Livy are distinguishable only as classes—the good all very good, the bad very bad, the indifferent very indifferent. You discover no important difference between a Fabius and a Marcellus, further than it lies on the face of their actions. In Tacitus, the characters are all individuals. Each stands out distinctly from the surrounding multitude, and not only performs his own proper actions, but is governed by his own peculiar motives. Livy places before us the statues of heroes and gods; Tacitus conducts us through the crowd of living men.

In an attempt to sketch the most striking features of Tacitus, as a writer, no critic can omit to mention his sage and pithy maxims. Apothegms abound on every page—sagacious, truthful, and profound in sentiment, in style concise, antithetic and sententious. Doubtless he is excessively fond of pointed antithesis. Perhaps he is too much given to moralizing and reflection. It was, as we have said, the fault of his age. But no one, who is familiar with Seneca, will severely censure Tacitus. He will only wonder that he should have risen so far above the faults of his contemporaries. Indeed, Tacitus interweaves his reflections with so much propriety, and clothes his apothegms with so much dignity—he is so manifestly competent to instruct the world by maxims, whether in civil, social, or individual life, that we are far from wishing he had indulged in it less. His reflections do not interrupt the thread of his narrative. They grow naturally out of his incidents. They break forth spontaneously from the lips of his men. His history is indeed philosophy teaching by examples; and his pithy sayings are truly lessons of wisdom, embodied in the form most likely to strike the attention, and impress the memory. We should love to see a collection of apothegms from the pen of Tacitus. It would make an admirable book of laconics. No book would give you more ideas in fewer words. Nowhere could you gain so much knowledge, and lose so little time. The reader of Tacitus, who will study him with pen in hand, to mark, or refer to the most striking passages, will soon find himself master of a text book in moral and political science, we might say a text book in human nature, singularly concise and sententious, and what is not always true even of concise and sententious writers, as singularly wise and profound. In such a book, many of the *speeches* would find a place entire; for many of them are little else than a series of condensed, well-timed, and most instructive apothegms.*

But the scholar, who is on the lookout, will find lurking in every section, and almost every sentence, some important truth in morals, in politics, in the individual or social nature of man. Neither the editor nor the teacher can be expected to develope these sentiments, nor even, in many instances, to point them out. That labor must be performed by the scholar; and his will be the reward.

No hasty perusal, no single reading of Tacitus, will give a just conception of the surpassing richness of his works. They must be studied profoundly to be duly appreciated. They are a mine of wisdom, of vast extent and unknown depth, whose treasures lie chiefly beneath the surface, imbedded in the solid rock which must be entered with mining implements, explored with strong lights, and its wealth brought up by severe toil and sweat.

* E g the speech of Galba to Piso. His. i. 15, 16.

C. CORN. TACITUS

DE

SITU, MORIBUS ET POPULIS GERMANIAE

BREVIARIUM LIBELLI.

Cap. 1. Germaniae situs: 2. incolae indigenae: auctores gentis: nominis origo: Hercules. 3. Baritus: ara Ulixis. 4. Germani, gens sincera: habitus corporum. 5. Terrae natura: non aurum, non argentum, nec aestimatum. 6. Germanorum arma, equitatus, peditatus, ordo militiae: 7. reges, duces, sacerdotes: 8. feminarum virtus et veneratio: Veleda: Aurinia. 9. dii, sacra, simulacra nulla. 10. Auspicia, sortes: ex equis, e captivo praesagia. 11. Consultationes publicae et conventus. 12. Accusationes, poenae, jus redditum. 13. Scuto frameaque ornati juvenes, principum comites: eorum virtus et fama. 14. Gentis bellica studia. 15. In pace, venatio, otium: Collata principibus munera. 16. Urbes nullae: vici, domus, specus suffugium hiemi et receptaculum frugibus. 17. Vestitus hominum, feminarum. 18. Matrimonia severa: dos a marito oblata. 19. Pudicitia. Adulterii poena: Monogamia: Liberorum numerus non finitus. 20. Liberorum educatio: Successionis leges. 21. Patris, propinqui, amicitiae, inimicitiaeque susceptae: homicidii pretium: Hospitalitas. 22. Lotio, victus, ebriorum rixae: consultatio in conviviis. 23. Potus, cibus. 24. Spectacula: aleae furor. 25. Servi, libertini. 26. Fenus ignotum: Agricultura: Anni tempora. 27. Funera, sepulcra, luctus.

28. Singularum gentium instituta: Galli, olim valida gens, in

Germaniam transgressi, Helvetii, Boii : Aravisci, Osi, incertum genus : Germanicae originis populi Treveri, Nervii, Vangiones, Triboci, Nemetes, Ubii. 29. Batavi, Cattorum proles : Mattiaci : Decumates agri. 30, 31. Cattorum regio, habitus, disciplina militaris ; vota, virtutis incentiva. 32. Usipii, Tencteri, equitatu praestantes. 33. Bructerorum sedes, a Chamavis et Angrivariis occupatae. 34. Dulgibini : Chasvari : Frisii. 35. Chauci, pacis studio, justitia, et virtute nobiles. 36. Cherusci et Fosi, a Cattis victi. 37. Cimbrorum parva civitas, gloria ingens : Romanorum clades : Germani triumphati magis quam victi. 38. Suevorum numerus, mores. 39. Semnonum religio, victimae humanae 40. Longobardi : Reudigni : Aviones : Angli : Varini : Eudoses : Suardones : Nuithones : Herthae cultus communis. 41. Hermunduri. 42. Narisci : Marcomanni : Quadi. 43. Marsigni : Gothini : Osi : Burii : Lygiorum civitates, Arii, Helvecones, Manimi, Elysii, Naharvali ; horum numen Alcis : Gotones : Rugii : Lemovii. 44. Suiones, classibus valentes. 45. Mare pigrum : Aestyi, Matris Deum cultores, succinum legunt : Sitonibus femina imperat. 46. Peucini, Venedi, Fenni, Germani, an Sarmatae ? Eorum feritas, paupertas : Hominum monstra, Hellusii, Oxiones.

I. Germania omnis a Gallis Rhaetisque et Pannoniis Rheno et Danubio fluminibus, a Sarmatis Dacisque mutuo metu aut montibus separatur : cetera Oceanus ambit, latos sinus et insularum immensa spatia complectens, nuper cognitis quibusdam gentibus ac regibus, quos bellum aperuit. Rhenus, Rhaeticarum Alpium inaccesso ac praecipiti vertice ortus, modico flexu in occidentem versus, septentrionali Oceano miscetur. Danubius, molli et clementer edito montis Abnobae jugo effusus, plures populos adit, donec in Ponticum mare sex meatibus erumpat : septimum os paludibus hauritur.

II. Ipsos Germanos indigenas crediderim, minimeque aliarum gentium adventibus et hospitiis mixtos; quia nec terra olim, sed classibus advehebantur, qui mutare sedes quaerebant, et immensus ultra, utque sic dixerim, adversus Oceanus raris ab orbe nostro navibus aditur. Quis porro, praeter periculum horridi et ignoti maris, Asia aut Africa aut Italia relicta, Germaniam peteret, informem terris, asperam coelo, tristem cultu aspectuque, nisi si patria sit? Celebrant carminibus antiquis (quod unum apud illos memoriae et annalium genus est) Tuisconem deum terra editum, et filium Mannum, originem gentis conditoresque. Manno tres filios assignant, e quorum nominibus proximi Oceano Ingaevones, medii Hermiones, ceteri Istaevones vocentur. Quidam autem, ut in licentia vetustatis, plures deo ortos pluresque gentis appellationes, Marsos, Gambrivios, Suevos, Vandalios, affirmant; eaque vera et antiqua nomina. Ceterum Germaniae vocabulum recens et nuper additum; quoniam, qui primi Rhenum transgressi Gallos expulerint, ac nunc Tungri, tunc Germani vocati sint: ita nationis nomen, non gentis evaluisse paulatim, ut omnes primum a victore ob metum, mox a seipsis invento nomine Germani vocarentur.

III. Fuisse apud eos et Herculem memorant, primumque omnium virorum fortium ituri in proelia canunt. Sunt illis haec quoque carmina, quorum relatu, quem baritum vocant, accendunt animos, futuraeque pugnae fortunam ipso cantu augurantur: terrent enim trepidantve, prout sonuit acies. Nec tam voces illae, quam virtutis concentus videntur. Affectatur praecipue asperitas soni et fractum murmur, objectis ad os scutis, quo plenior et gravior vox repercussu intumescat. Ceterum et Ulixem quidam opinantur longo illo et fabuloso errore in hunc Oceanum delatum, adisse Germaniae terras, Asciburgiumque, quod in ripa Rheni situm hodieque incolitur, ab illo constitutum nominatumque. Aram quin etiam Ulixi consecratam, adjecto Laertae patris nomine, eodem loco olim repertam, monumentaque et tumulos quosdam Graecis litteris inscriptos in confinio Germaniae Rhaetiaeque adhuc exstare : quae neque confirmare argumentis, neque refellere in animo est : ex ingenio suo quisque demat, vel addat fidem.

IV. Ipse eorum opinionibus accedo, qui Germaniae populos nullis aliis aliarum nationum connubiis infectos propriam et sinceram et tantum sui similem gentem exstitisse arbitrantur : unde habitus quoque corporum, quanquam in tanto hominum numero, idem omnibus ; truces et caerulei oculi, rutilae comae, magna corpora et tantum ad impetum valida ; laboris atque operum non eadem patientia : minimeque sitim aestumque tolerare, frigora atque inediam coelo solove assueverunt.

V. Terra, etsi aliquanto specie differt, in universum tamen aut silvis horrida aut paludibus foeda : humidior, qua Gallias ; ventosior, qua Noricum ac Pannoniam aspicit : satis ferax ; frugiferarum arborum impatiens : pecorum fecunda, sed plerumque improcera ; ne armentis quidem suus honor, aut gloria frontis : numero gaudent ; eaeque solae et gratissimae opes sunt. Argentum et aurum propitii an irati dii negaverint, dubito. Nec tamen affirmaverim, nullam Germaniae venam argentum aurumve gignere : quis enim scrutatus est ? possessione et usu haud perinde afficiuntur. Est videre apud illos argentea vasa, legatis et principibus eorum muneri data, non in alia vilitate, quam quae humo finguntur · quanquam proximi, ob usum commerciorum, aurum et argentum in pretio habent, formasque quasdam nostrae pecuniae agnoscunt atque eligunt : interiores simplicius et antiquius permutatione mercium utuntur. Pecuniam probant veterem et diu notam, serratos bigatosque. Argentum quoque, magis quam aurum sequuntur, nulla affectione animi, sed quia numerus argenteorum facilior usui est promiscua ac vilia mercantibus.

VI. Ne ferrum quidem superest, sicut ex genere telorum colligitur. Rari gladiis aut majoribus lanceis utuntur : hastas, vel ipsorum vocabulo frameas gerunt, angusto et brevi ferro sed ita acri et ad usum habili, ut eodem telo, prout ratio poscit, vel cominus vel eminus pugnent : et eques quidem scuto frameaque contentus est : pedites et missilia spargunt, plura singuli, atque in immensum vibrant, nudi aut sagulo leves. Nulla cultus jactatio ; scuta tantum lectissimis coloribus distinguunt : paucis loricae : vix uni alterive cassis aut galea. Equi non forma, non velocitate conspicui : sed nec variare gyros in morem nostrum docentur. In rectum, aut uno flexu dextros agunt ita conjuncto orbe, ut nemo posterior sit. In universum aestimanti, plus penes peditem roboris : eoque mixti proeliantur, apta et congruente ad equestrem pugnam velocitate peditum, quos ex omni juventute delectos ante aciem locant. Definitur et numerus : centeni ex singulis pagis sunt : idque ipsum inter suos vocantur ; et quod primo numerus fuit, jam nomen et honor est. Acies per cuneos componitur Cedere loco, dummodo rursus instes, consilii quam formidinis arbitrantur. Corpora suorum etiam in dubiis proeliis referunt. Scutum reliquisse, praecipuum flagitium; nec aut sacris adesse, aut concilium inire, ignominioso fas; multique superstites bellorum infamiam laqueo finierunt.

VII. Reges ex nobilitate, duces ex virtute sumunt Nec regibus infinita aut libera potestas: et duces exemplo potius, quam imperio, si prompti, si conspicui, si ante aciem agant, admiratione praesunt. Ceterum neque animadvertere neque vincire, ne verberare quidem, nisi sacerdotibus permissum; non quasi in poenam, nec ducis jussu, sed velut deo imperante, quem adesse bellantibus credunt: effigiesque et signa quaedam, detracta lucis, in proelium ferunt. Quodque praecipuum fortitudinis incitamentum est, non casus nec fortuita conglobatio turmam aut cuneum facit, sed familiae et propinquitates, et in proximo pignora, unde feminarum ululatus audiri, unde vagitus infantium: hi cuique sanctissimi testes, hi maximi laudatores. Ad matres, ad conjuges vulnera ferunt; nec illae numerare, aut exigere plagas pavent; cibosque et hortamina pugnantibus gestant.

VIII. Memoriae proditur, quasdam acies, inclinatas jam et labantes, a feminis restitutas, constantia precum et objectu pectorum et monstrata cominus captivitate, quam longe impatientius feminarum suarum nomine timent: adeo ut efficacius obligentur animi civitatum, quibus inter obsides puellae quoque nobiles imperantur. Inesse quin etiam sanctum aliquid et providum putant: nec aut consilia earum aspernantur, aut responsa negligunt. Vidimus sub divo Vespasiano Veledam diu apud plerosque numinis loco habitam. Sed et olim Auriniam et complures alias venerati sunt non adulatione, nec tanquam facerent deas.

IX. Deorum maxime Mercurium colunt, cui certis diebus humanis quoque hostiis litare fas habent. Herculem ac Martem concessis animalibus placant: pars Suevorum et Isidi sacrificat. Unde causa et origo peregrino sacro parum comperi, nisi quod signum ipsum, in modum liburnae figuratum, docet advectam religionem. Ceterum nec cohibere parietibus deos, neque in ullam humani oris speciem assimulare, ex magnitudine coelestium arbitrantur: lucos ac nemora consecrant, deorumque nominibus appellant secretum illud, quod sola reverentia vident.

X. Auspicia sortesque, ut qui maxime, observant. Sortium consuetudo simplex: virgam, frugiferae arbori decisam, in surculos amputant, eosque, notis quibusdam discretos, super candidam vestem temere ac fortuito spargunt: mox, si publice consuletur, sacerdos civitatis, sin privatim, ipse paterfamiliae, precatus deos coelumque suspiciens, ter singulos tollit, sublatos secundum impressam ante notam interpretatur. Si prohibuerunt, nulla de eadem re in eundem diem consultatio; sin permissum, auspiciorum adhuc fides exigitur. Et illud quidem etiam hic notum, avium voces volatusque interrogare: proprium gentis, equorum quoque praesagia ac monitus experiri; publice aluntur iisdem nemoribus ac lucis candidi et nullo mortali opere contacti: quos pressos sacro curru sacerdos ac rex vel princeps civitatis comitantur, hinnitusque ac fremitus observant. Nec ulli auspicio major fides non solum apud plebem, sed apud proceres, apud sacerdotes; se enim ministros deorum, illos conscios putant. Est et alia observatio auspiciorum, qua gravium bellorum eventus explorant; ejus gentis, cum qua bellum est, captivum, quoquo modo interceptum, cum electe popularium suorum, patriis quemque armis, committunt: victoria hujus vel illius pro praejudicio accipitur.

XI. De minoribus rebus principes consultant; de majoribus omnes: ita tamen, ut ea quoque, quorum penes plebem arbitrium est, apud principes pertractentur. Coeunt, nisi quid fortuitum et subitum inciderit, certis diebus, cum aut inchoatur luna aut impletur: nam agendis rebus hoc auspicatissimum initium credunt. Nec dierum numerum, ut nos, sed noctium computant. Sic constituunt, sic condicunt: nox ducere diem videtur. Illud ex libertate vitium, quod non simul, nec ut jussi conveniunt, sed et alter et tertius dies cunctatione coeuntium absumitur. Ut turbae placuit, considunt armati. Silentium per sacerdotes, quibus tum et coercendi jus est, imperatur Mox rex vel princeps, prout aetas cuique, prout nobilitas, prout decus bellorum, prout facundia est, audiuntur, auctoritate suadendi magis, quam jubendi potestate. Si displicuit sententia, fremitu aspernantur; sin placuit, frameas concutiunt. Honoratissimum assensus genus est, armis laudare.

XII. Licet apud concilium accusare quoque et discrimen capitis intendere. Distinctio poenarum ex delicto: proditores et transfugas arboribus suspendunt; ignavos et imbelles et corpore infames coeno ac palude, injecta insuper crate, mergunt. Diversitas supplicii illuc respicit, tanquam scelera ostendi oporteat, dum puniuntur, flagitia abscondi. Sed et levioribus delictis, pro modo poenarum, equorum pecorumque numero convicti mulctantur: pars mulctae regi vel civitati, pars ipsi, qui vindicatur, vel propinquis ejus exsolvitur. Eliguntur in iisdem conciliis et principes, qui jura per pagos vicosque reddunt. Centeni singulis ex plebe comites, consilium simul et auctoritas, adsunt.

XIII. Nihil autem neque publicae neque privatae rei, nisi armati agunt. Sed arma sumere non ante cuiquam moris, quam civitas suffecturum probaverit. Tum in ipso concilio, vel principum aliquis vel pater vel propinquus scuto frameaque juvenem ornant: haec apud illos toga, hic primus juventae honos: ante hoc domus pars videntur, mox reipublicae. Insignis nobilitas, aut magna patrum merita, principis dignationem etiam adolescentulis assignant: ceteris robustioribus ac jampridem probatis aggregantur; nec rubor, inter comites aspici. Gradus quin etiam et ipse comitatus habet judicio ejus, quem sectantur: magnaque et comitum aemulatio, quibus primus apud principem suum locus, et principum, cui plurimi et acerrimi comites. Haec dignitas, hae vires, magno semper electorum juvenum globo circumdari, in pace decus, in bello praesidium. Nec solum in sua gente cuique, sed apud finitimas quoque civitates id nomen, ea gloria est, si numero ac virtute comitatus emineat: expetuntur enim legationibus et muneribus ornantur et ipsa plerumque fama bella profligant.

XIV. Cum ventum in aciem, turpe principi virtute vinci, turpe comitatui, virtutem principis non adaequare. Jam vero infame in omnem vitam ac probrosum, superstitem principi suo ex acie recessisse. Illum defendere, tueri, sua quoque fortia facta gloriae ejus assignare, praecipuum sacramentum est. Principes pro victoria pugnant; comites pro principe. Si civitas, in qua orti sunt, longa pace et otio torpeat plerique nobilium adolescentium petunt ultro eas nationes, quae tum bellum aliquod gerunt; quia et ingrata genti quies, et facilius inter ancipitia clarescunt, magnumque comitatum non nisi vi belloque tuentur: exigunt enim principis sui liberalitate illum bellatorem equum, illam cruentam victricemque frameam. Nam epulae et, quanquam incompti, largi tamen apparatus pro stipendio cedunt: materia munificentiae per bella et raptus. Nec arare terram, aut expectare annum, tam facile persuaseris, quam vocare hostes et vulnera mereri. Pigrum quinimmo et iners videtur, sudore acquirere, quod possis sanguine parare.

XV. Quotiens bella non ineunt, non multum venatibus, plus per otium transigunt, dediti somno ciboque, fortissimus quisque ac bellicosissimus nihil agens, delegata domus et penatium et agrorum cura feminis senibusque et infirmissimo cuique ex familia: ipsi hebent; mira diversitate naturae, cum iidem homines sic ament inertiam et oderint quietem. Mos est civitatibus ultro ac viritim conferre principibus vel armentorum vel frugum, quod pro honore acceptum, etiam necessitatibus subvenit. Gaudent praecipue finitimarum gentium donis, quae non modo a singulis, sed publice mittuntur: electi equi, magna arma, phalerae, torquesque. Jam et pecuniam accipere docuimus.

XVI. Nullas Germanorum populis urbes habitari, satis notum est: ne pati quidem inter se junctas sedes. Colunt discreti ac diversi, ut fons, ut campus, ut nemus placuit. Vicos locant, non in nostrum morem, connexis et cohaerentibus aedificiis: suam quisque domum spatio circumdat, sive adversus casus ignis remedium, sive inscitia aedificandi Ne caementorum quidem apud illos aut tegularum usus : materia ad omnia utuntur informi et citra speciem aut delectationem. Quaedam loca diligentius illinunt terra ita pura ac splendente, ut picturam ac lineamenta colorum imitetur. Solent et subterraneos specus aperire, eosque multo insuper fimo onerant, suffugium hiemi et receptaculum frugibus : quia rigorem frigorum ejusmodi locis molliunt : et, si quando hostis advenit, aperta populatur, abdita autem et defossa aut ignorantur, aut eo ipso fallunt, quod quaerenda sunt.

XVII. Tegumen omnibus sagum, fibula, aut, si desit, spina consertum : cetera intecti totos dies juxta focum atque ignem agunt. Locupletissimi veste distinguuntur, non fluitante, sicut Sarmatae ac Parthi, sed stricta et singulos artus exprimente. Gerunt et ferarum pelles, proximi ripae negligenter, ulteriores exquisitius, ut quibus nullus per commercia cultus. Eligunt feras, et detracta velamina spargunt maculis pellibusque belluarum, quas exterior Oceanus atque ignotum mare gignit. Nec alius feminis quam viris habitus, nisi quod feminae saepius lineis amictibus velantur, eosque purpura variant, partemque vestitus superioris in manicas non extendunt, nudae brachia ac lacertos : sed et proxima pars pectoris patet.

XVIII. Quanquam severa illic matrimonia ; nec ullam morum partem magis laudaveris : nam prope soli barbarorum singulis uxoribus contenti sunt, exceptis admodum paucis, qui non libidine, sed ob nobilitatem, plurimis nuptiis ambiuntur. Dotem non uxor marito, sed uxori maritus offert. Intersunt parentes et propinqui, ac munera probant : munera non ad delicias muliebres quaesita, nec quibus nova

3

nupta comatur: sed boves et frenatum equum et scutum cum framea gladioque. In haec munera uxor accipitur; atque invicem ipsa armorum aliquid viro affert: hoc maximum vinculum, haec arcana sacra, hos conjugales deos arbitrantur. Ne se mulier extra virtutum cogitationes extraque bellorum casus putet, ipsis incipientis matrimonii auspiciis admonetur, venire se laborum periculorumque sociam, idem in pace, idem in proelio passuram ausuramque: hoc juncti boves, hoc paratus equus, hoc data arma denuntiant; sic vivendum, sic pereundum: accipere se, quae liberis inviolata ac digna reddat, quae nurus accipiant rursus, quae ad nepotes referantur.

XIX. Ergo septa pudicitia agunt, nullis spectaculorum illecebris, nullis conviviorum irritationibus corruptae. Litterarum secreta viri pariter ac feminae ignorant. Paucissima in tam numerosa gente adulteria; quorum poena praesens et maritis permissa. Accisis crinibus, nudatam, coram propinquis, expellit domo maritus, ac per omnem vicum verbere agit: publicatae enim pudicitiae nulla venia: non forma, non aetate, non opibus maritum invenerit. Nemo enim illic vitia ridet: nec corrumpere et corrumpi saeculum vocatur. Melius quidem adhuc eae civitates, in quibus tantum virgines nubunt, et cum spe votoque uxoris semel transigitur. Sic unum accipiunt maritum, quo modo unum corpus unamque vitam, ne ulla cogitatio ultra, ne longior cupiditas, ne tanquam maritum, sed tanquam matrimonium ament Numerum liberorum finire, aut quenquam ex agnatis necare, flagitium habetur: plusque ibi boni mores valent, quam alibi bonae leges.

XX. In omni domo nudi ac sordidi, in hos artus, in

haec corpora, quae miramur, excrescunt. Sua quemque mater uberibus alit, nec ancillis ac nutricibus delegantur. Dominum ac servum nullis educationis deliciis dignoscas: inter eadem pecora, in eadem humo degunt; donec aetas separet ingenuos, virtus agnoscat. Sera juvenum Venus; eoque inexhausta pubertas: nec virgines festinantur; eadem juventa, similis proceritas: pares validaeque miscentur; ac robora parentum liberi referunt. Sororum filiis idem apud avunculum, qui ad patrem honor. Quidam sanctiorem arctioremque hunc nexum sanguinis arbitrantur, et in accipiendis obsidibus magis exigunt; tanquam et in animum firmius, et domum latius teneant. Heredes tamen successoresque sui cuique liberi: et nullum testamentum. Si liberi non sunt, proximus gradus in possessione fratres, patrui, avunculi. Quanto plus propinquorum, quo major affinium numerus, tanto gratiosior senectus, nec ulla orbitatis pretia.

XXI. Suscipere tam inimicitias, seu patris, seu propinqui, quam amicitias, necesse est: nec implacabiles durant. Luitur enim etiam homicidium certo armentorum ac pecorum numero, recipitque satisfactionem universa domus: utiliter in publicum; quia periculosiores sunt inimicitiae juxta libertatem. Convictibus et hospitiis non alia gens effusius indulget. Quemcunque mortalium arcere tecto, nefas habetur: pro fortuna quisque apparatis epulis excipit. Cum defecere, qui modo hospes fuerat, monstrator hospitii et comes: proximam domum non invitati adeunt: nec interest; pari humanitate accipiuntur. Notum ignotumque, quantum ad jus hospitis, nemo discernit. Abeunti, si quid poposcerit, concedere moris: et poscendi invicem eadem facilitas. Gaudent muneribus: sed nec data imputant, nec acceptis obligantur. Victus inter hospites comis.

XXII. Statim e somno, quem plerumque in diem extrahunt, lavantur, saepius calida, ut apud quos plurimum hiems occupat. Lauti cibum capiunt: separatae singulis sedes et sua cuique mensa: tum ad negotia, nec minus saepe ad convivia, procedunt armati. Diem noctemque continuare potando, nulli probrum. Crebrae, ut inter vinolentos, rixae, raro conviciis, saepius caede et vulneribus transiguntur. Sed et de reconciliandis invicem inimicis et jungendis affinitatibus et asciscendis principibus, de pace denique ac bello plerumque in conviviis consultant: tanquam nullo magis tempore aut ad simplices cogitationes pateat animus, aut ad magnas incalescat. Gens non astuta nec callida aperit adhuc secreta pectoris licentia joci. Ergo detecta et nuda omnium mens postera die retractatur, et salva utriusque temporis ratio est: deliberant, dum fingere nesciunt; constituunt, dum errare non possunt.

XXIII. Potui humor ex hordeo aut frumento, in quandam similitudinem vini corruptus. Proximi ripae et vinum mercantur. Cibi simplices; agrestia poma, recens fera, aut lac concretum. Sine apparatu, sine blandimentis, expellunt famem. Adversus sitim non eadem temperantia. Si indulseris ebrietati suggerendo quantum concupiscunt, haud minus facile vitiis, quam armis vincentur.

XXIV. Genus spectaculorum unum atque in omni coetu idem. Nudi juvenes, quibus id ludicrum est, inter gladios se atque infestas frameas saltu jaciunt. Exercitatio artem paravit, ars decorem: non in quaesum tamen aut mercedem; quamvis audacis lasciviae pretium est voluptas spectantium Aleam, quod mirere, sobrii inter seria exercent tanta lucrandi perdendive temeritate, ut, cum omnia defecerunt, extremo ac novissimo jactu de libertate ac de corpore contendant. Victus voluntariam servitutem adit: quamvis juvenior, quamvis robustior, alligari se ac venire patitur: ea est in re prava pervicacia: ipsi fidem vocant. Servos conditionis hujus per commercia tradunt, ut se quoque pudore victoriae exsolvant.

XXV. Ceteris servis, non in nostrum morem descriptis per familiam ministeriis, utuntur. Suam quisque sedem, suos penates regit. Frumenti modum dominus, aut pecoris aut vestis, ut colono, injungit: et servus hactenus paret; cetera domus officia uxor ac liberi exsequuntur. Verberare servum ac vinculis et opere coercere, rarum. Occidere solent, non disciplina et severitate, sed impetu et ira, ut inimicum, nisi quod impune. Liberti non multum supra servos sunt, raro aliquod momentum in domo, nunquam in civitate; exceptis duntaxat iis gentibus, quae regnantur: ibi enim et super ingenuos et super nobiles ascendunt: apud ceteros impares libertini libertatis argumentum sunt.

XXVI. Fenus agitare et in usuras extendere, ignotum: ideoque magis servatur, quam si vetitum esset Agri pro numero cultorum ab universis in vices occupantur, quos mox inter se secundum dignationem partiuntur: facilitatem partiendi camporum spatia praestant. Arva per annos mutant: et superest ager; nec enim cum ubertate et amplitudine soli labore contendunt, ut pomaria conserant et prata separent et hortos rigent: sola terrae seges imperatur. Unde annum quoque ipsum non in totidem digerunt species hiems et ver et aestas intellectum ac vocabula habent autumni perinde nomen ac bona ignorantur.

XXVII. Funerum nulla ambitio; id solum observatur, ut corpora clarorum virorum certis lignis crementur. Struem rogi nec vestibus nec odoribus cumulant: sua cuique arma, quorundam igni et equus adjicitur. Sepulcrum caespes erigit; monumentorum arduum et operosum honorem, ut gravem defunctis, aspernantur. Lamenta ac lacrimas cito, dolorem et tristitiam tarde ponunt. Feminis lugere honestum est; viris meminisse. Haec in commune de omnium Germanorum origine ac moribus accepimus: nunc singularum gentium instituta ritusque, quatenus differant, quae nationes e Germania in Gallias commigraverint, expediam.

XXVIII Validiores olim Gallorum res fuisse, summus auctorum divus Julius tradit: eoque credibile est etiam Gallos in Germaniam transgressos. Quantulum enim amnis obstabat, quo minus, ut quaeque gens evaluerat, occuparet permutaretque sedes, promiscuas adhuc et nulla regnorum potentia divisas? Igitur inter Hercyniam sylvam Rhenumque et Moenum amnes Helvetii, ulteriora Boii, Gallica utraque gens, tenuere. Manet adhuc *Boihemi* nomen, signatque loci veterem memoriam, quamvis mutatis cultoribus. Sed utrum Aravisci in Pannoniam ab Osis, Germanorum natione, an Osi ab Araviscis in Germaniam commigraverint, cum eodem adhuc sermone, institutis, moribus utantur, incertum est: quia, pari olim inopia ac libertate, eadem utriusque ripae bona malaque erant. Treveri et Nervii circa affectationem Germanicae originis ultro ambitiosi sunt, tanquam per hanc gloriam sanguinis a similitudine et inertia Gallorum separentur. Ipsam Rheni ripam haud dubie Germanorum populi colunt, Vangiones, Triboci, Nemetes. Ne Ubii quidem, quanquam Romana colonia esse meruerint ac libentius Agrippinenses conditoris sui nomine vocentur, origine erubescunt, transgressi olim et experimento fidei super ipsam Rheni ripam collocati, ut arcerent, non ut custodirentur.

XXIX. Omnium harum gentium virtute praecipui Batavi, non multum ex ripa, sed insulam Rheni amnis colunt, Chattorum quondam populus et seditione domestica in eas sedes transgressus, in quibus pars Romani imperii fierent. Manet honos et antiquae societatis insigne: nam nec tributis contemnuntur, nec publicanus atterit: exempti oneribus et collationibus et tantum in usum proeliorum sepositi, velut tela atque arma, bellis reservantur. Est in eodem obsequio et Mattiacorum gens; protulit enim magnitudo populi Romani ultra Rhenum, ultraque veteres terminos, imperii reverentiam. Ita sede finibusque in sua ripa, mente animoque nobiscum agunt, cetera similes Batavis, nisi quod ipso adhuc terrae suae solo et coelo acrius animantur. Non numeraverim inter Germaniae populos, quanquam trans Rhenum Danubiumque consederint, eos, qui Decumates agros exercent. Levissimus quisque Gallorum et inopia audax, dubiae possessionis solum occupavere. Mox limite acto promotisque praesidiis, sinus imperii et pars provinciae habentur.

XXX. Ultra hos Chatti initium sedis ab Hercynio saltu inchoant, non ita effusis ac palustribus locis ut ceterae civitates, in quas Germania patescit; durant siquidem colles, paulatim rarescunt, et Chattos suos saltus Hercynius prosequitur simul atque deponit. Duriora genti corpora, stricti artus, minax vultus et major animi vigor. Multum, ut inter Germanos, rationis ac solertiae: praeponere electos, audire praepositos, nosse ordines, intelligere occasiones, differre impetus, disponere diem, vallare noctem, fortunam inter dubia, virtutem inter certa numerare: quodque rarissimum nec nisi ratione disciplinae concessum, plus reponere in duce, quam exercitu. Omne robur in pedite, quem, super arma, ferramentis quoque et copiis onerant. Alios ad proelium ire videas, Chattos ad bellum. Rari excursus et fortuita pugna; equestrium sane virium id proprium, cito parare victoriam, cito cedere: velocitas juxta formidinem, cunctatio propior constantiae est.

XXXI. Et aliis Germanorum populis usurpatum rara et privata cujusque audentia apud Chattos in consensum vertit, ut primum adoleverint, crinem barbamque submittere, nec, nisi hoste caeso, exuere votivum obligatumque virtuti oris habitum. Super sanguinem et spolia revelant frontem, seque tum demum pretia nascendi retulisse, dignosque patria ac parentibus ferunt. Ignavis et imbellibus manet squalor. Fortissimus quisque ferreum insuper annulum (ignominiosum id genti) velut vinculum gestat, donec se caede hostis absolvat. Plurimis Chattorum hic placet habitus. Jamque canent insignes, et hostibus simul suisque monstrati. Omnium penes hos initia pugnarum: haec prima semper acies, visu nova; nam ne in pace quidem vultu mitiore mansuescunt. Nulli domus aut ager aut aliqua cura: prout ad quemque venere, aluntur: prodigi alieni, contemptores sui donec exsanguis senectus tam durae virtuti impares faciat.

XXXII. Proximi Chattis certum jam alveo Rhenum, quique terminus esse sufficiat, Usipii ac Tencteri colunt. Tencteri, super solitum bellorum decus, equestris disciplinae arte praecellunt: nec major apud Chattos peditum laus, quam Tencteris equitum. Sic instituere majores, posteri imitantur; hi lusus infantium, haec juvenum aemulatio, perseverant senes · inter familiam et penates et jura successionum equi traduntur; excipit filius, non, ut cetera, maximus natu, sed prout ferox bello et melior.

XXXIII. Juxta Tencteros Bructeri olim occurrebant: nunc Chamavos et Angrivarios immigrasse narratur, pulsis Bructeris ac penitus excisis vicinarum consensu nationum, seu superbiae odio, seu praedae dulcedine, seu favore quodam erga nos deorum: nam ne spectaculo quidem proelii invidere: super sexaginta millia, non armis telisque Romanis, sed, quod magnificentius est, oblectationi oculisque ceciderunt. Maneat, quaeso, duretque gentibus, si non amor nostri, at certe odium sui: quando, urgentibus imperii fatis, nihil jam praestare fortuna majus potest, quam hostium discordiam.

XXXIV. Angrivarios et Chamavos a tergo Dulgibini et Chasuarii cludunt aliaeque gentes, haud perinde memoratae. A fronte Frisii excipiunt. Majoribus minoribusque Frisiis vocabulum est ex modo virium: utraeque nationes usque ad Oceanum Rheno praetexuntur, ambiuntque immensos insuper lacus et Romanis classibus navigatos. Ipsum quin etiam Oceanum illa tentavimus: et superesse adhuc Herculis columnas fama vulgavit; sive adiit Hercules, seu, quicquid ubique magnificum est, in claritatem ejus referre consensimus. Nec defuit audentia Druso Germanico: sed obstitit Oceanus in se simul atque in Herculem inquiri. Mox nemo tentavit; sanctiusque ac reverentius visum, de actis deorum credere, quam scire.

XXXV. Hactenus in Occidentem Germaniam novimus. In Septentrionem ingenti flexu redit. Ac primo statim Chaucorum gens, quanquam incipiat a Frisiis ac partem littoris occupet, omnium, quas exposui, gentium lateribus obtenditur, donec in Chattos usque sinuetur. Tam immensum terrarum spatium non tenent tantum Chauci, sed et implent: populus inter Germanos nobilissimus, quique magnitudinem suam malit justitia tueri: sine cupiditate, sine impotentia, quieti secretique, nulla provocant bella, nullis raptibus aut latrociniis populantur. Id praecipuum virtutis ac virium argumentum est, quod, ut superiores agant, non per injurias assequuntur. Prompta tamen omnibus arma, ac, si res poscat, exercitus, plurimum virorum equorumque: et quiescentibus eadem fama.

XXXVI. In latere Chaucorum Chattorumque Cherusci nimiam ac marcentem diu pacem illacessiti nutrierunt; idque jucundius, quam tutius, fuit: quia inter impotentes et validos falso quiescas; ubi manu agitur, modestia ac probitas nomina superioris sunt. Ita, qui olim boni aequique Cherusci, nunc inertes ac stulti vocantur: Chattis victoribus fortuna in sapientiam cessit. Tracti ruina Cheruscorum et Fosi, contermina gens, adversarum rerum ex aequo socii, cum in secundis minores fuissent.

XXXVII. Eundem Germaniae sinum proximi Oceano Cimbri tenent, parva nunc civitas, sed gloria ingens; veterisque famae lata vestigia manent, utraque ripa castra ac spatia, quorum ambitu nunc quoque metiaris molem manusque gentis et tam magni exitus fidem. Sexcentesimum et quadragesimum annum urbs nostra agebat, cum primum Cimbrorum audita sunt arma, Caecilio Metello et Papirio Carbone consulibus. Ex quo si ad alterum Imperatoris Trajani consulatum computemus, ducenti ferme et decem anni colliguntur; tamdiu Germania vincitur. Medio tam longi aevi spatio, multa invicem damna: non Samnis, non Poeni, non Hispaniae Galliaeve, ne Parthi quidem saepius admonuere: quippe regno Arsacis acrior est Germanorum libertas. Quid enim aliud nobis, quam caedem Crassi, amisso et ipse Pacoro, infra Ventidium dejectus Oriens objecerit? At Germani, Carbone et Cassio et Scauro Aurelio et Servilio Caepione, M. quoque Manlio fusis vel captis, quinque simul consulares exercitus Populo Romano, Varum, tresque cum eo legiones, etiam Caesari abstulerunt: nec impune C. Marius in Italia, divus Julius in Gallia, Drusus ac Nero et Germanicus in suis eos sedibus perculerunt. Mox ingentes C. Caesaris minae in ludibrium versae. Inde otium, donec occasione discordiae nostrae et civilium armorum, expugnatis legionum hibernis, etiam Gallias affectavere: ac rursus pulsi, inde proximis temporibus triumphati magis quam victi sunt.

XXXVIII. Nunc de Suevis dicendum est, quorum non una, ut Chattorum Tencterorumve, gens: majorem enim Germaniae partem obtinent, propriis adhuc nationibus nominibusque discreti, quanquam in commune Suevi vocentur. Insigne gentis obliquare crinem nodoque substringere: sic Suevi a ceteris

Germanis, sic Suevorum ingenui a servis separantur: in aliis gentibus, seu cognatione aliqua Suevorum, seu quod saepe accidit, imitatione, rarum et intra juventae spatium; apud Suevos, usque ad canitiem, horrentem capillum retro sequuntur, ac saepe in ipso solo vertice religant. Principes et ornatiorem habent: ea cura formae, sed innoxiae: neque enim ut ament amenturve; in altitudinem quandam et terrorem, adituri bella, compti, ut hostium oculis, ornantur.

XXXIX. Vetustissimos se nobilissimosque Suevorum Semnones memorant. Fides antiquitatis religione firmatur. Stato tempore in silvam auguriis patrum et prisca formidine sacram, omnes ejusdem sanguinis populi legationibus coeunt, caesoque publice homine celebrant barbari ritus horrenda primordia. Est et alia luco reverentia. Nemo nisi vinculo ligatus ingreditur, ut minor et potestatem numinis prae se ferens. Si forte prolapsus est, attolli et insurgere haud licitum: per humum evolvuntur: eoque omnis superstitio respicit, tanquam inde initia gentis, ibi regnator omnium deus, cetera subjecta atque parentia. Adjicit auctoritatem fortuna Semnonum: centum pagis habitantur; magnoque corpore efficitur, ut se Suevorum caput credant.

XL. Contra Langobardos paucitas nobilitat: plurimis ac valentissimis nationibus cincti, non per obsequium, sed proeliis et periclitando tuti sunt. Reudigni deinde et Aviones et Anglii et Varini et Eudoses et Suardones et Nuithones fluminibus aut silvis muniuntur: nec quidquam notabile in singulis, nisi quod in commune Nerthum, id est Terram matrem colunt, eamque intervenire rebus hominum, invehi populis arbitrantur. Est in insula Oceani castum nemus, dicatumque in eo vehiculum, veste contectum · attingere uni sacerdoti concessum. Is adesse penetrali deam intelligit, vectamque bubus feminis multa cum veneratione prosequitur. Laeti tunc dies, festa loca, quaecumque adventu hospitioque dignatur. Non bella ineunt, non arma sumunt; clausum omne ferrum: pax et quies tunc tantum nota, tunc tantum amata, donec idem sacerdos satiatam conversatione mortalium deam templo reddat. Mox vehiculum et vestes, et, si credere velis, numen ipsum secreto lacu abluitur. Servi ministrant, quos statim idem lacus haurit; arcanus hinc terror sanctaque ignorantia, quid sit illud, quod tantum perituri vident.

XLI. Et haec quidem pars Suevorum in secretiora Germaniae porrigitur. Propior, ut quo modo paulo ante Rhenum, sic nunc Danubium sequar, Hermundurorum civitas, fida Romanis, eoque solis Germanorum non in ripa commercium, sed penitus, atque in splendidissima Rhaetiae provinciae colonia. Passim et sine custode transeunt: et, cum ceteris gentibus arma modo castraque nostra ostendamus, his domos villasque patefecimus non concupiscentibus. In Hermunduris Albis oritur, flumen inclitum et notum olim; nunc tantum auditur.

XLII. Juxta Hermunduros Narisci, ac deinde Marcomanni et Quadi agunt. Praecipua Marcomannorum gloria viresque, atque ipsa etiam sedes, pulsis olim Boiis, virtute parta. Nec Narisci Quadive degenerant. Eaque Germaniae velut frons est, quatenus Danubio peragitur. Marcomannis Quadisque usque ad nostram memoriam reges manserunt ex gente ipsorum, nobile Marobodui et Tudri genus: jam et externos patiuntur. Sed vis et potentia regibus ex auctoritate Romana: raro armis nostris, saepius pecunia juvantur, nec minus valent.

XLIII. Retro Marsigni, Gothini, Osi, Burii, terga Marcomannorum Quadorumque claudunt: e quibus Marsigni et Burii sermone cultuque Suevos referunt Gothinos Gallica, Osos Pannonica lingua coarguit non esse Germanos, et quod tributa patiuntur. Partem tributorum Sarmatae, partem Quadi, ut alienigenis, imponunt. Gothini, quo magis pudeat, et ferrum effodiunt. Omnesque hi populi pauca campestrium, ceterum saltus et vertices montium jugumque insederunt. Dirimit enim scinditque Sueviam continuum montium jugum, ultra quod plurimae gentes agunt: ex quibus latissime patet Lygiorum nomen in plures civitates diffusum. Valentissimas nominasse sufficiet, Arios, Helvecónas, Manimos, Elysios, Naharválos Apud Naharvalos antiquae religionis lucus ostenditur. Praesidet sacerdos muliebri ornatu: sed deos, interpretatione Romana, Castorem Pollucemque memorant: ea vis numini; nomen Alcis. Nulla simulacra, nullum peregrinae superstitionis vestigium: ut fratres tamen, ut juvenes, venerantur. Ceterum Arii super vires, quibus enumeratos paulo ante populos antecedunt, truces, insitae feritati arte ac tempore lenocinantur. Nigra scuta, tincta corpora: atras ad proelia noctes legunt: ipsaque formidine atque umbra feralis exercitus terrorem inferunt, nullo hostium sustinente novum ac velut infernum aspectum: nam primi in omnibus proeliis oculi vincuntur. Trans Lygios Gothónes regnantur, paulo jam adductius, quam ceterae Germanorum gentes, nondum tamen supra libertatem. Protinus deinde ab Oceano

Rugii et Lemovii · omniumque harum gentium insigne, rotunda scuta, breves gladii, et erga reges obsequium.

XLIV. Suionum hinc civitates, ipso in Oceano, praeter viros armaque classibus valent: forma navium eo differt, quod utrimque prora paratam semper appulsui frontem agit: nec velis ministrantur, nec remos in ordinem lateribus adjungunt. Solutum, ut in quibusdam fluminum, et mutabile, ut res poscit, hinc vel illinc remigium. Est apud illos et opibus honos; eoque unus imperitat, nullis jam exceptionibus, non precario jure parendi. Nec arma, ut apud ceteros Germanos, in promiscuo, sed clausa sub custode et quidem servo: quia subitos hostium incursus prohibet Oceanus, otiosa porro armatorum manus facile lasciviunt: enimvero neque nobilem neque ingenuum, ne libertinum quidem, armis praeponere regia utilitas est.

XLV. Trans Suionas aliud mare, pigrum ac prope immotum, quo cingi cludique terrarum orbem hinc fides, quod extremus cadentis jam solis fulgor in ortus edurat adeo clarus, ut sidera hebetet; sonum insuper audiri, formasque deorum et radios capitis aspici persuasio adjicit. Illuc usque, et fama vera, tantum natura. Ergo jam dextro Suevici maris littore Aestyorum gentes alluuntur: quibus ritus habitusque Suevorum; lingua Britannicae propior. Matrem deum venerantur: insigne superstitionis, formas aprorum gestant; id pro armis omnique tutela: securum deae cultorem etiam inter hostes praestat. Rarus ferri, frequens fustium usus. Frumenta ceterosque fructus patientius, quam pro solita Germanorum inertia, laborant. Sed et mare scrutantur, ac soli omnium succinum, quod ipsi glesum vocant, inter vada atque in ipso littore legunt. Nec, quae natura quaeve ratio gignat, ut barbaris, quaesitum compertumve. Diu quin etiam inter cetera ejectamenta maris jacebat, donec luxuria nostra dedit nomen: ipsis in nullo usu: rude legitur, informe perfertur, pretiumque mirantes accipiunt. Succum tamen arborum esse intelligas, quia terrena quaedam atque etiam volucria animalia plerumque interlucent, quae implicata humore, mox, durescente materia, cluduntur. Fecundiora igitur nemora lucosque, sicut Orientis secretis, ubi thura balsamaque sudantur, ita Occidentis insulis terrisque inesse, crediderim; quae vicini solis radiis expressa atque liquentia in proximum mare labuntur, ac vi tempestatum in adversa littora exundant. Si naturam succini admoto igne tentes, in modum taedae accenditur, alitque flammam pinguem et olentem: mox ut in picem resinamve lentescit. Suionibus Sitonum gentes continuantur. Cetera similes, uno differunt, quod femina dominatur: in tantum non modo a libertate, sed etiam a servitute degenerant.

XLVI. Hic Sueviae finis. Peucinorum Venedorumque et Fennorum nationes Germanis an Sarmatis ascribam, dubito: quanquam Peucini, quos quidam Bastarnas vocant, sermone, cultu, sede ac domiciliis, ut Germani, agunt. Sordes omnium ac torpor procerum: connubiis mixtis, nonnihil in Sarmatarum habitum foedantur Venedi multum ex moribus traxerunt. Nam quidquid inter Peucinos Fennosque silvarum ac montium erigitur, latrociniis pererrant. Hi tamen inter Germanos potius referuntur, quia et domos figunt et scuta gestant et pedum usu ac pernicitate gaudent; quae omnia diversa Sarmatis sunt, in plaustro equoque viventibus. Fennis mira feritas, foeda paupertas: non arma, non equi, non penates: victui herba, vestitui pelles, cubile humus: sola in sagittis spes, quas, inopia ferri, ossibus asperant. Idemque venatus viros pariter ac feminas alit. Passim enim comitantur, partemque praedae petunt. Nec aliud infantibus ferarum imbriumque suffugium, quam ut in aliquo ramorum nexu contegantur: huc redeunt juvenes, hoc senum receptaculum. Sed beatius arbitrantur, quam ingemere agris, illaborare domibus, suas alienasque fortunas spe metuque versare. Securi adversus homines, securi adversus deos, rem difficillimam assecuti sunt, ut illis ne voto quidem opus esset. Cetera jam fabulosa: Hellusios et Oxionas ora hominum vultusque, corpora atque artus ferarum, gerere: quod ego, ut incompertum, in medium relinquam.

CN. JULII AGRICOLAE
VITA.

BREVIARIUM.

Cap. 1. Scribendi clarorum virorum vitam mos antiquus, 2. sub malis principibus periculosus, 3. sub Trajano in honorem Agricolae repetitus a Tacito, qui non eloquentiam, at pietatem pollicetur. 4. Agricolae stirps, educatio, studia. 5. Positis in Britannia primis castrorum rudimentis, 6. uxorem ducit: fit quaestor, tribunus, praetor: recognoscendis templorum donis praefectus. 7. Othoniano bello matrem partemque patrimonii amittit. 8. In Vespasiani partes transgressus, legioni vicesimae in Britannia praepositus, alienae famae cura promovet suam. 9. Redux inter patricios ascitus Aquitaniam regit. Consul factus Tacito filiam despondet. Britanniae praeficitur.

10. Britanniae descriptio. Thule cognita: mare pigrum. 11. Britannorum origo, habitus, sacra, sermo, mores, 12. militia, regimen, rarus conventus: coelum, solum, metalla, margarita. 13. Victae gentis ingenium. Caesarum in Britanniam expeditiones. 14. Consularium legatorum res gestae. 15. Britanniae rebellio, 16. Boadicea duce coepta, a Suet. Paullino compressa. Huic succedunt ignavi. 17. Rem restituunt Petilius Cerialis et Julius Frontinus; hic Silures, ille Brigantes vincit; 18. Agricola Ordovices et Monam. Totam provinciam pacat, et 19, 20. moderatione, prudentia, abstinentia, aequitate in obsequio retinet, 21. animosque artibus et voluptatibus mollit.

22, 23. Nova expeditio novas gentes aperit, quae praesidio firmantur. Agricolae candor in communicanda gloria. 24. Consilium de occupanda Hibernia. 25—27. Civitates trans Bodotriam sitae explorantur. Caledonii, Romanos aggressi, consilio ductuque Agricolae pulsi, sacrificiis conspirationem civitatum sanciunt. 28. Usipiorum cohors miro casu Britanniam circumvecta. Agricolae filius obit. 29. Bellum Britanni reparant Calgaco duce, cujus 30—32. oratio ad suos. 33, 34. Romanos quoque hortatur Agricola. 35—37. Atrox et cruentum proelium. 38. Penes Romanos victoria. Agricola Britanniam circumvehi praecipit.

39. Domitianus, fronte laetus, pectore anxius, nuntium victoriae excipit. 40. Honores tamen Agricolae decerni jubet, condito odio, donec provincia decedat Agricola. Is redux modeste agit. 41. Periculum ab accusatoribus et laudatoribus. 42. Excusat se, ne provinciam sortiatur proconsul. 43. Obit non sine veneni suspicione, a Domitiano dati. 44. Ejus aetas, habitus, honores, opes. 45. Mortis opportunitas ante Domitiani atrocitates. 46. Questus auctoris et ex virtute solatia. Fama Agricolae ad posteros transmissa.

I. Clarorum virorum facta moresque posteris tradere, antiquitus usitatum, ne nostris quidem temporibus, quanquam incuriosa suorum aetas omisit, quotiens magna aliqua ac nobilis virtus vicit ac supergressa est vitium parvis magnisque civitatibus commune, ignorantiam recti et invidiam. Sed apud priores, ut agere digna memoratu pronum magisque in aperto erat, ita celeberrimus quisque ingenio ad prodendam virtutis memoriam, sine gratia aut ambitione, bonae tantum conscientiae pretio ducebatur. Ac plerique suam ipsi vitam narrare fiduciam potius morum, quam arrogantiam arbitrati sunt: nec id Rutilio et Scauro citra fidem aut obtrectationi fuit: adeo virtutes iisdem temporibus optime aestimantur, quibus facillime gignuntur. At nunc narraturo mihi vitam defuncti hominis, venia opus fuit: quam non petissem incursaturus tam saeva et infesta virtutibus tempora.

II. Legimus, cum Aruleno Rustico Paetus Thrasea, Herennio Senecioni Priscus Helvidius laudati essent, capitale fuisse: neque in ipsos modo auctores, sed in libros quoque eorum saevitum, delegato triumviris ministerio, ut monumenta clarissimorum ingeniorum in comitio ac foro urerentur. Scilicet illo igne vocem populi Romani et libertatem senatus et conscientiam generis humani aboleri arbitrabantur, expulsis insuper sapientiae professoribus atque omni bona arte in exilium acta, ne quid usquam honestum occurreret. Dedimus profecto grande patientiae documentum: et sicut vetus aetas vidit, quid ultimum in libertate esset, ita nos, quid in servitute, adempto per inquisitiones et loquendi audiendique commercio. Memoriam quoque ipsam cum voce perdidissemus, si tam in nostra potestate esset oblivisci, quam tacere.

III. Nunc demum redit animus: et quanquam primo statim beatissimi saeculi ortu Nerva Caesar res olim dissociabiles miscuerit, principatum ac libertatem, augeatque quotidie felicitatem imperii Nerva Trajanus, nec spem modo ac votum securitas publica, sed ipsius voti fiduciam ac robur assumpserit; natura tamen infirmitatis humanae tardiora sunt remedia, quam mala; et, ut corpora nostra lente augescunt, cito exstinguuntur, sic ingenia studiaque oppresseris facilius, quam revocaveris. Subit quippe etiam ipsius inertiae dulcedo: et invisa primo desidia postremo amatur. Quid, si per quindecim annos, grande mortalis aevi spatium, multi fortuitis casibus, promptissimus quisque saevitia principis interciderunt? Pauci, et, ut ita dixerim, non modo aliorum, sed etiam nostri superstites sumus, exemptis e media vita tot annis, quibus juvenes ad senectutem, senes prope ad ipsos exactae aetatis terminos per silentium venimus. Non tamen pigebit vel incondita ac rudi voce memoriam prioris servitutis ac testimonium praesentium bonorum composuisse. Hic interim liber honori Agricolae soceri mei destinatus, professione pietatis aut laudatus erit aut excusatus.

IV. Cnaeus Julius Agricola, veteri et illustri Forojuliensium colonia ortus, utrumque avum procuratorem Caesarum habuit: quae equestris nobilitas est. Pater Julius Graecinus, senatorii ordinis, studio eloquentiae sapientiaeque notus, iisque ipsis virtutibus iram Caii Caesaris meritus : namque M. Silanum accusare jussus et, quia abnuerat, interfectus est. Mater Julia Procilla fuit, rarae castitatis : in hujus sinu indulgentiaque educatus, per omnem honestarum artium cultum pueritiam adolescentiamque transegit. Arcebat eum ab illecebris peccantium, praeter ipsius bonam integramque naturam, quod statim parvulus sedem ac magistram studiorum Massiliam habuit, locum Graeca comitate et provinciali parsimonia mistum ac bene compositum. Memoria teneo solitum ipsum narrare, se in prima juventa studium philosophiae acrius, ultra quam concessum Romano ac senatori, hausisse, ni prudentia matris incensum ac flagrantem animum coercuisset. Scilicet sublime et erectum ingenium pulchritudinem ac speciem excelsae magnaeque gloriae vehementius, quam caute, appetebat : mox mitigavit ratio et aetas: retinuitque, quod est difficillimum, ex sapientia modum.

V. Prima castrorum rudimenta in Britannia Suetonio Paullino, diligenti ac moderato duci, approbavit, electus, quem contubernio aestimaret. Nec Agricola licenter more juvenum, qui militiam in lasciviam vertunt, neque segniter ad voluptates et commeatus titulum tribunatus et inscitiam retulit: sed noscere provinciam, nosci exercitui, discere a peritis, sequi optimos, nihil appetere jactatione, nihil ob formidinem recusare, simulque et anxius et intentus agere. Non sane alias exercitatior magisque in ambiguo Britannia fuit: trucidati veterani, incensae coloniae, intercepti exercitus; tum de salute, mox de victoria, certavere. Quae cuncta, etsi consiliis ductuque alterius agebantur ac summa rerum et recuperatae provinciae gloria in ducem cessit, artem et usum et stimulos addidere juveni; intravitque animum militaris gloriae cupido ingrata temporibus, quibus sinistra erga eminentes interpretatio, nec minus periculum ex magna fama, quam ex mala.

VI. Hinc ad capessendos magistratus in urbem digressus, Domitiam Decidianam, splendidis natalibus ortam, sibi junxit; idque matrimonium ad majora nitenti decus ac robur fuit; vixeruntque mira concordia, per mutuam caritatem et invicem se anteponendo: nisi quod in bona uxore tanto major laus, quanto in mala plus culpae est. Sors quaesturae provinciam Asiam, proconsulem Salvium Titianum dedit: quorum neutro corruptus est; quanquam et provincia dives ac parata peccantibus, et proconsul in omnem aviditatem pronus, quantalibet facilitate redempturus esset mutuam dissimulationem mali. Auctus est ibi filia, in subsidium simul et solatium: nam filium ante sublatum brevi amisit. Mox inter quaesturam ac tribunatum plebis atque etiam ipsum tribunatus annum quiete et otio transiit, gnarus sub

Nerone temporum, quibus inertia pro sapientia fuit Idem praeturae tenor et silentium ; nec enim jurisdictio obvenerat: ludos et inania honoris medio rationis atque abundantiae duxit, uti longe a luxuria, ita famae propior. Tum electus a Galba ad dona templorum recognoscenda, diligentissima conquisitione fecit, ne cujus alterius sacrilegium respublica, quam Neronis sensisset.

VII. Sequens annus gravi vulnere animum domumque ejus afflixit: nam classis Othoniana, licenter vaga, dum Intemelios (Liguriae pars est) hostiliter populatur, matrem Agricolae in praediis suis interfecit: praediaque ipsa et magnam patrimonii partem diripuit, quae causa caedis fuerat. Igitur ad solemnia pietatis profectus Agricola, nuntio affectati a Vespasiano imperii deprehensus ac statim in partes transgressus est. Initia principatus ac statum urbis Mucianus regebat, juvene admodum Domitiano et ex paterna fortuna tantum licentiam usurpante. Is missum ad delectus agendos Agricolam integreque ac strenue versatum, vicesimae legioni, tarde ad sacramentum transgressae, praeposuit, ubi decessor seditiose agere narrabatur: quippe legatis quoque consularibus nimia ac formidolosa erat. Nec legatus praetorius ad cohibendum potens, incertum, suo an militum ingenio: ita successor simul et ultor electus, rarissima moderatione maluit videri invenisse bonos, quam fecisse.

VIII. Praeerat tunc Britanniae Vettius Bolanus placidius, quam feroci provincia dignum est: temperavit Agricola vim suam ardoremque compescuit, ne incresceret; peritus obsequi eruditusque utilia honestis miscere. Brevi deinde Britannia consularem Petilium Cerialem accepit. Habuerunt virtutes spatium exemplorum. Sed primo Cerialis labores modo et discrimina, mox et gloriam communicabat: saepe parti exercitus in experimentum, aliquando majoribus copiis ex eventu praefecit: nec Agricola unquam in suam famam gestis exsultavit; ad auctorem et ducem, ut minister, fortunam referebat: ita virtute in obsequendo, verecundia in praedicando, extra invidiam, nec extra gloriam erat.

IX. Revertentem ab legatione legionis divus Vespasianus inter patricios ascivit, ac deinde provinciae Aquitaniae praeposuit, splendidae in primis dignitatis administratione ac spe consulatus, cui destinarat. Credunt plerique militaribus ingeniis subtilitatem deesse, quia castrensis jurisdictio secura et obtusior ac plura manu agens calliditatem fori non exerceat. Agricola naturali prudentia, quamvis inter togatos, facile justeque agebat. Jam vero tempora curarum remissionumque divisa: ubi conventus ac judicia poscerent, gravis, intentus, severus, et saepius misericors; ubi officio satisfactum, nulla ultra potestatis persona: tristitiam et arrogantiam et avaritiam exuerat: nec illi, quod est rarissimum, aut facilitas auctoritatem aut severitas amorem deminuit. Integritatem atque abstinentiam in tanto viro referre, injuria virtutum fuerit. Ne famam quidem, cui etiam saepe boni indulgent, ostentanda virtute, aut per artem quaesivit: procul ab aemulatione adversus collegas, procul a contentione adversus procuratores, et vincere inglorium, et atteri sordidum arbitrabatur. Minus triennium in ea legatione detentus ac statim ad spem consulatus revocatus est, comitante opinione Britanniam ei provinciam dari nullis in hoc suis sermonibus sed quia par videbatur. Haud semper errat fama aliquando et elegit. Consul egregiae tum spei filiam juveni mihi despondit ac post Consulatum collocavit, et statim Britanniae praepositus est, adjecto pontificatus sacerdotio.

X. Britanniae situm populosque, multis scriptoribus memoratos non in comparationem curae ingeniive referam; sed quia tum primum perdomita est. Ita quae priores nondum comperta eloquentia percoluere, rerum fide tradentur. Britannia, insularum quas Romana notitia complectitur, maxima, spatio ac coelo in orientem Germaniae, in occidentem Hispaniae obtenditur: Gallis in meridiem etiam inspicitur: septemtrionalia ejus, nullis contra terris, vasto atque aperto mari pulsantur. Formam totius Britanniae Livius veterum, Fabius Rusticus recentium eloquentissimi auctores, oblongae scutulae vel bipenni assimulavere: et est ea facies citra Caledoniam, unde et in universum fama est transgressa: sed immensum et enorme spatium procurrentium extremo jam littore terrarum, velut in cuneum tenuatur. Hanc oram novissimi maris tunc primum Romana classis circumvecta insulam esse Britanniam affirmavit, ac simul incognitas ad id tempus insulas, quas Orcadas vocant, invenit domuitque. Dispecta est et Thule, nam hactenus jussum, et hiems appetebat; sed mare pigrum et grave remigantibus; perhibent ne ventis quidem perinde attolli: credo, quod rariores terrae montesque, causa ac materia tempestatum, et profunda moles continui maris tardius impellitur. Naturam Oceani atque aestus neque quaerere hujus operis est, ac multi retulere; unum addiderim: nusquam latius dominari mare, multum fluminum huc atque illuc ferre, nec littore tenus accrescere aut resorberi, sed influere penitus atque ambire, et jugis etiam atque montibus inseri velut in suo.

XI. Ceterum Britanniam qui mortales initio coluerint, indigenae an advecti, ut inter barbaros, parum compertum. Habitus corporum varii: atque ex eo argumenta; namque rutilae Caledoniam habitantium comae, magni artus, Germanicam originem asseverant. Silurum colorati vultus et torti plerumque crines et posita contra Hispania Iberos veteres trajecisse easque sedes occupasse fidem faciunt. Proximi Gallis et similes sunt; seu durante originis vi, seu, procurrentibus in diversa terris, positio coeli corporibus habitum dedit: in universum tamen aestimanti, Gallos vicinam insulam occupasse credibile est. Eorum sacra deprehendas superstitionum persuasione: sermo haud multum diversus; in deposcendis periculis eadem audacia et, ubi advenere, in detrectandis eadem formido. Plus tamen ferociae Britanni praeferunt, ut quos nondum longa pax emollierit: nam Gallos quoque in bellis floruisse accepimus: mox segnitia cum otio intravit, amissa virtute pariter ac libertate; quod Britannorum olim victis evenit: ceteri manent, quales Galli fuerunt.

XII. In pedite robur: quaedam nationes et curru proeliantur: honestior auriga, clientes propugnant. Olim regibus parebant, nunc per principes factionibus et studiis trahuntur: nec aliud adversus validissimas gentes pro nobis utilius, quam quod in commune non consulunt. Rarus duabus tribusve civitatibus ad propulsandum commune periculum conventus: ita, dum singuli pugnant, universi vincuntur. Coelum crebris imbribus ac nebulis foedum: asperitas frigorum abest. Dierum spatia ultra nostri orbis mensuram, et nox clara et extrema Britanniae parte brevis, ut finem atque initium lucis exiguo discrimine internoscas. Quod si nubes non officiant, aspici per noctem solis fulgorem, nec occidere et exsurgere, sed transire affirmant. Scilicet extrema et plana terrarum, humili umbra, non erigunt tenebras, infraque coelum et sidera nox cadit. Solum, praeter oleam vitemque et cetera calidioribus terris oriri sueta, patiens frugum, fecundum Tarde mitescunt, cito proveniunt: eadem utriusque rei causa, multus humor terrarum coelique Fert Britannia aurum et argentum et alia metalla, pretium victoriae: gignit et Oceanus margarita, sed subfusca ac liventia. Quidam artem abesse legentibus arbitrantur: nam in Rubro mari viva ac spirantia saxis avelli, in Britannia, prout expulsa sint, colligi: ego facilius crediderim naturam margaritis deesse, quam nobis avaritiam.

XIII. Ipsi Britanni delectum ac tributa et injuncta imperii munera impigre obeunt, si injuriae absint: has aegre tolerant, jam domiti ut pareant, nondum ut serviant. Igitur primus omnium Romanorum divus Julius cum exercitu Britanniam ingressus, quanquam prospera pugna terruerit incolas ac littore potitus sit, potest videri ostendisse posteris, non tradidisse. Mox bella civilia et in rempublicam versa principum arma, ac longa oblivio Britanniae etiam in pace. Consilium id divus Augustus vocabat, Tiberius praeceptum. Agitasse C. Caesarem de intranda Britannia satis constat, ni velox ingenio, mobilis poenitentiae, et ingentes adversus Germaniam conatus frustra fuissent. Divus Claudius auctor operis, transvectis legionibus auxiliisque et assumpto in partem rerum Vespasiano:

quod initium venturae mox fortunae fuit: domitae gentes, capti reges, et monstratus fatis Vespasianus.

XIV. Consularium primus Aulus Plautius praepositus, ac subinde Ostorius Scapula, uterque bello egregius: redactaque paulatim in formam provinciae proxima pars Britanniae: addita insuper veteranorum colonia: quaedam civitates Cogiduno regi donatae (is ad nostram usque memoriam fidissimus mansit) ut vetere ac jam pridem recepta populi Romani consuetudine, haberet instrumenta servitutis et reges. Mox Didius Gallus parta a prioribus continuit, paucis admodum castellis in ulteriora promotis, per quae fama aucti officii quaereretur. Didium Veranius excepit, isque intra annum exstinctus est. Suetonius hinc Paullinus biennio prosperas res habuit, subactis nationibus firmatisque praesidiis: quorum fiducia Monam insulam, ut vires rebellibus ministrantem, aggressus, terga occasioni patefecit.

XV. Namque absentia legati remoto metu, Britanni agitare inter se mala servitutis, conferre injurias et interpretando accendere: nihil profici patientia, nisi ut graviora, tanquam ex facili tolerantibus, imperentur: singulos sibi olim reges fuisse, nunc binos imponi: e quibus legatus in sanguinem, procurator in bona saeviret. Aeque discordiam praepositorum, aeque concordiam, subjectis exitiosam: alterius manus centuriones, alterius servos vim et contumelias miscere. Nihil jam cupiditati, nihil libidini exceptum: in proelio fortiorem esse, qui spoliet; nunc ab ignavis plerumque et imbellibus eripi domos, abstrahi liberos, injungi delectus, tanquam mori tantum pro patria nescientibus: quantulum enim transisse militum, si sese Britanni numerent? sic Germanias excussisse jugum: et flumine, non Oceano, defendi: sibi patriam, conjuges, parentes, illis avaritiam et luxuriam causas belli esse. Recessuros, ut divus Julius recessisset, modo virtutes majorum suorum aemularentur. Neve proelii unius aut alterius eventu pavescerent: plus impetus, majorem constantiam, penes miseros esse. Jam Britannorum etiam deos misereri, qui Romanum ducem absentem, qui relegatum in alia insula exercitum detinerent: jam ipsos, quod difficillimum fuerit, deliberare: porro in ejusmodi consiliis periculosius esse deprehendi, quam audere.

XVI. His atque talibus invicem instincti, Boudicea, generis regii femina, duce (neque enim sexum in imperiis discernunt) sumpsere universi bellum: ac sparsos per castella milites consectati, expugnatis praesidiis, ipsam coloniam invasere, ut sedem servitutis: nec ullum in barbaris saevitiae genus omisit ira et victoria. Quod nisi Paullinus, cognito provinciae motu, propere subvenisset, amissa Britannia foret: quam unius proelii fortuna veteri patientiae restituit, tenentibus arma plerisque, quos conscientia defectionis et propius ex legato timor agitabat, ne, quanquam egregius cetera, arroganter in deditos et, ut suae quoque injuriae ultor, durius consuleret. Missus igitur Petronius Turpilianus, tanquam exorabilior: et delictis hostium novus, eoque poenitentiae mitior, compositis prioribus, nihil ultra ausus, Trebellio Maximo provinciam tradidit. Trebellius segnior, et nullis castrorum experimentis, comitate quadam curandi provinciam tenuit. Didicere jam barbari quoque ignoscere vitiis blandientibus: et interventus civilium armorum praebuit justam segnitiae excusationem: sed discordia laboratum, cum assuetus expeditionibus miles otio lasciviret. Trebellius fuga ac latebris vitata exercitus ira, indecorus atque humilis, precario mox praefuit: ac velut pacti, exercitus licentiam, dux salutem; et seditio sine sanguine stetit. Nec Vettius Bolanus, manentibus adhuc civilibus bellis, agitavit Britanniam disciplina: eadem inertia erga hostes, similis petulantia castrorum: nisi quod innocens Bolanus et nullis delictis invisus, caritatem paraverat loco auctoritatis.

XVII. Sed, ubi cum cetero orbe Vespasianus et Britanniam recuperavit, magni duces, egregii exercitus, minuta hostium spes. Et terrorem statim intulit Petilius Cerialis, Brigantum civitatem, quae numerosissima provinciae totius perhibetur, aggressus. Multa proelia, et aliquando non incruenta · magnamque Brigantum partem aut victoria amplexus est aut bello. Et, cum Cerialis quidem alterius successoris curam famamque obruisset, sustinuit quoque molem Julius Frontinus, vir magnus quantum licebat, validamque et pugnacem Silurum gentem armis subegit, super virtutem hostium, locorum quoque difficultates eluctatus.

XVIII. Hunc Britanniae statum, has bellorum vices media jam aestate transgressus Agricola invenit, cum et milites, velut omissa expeditione, ad securitatem, et hostes ad occasionem verterentur. Ordovicum civitas, haud multo ante adventum ejus, alam, in finibus suis agentem, prope universam obtriverat. eoque initio erecta provincia: et, quibus bellum volentibus erat, probare exemplum, ac recentis legati animum opperiri, cum Agricola, quanquam transvecta aestas, sparsi per provinciam numeri, praesumpta apud militem illius anni quies. tarda et contraria bellum inchoaturo, et plerisque custodiri suspecta potius videbatur, ire obviam discrimini statuit: contractisque legionum vexillis et modica auxiliorum manu, quia in aequum degredi Ordovices non audebant, ipse ante agmen, quo ceteris par animus simili periculo esset, erexit aciem: caesaque prope universa gente, non ignarus instandum famae, ac, prout prima cessissent, terrorem ceteris fore, Monam insulam, cujus possessione revocatum Paullinum rebellione totius Britanniae supra memoravi, redigere in potestatem animo intendit. Sed, ut in dubiis consiliis, naves deerant: ratio et constantia ducis transvexit. Depositis omnibus sarcinis, lectissimos auxiliarium, quibus nota vada et patrius nandi usus, quo simul seque et arma et equos regunt, ita repente immisit, ut obstupefacti hostes, qui classem, qui naves, qui mare expectabant, nihil arduum aut invictum crediderint sic ad bellum venientibus. Ita petita pace ac dedita insula, clarus ac magnus haberi Agricola: quippe cui ingredienti provinciam, quod tempus alii per ostentationem aut officiorum ambitum transigunt, labor et periculum placuisset. Nec Agricola, prosperitate rerum in vanitatem usus, expeditionem aut victoriam vocabat victos continuisse: ne laureatis quidem gesta prosecutus est: sed ipsa dissimulatione famae famam auxit, aestimantibus, quanta futuri spe tam magna tacuisset.

XIX. Ceterum animorum provinciae prudens, simulque doctus per aliena experimenta parum profici armis, si injuriae sequerentur, causas bellorum statuit excidere. A se suisque orsus, primum domum suam coercuit; quod plerisque haud minus arduum est, quam provinciam regere. Nihil per libertos servosque publicae rei: non studiis privatis nec ex commendatione aut precibus centurionum milites ascire, sed optimum quemque fidissimum putare: omnia scire, non omnia exsequi: parvis peccatis veniam, magnis severitatem commodare: nec poena semper, sed saepius poenitentia contentus esse: officiis et administrationibus potius non peccaturos praeponere, quam damnare, cum peccassent. Frumenti et tributorum auctionem aequalitate munerum mollire, circumcisis, quae, in quaestum reperta, ipso tributo gravius tolerabantur: namque per ludibrium assidere clausis horreis et emere ultro frumenta, ac vendere pretio cogebantur: devortia itinerum et longinquitas regionum indicebatur, ut civitates a proximis hibernis in remota et avia referrent, donec, quod omnibus in promptu erat, paucis lucrosum fieret.

XX. Haec primo statim anno comprimendo, egregiam famam paci circumdedit; quae vel incuria vel intolerantia priorum haud minus quam bellum timebatur. Sed, ubi aestas advenit, contracto exercitu, multus in agmine laudare modestiam, disjectos coercere: loca castris ipse capere, aestuaria ac silvas ipse praetentare; et nihil interim apud hostes quietum pati, quo minus subitis excursibus popularetur: atque, ubi satis terruerat, parcendo rursus irritamenta pacis ostentare. Quibus rebus multae civitates, quae in illum diem ex aequo egerant, datis obsidibus, iram posuere, et praesidiis castellisque circumdatae tanta ratione curaque, ut nulla ante Britanniae nova pars illacessita transierit.

XXI. Sequens hiems saluberrimis consiliis absumpta: namque, ut homines dispersi ac rudes, eoque in bella faciles, quieti et otio per voluptates assuescerent, hortari privatim, adjuvare publice, ut templa, fora, domus exstruerent, laudando promptos et castigando segnes: ita honoris aemulatio pro necessitate erat. Jam vero principum filios liberalibus artibus erudire, et ingenia Britannorum studiis Gallorum anteferre, ut, qui modo linguam Romanam abnuebant, eloquentiam concupiscerent. Inde etiam habitus nostri honor et frequens toga: paulatimque discessum ad delenimenta vitiorum, porticus et balnea et conviviorum elegantiam: idque apud imperitos humanitas vocabatur, cum pars servitutis esset.

XXII. Tertius expeditionum annus novas gentes aperuit, vastatis usque ad Taum (aestuario nomen est) nationibus: qua formidine territi hostes quanquam conflictatum saevis tempestatibus exercitum lacessere non ausi; ponendisque insuper castellis spatium fuit. Annotabant periti non alium ducem opportunitates locorum sapientius legisse: nullum ab Agricola positum castellum aut vi hostium expugnatum aut pactione ac fuga desertum. Crebrae eruptiones: nam adversus moras obsidionis annuis copiis firmabantur: ita intrepida ibi hiems, et sibi quisque praesidio, irritis hostibus eoque desperantibus, quia soliti plerumque damna aestatis hibernis eventibus pensare, tum aestate atque hieme juxta pellebantur. Nec Agricola unquam per alios gesta avidus intercepit: seu centurio seu praefectus, incorruptum facti testem habebat. Apud quosdam acerbior in conviciis narrabatur; ut erat comis bonis, adversus malos injucundus: ceterum ex iracundia nihil supererat; secretum et silentium ejus non timeres: honestius putabat offendere, quam odisse.

XXIII. Quarta aestas obtinendis, quae percurrerat,

insumpta: ac, si virtus exercituum et Romani nominis gloria pateretur, inventus in ipsa Britannia terminus. Nam Clota et Bodotria, diversi maris aestibus per immensum revectae, angusto terrarum spatio dirimuntur: quod tum praesidiis firmabatur: atque omnis propior sinus tenebatur, summotis velut in aliam insulam hostibus.

XXIV. Quinto expeditionum anno, nave prima transgressus, ignotas ad id tempus gentes crebris simul ac prosperis proeliis domuit: eamque partem Britanniae, quae Hiberniam aspicit, copiis instruxit in spem magis quam ob formidinem; si quidem Hibernia, medio inter Britanniam atque Hispaniam sita et Gallico quoque mari opportuna, valentissimam imperii partem magnis invicem usibus miscuerit. Spatium ejus, si Britanniae comparetur, angustius, nostri maris insulas superat. Solum coelumque et ingenia cultusque hominum haud multum a Britannia differunt: in melius aditus portusque per commercia et negotiatores cogniti. Agricola expulsum seditione domestica unum ex regulis gentis exceperat ac specie amicitiae in occasionem retinebat. Saepe ex eo audivi, legione una et modicis auxiliis debellari obtinerique Hiberniam posse. Idque etiam adversus Britanniam profuturum, si Romana ubique arma, et velut e conspectu libertas tolleretur.

XXV. Ceterum aestate, qua sextum officii annum inchoabat, amplexus civitates trans Bodotriam sitas, quia motus universarum ultra gentium et infesta hostilis exercitus itinera timebantur, portus classe exploravit: quae, ab Agricola primum assumpta in partem virium, sequebatur egregia specie, cum simul terra, simul mari bellum impelleretur, ac saepe iisdem castris pedes equesque et nauticus miles, mixti copiis et laetitia, sua quisque facta, suos casus attollerent: ac modo silvarum ac montium profunda, modo tempestatum ac fluctuum adversa, hinc terra et hostis, hinc victus Oceanus militari jactantia compararentur. Britannos quoque, ut ex captivis audiebatur, visa classis obstupefaciebat, tanquam, aperto maris sui secreto, ultimum victis perfugium clauderetur. Ad manus et arma conversi Caledoniam incolentes populi, paratu magno, majore fama, uti mos est de ignotis, oppugnasse ultro, castella adorti, metum, ut provocantes, addiderant: regrediendumque citra Bodotriam, et excedendum potius, quam pellerentur, specie prudentium ignavi admonebant: cum interim cognoscit hostes pluribus agminibus irrupturos. Ac, ne superante numero et peritia locorum circumiretur, diviso et ipse in tres partes exercitu incessit.

XXVI. Quod ubi cognitum hosti, mutato repente consilio, universi nonam legionem, ut maxime invalidam, nocte aggressi, inter somnum ac trepidationem caesis vigilibus, irrupere. Jamque in ipsis castris pugnabant, cum Agricola, iter hostium ab exploratoribus edoctus et vestigiis insecutus, velocissimos equitum peditumque assultare tergis pugnantium jubet, mox ab universis adjici clamorem; et propinqua luce fulsere signa: ita ancipiti malo territi Britanni: et Romanis redit animus, ac, securi pro salute, de gloria certabant. Ultro quin etiam erupere: et fuit atrox in ipsis portarum angustiis proelium, donec pulsi hostes; utroque exercitu certante, his, ut tulisse opem illis, ne eguisse auxilio viderentur. Quod nisi paludes et silvae fugientes texissent, debellatum illa victoria foret.

XXVII. Cujus conscientia ac fama ferox exerc tus, nihil virtuti suae invium: penetrandam Caledoniam, inveniendumque tandem Britanniae terminum continuo proeliorum cursu, fremebant: atque illi modo cauti ac sapientes, prompti post eventum ac magniloqui erant. Iniquissima haec bellorum conditio est: prospera omnes sibi vindicant, adversa uni imputantur. At Britanni non virtute, sed occasione et arte ducis rati, nihil ex arrogantia remittere, quo minus juventutem armarent, conjuges ac liberos in loca tuta transferrent, coetibus ac sacrificiis conspirationem civitatum sancirent: atque ita irritatis utrimque animis discessum.

XXVIII. Eadem aestate cohors Usipiorum, per Germanias conscripta, in Britanniam transmissa magnum ac memorabile facinus ausa est. Occiso centurione ac militibus, qui ad tradendam disciplinam immixti manipulis exemplum et rectores habebantur, tres liburnicas, adactis per vim gubernatoribus, ascendere: et uno remigante, suspectis duobus eoque interfectis, nondum vulgato rumore ut miraculum praevehebantur: mox hac atque illa rapti, et cum plerisque Britannorum, sua defensantium, proelio congressi, ac saepe victores, aliquando pulsi, eo ad extremum inopiae venere, ut infirmissimos suorum, mox sorte ductos, vescerentur. Atque circumvecti Britanniam, amissis per inscitiam regendi navibus, pro praedonibus habiti, primum a Suevis, mox a Frisiis intercepti sunt: ac fuere, quos per commercia venumdatos et in nostram usque ripam mutatione ementium adductos, indicium tanti casus illustravit.

XXIX. Initio aestatis Agricola, domestico vulnere ctus, anno ante natum filium amisit. Quem casum neque, ut plerique fortium virorum, ambitiose, neque per lamenta rursus ac moerorem muliebriter tulit: et in luctu bellum inter remedia erat. Igitur praemissa classe, quae pluribus locis praedata, magnum et incertum terrorem faceret, expedito exercitu, cui ex Britannis fortissimos et longa pace exploratos addiderat, ad montem Grampium pervenit, quem jam hostis insederat. Nam Britanni, nihil fracti pugnae prioris eventu, et ultionem aut servitium exspectantes, tandemque docti commune periculum concordia propulsandum, legationibus et foederibus omnium civitatum vires exciverant. Jamque super triginta millia armatorum aspiciebantur, et adhuc affluebat omnis juventus et quibus cruda ac viridis senectus, clari bello et sua quisque decora gestantes: cum inter plures duces virtute et genere praestans, nomine Calgacus, apud contractam multitudinem proelium poscentem, in hunc modum locutus fertur:

XXX. "Quotiens causas belli et necessitatem nostram intueor, magnus mihi animus est hodiernum diem consensumque vestrum initium libertatis totius Britanniae fore. Nam et universi servitutis expertes, et nullae ultra terrae, ac ne mare quidem securum, imminente nobis classe Romana: ita proelium atque arma, quae fortibus honesta, eadem etiam ignavis tutissima sunt. Priores pugnae, quibus adversus Romanos varia fortuna certatum est, spem ac subsidium in nostris manibus habebant: quia nobilissimi totius Britanniae eoque in ipsis penetralibus siti, nec servientium littora aspicientes, oculos quoque a contactu dominationis inviolatos habebamus. Nos terrarum ac libertatis extremos, recessus ipse ac sinus famae in hunc diem defendit: nunc terminus Britanniae patet; atque omne ignotum pro magnifico est. Sed nulla jam ultra gens, nihil nisi fluctus et saxa, et infestiores Romani: quorum superbiam frustra per obsequium et modestiam effugeris. Raptores orbis, postquam cuncta vastantibus defuere terrae, et mare scrutantur: si locuples hostis est, avari; si pauper, ambitiosi: quos non Oriens, non Occidens, satiaverit. Soli omnium opes atque inopiam pari affectu concupiscunt. Auferre, trucidare, rapere, falsis nominibus imperium; atque, ubi solitudinem faciunt, pacem appellant."

XXXI. "Liberos cuique ac propinquos suos natura carissimos esse voluit; hi per delectus, alibi servituri, auferuntur: conjuges sororesque, etsi hostilem libidinem effugiant, nomine amicorum atque hospitum polluuntur. Bona fortunasque in tributum egerunt, annos in frumentum: corpora ipsa ac manus silvis ac paludibus emuniendis inter verbera ac contumelias conterunt. Nata servituti mancipia semel veneunt, atque ultro a dominis aluntur: Britannia servitutem suam quotidie emit, quotidie pascit. Ac, sicut in familia recentissimus quisque servorum et conservis ludibrio est, sic in hoc orbis terrarum vetere famulatu novi nos et viles in excidium petimur. Neque enim arva nobis aut metalla aut portus sunt, quibus exercendis reservemur. Virtus porro ac ferocia subjectorum ingrata imperantibus: et longinquitas ac secretum ipsum quo tutius, eo suspectius. Ita, sublata spe veniae, tandem sumite animum, tam quibus salus, quam quibus gloria carissima est. Trinobantes, femina duce, exurere coloniam, expugnare castra, ac, nisi felicitas in socordiam vertisset, exuere jugum potuere: nos integri et indomiti et libertatem non in poenitentiam laturi, primo statim congressu nonne ostendamus, quos sibi Caledonia viros seposuerit? An eandem Romanis in bello virtutem, quam in pace lasciviam adesse creditis?"

XXXII. "Nostris illi dissensionibus ac discordiis clari, vitia hostium in gloriam exercitus sui vertunt: quem contractum ex diversissimis gentibus, ut secundae res tenent, ita adversae dissolvent: nisi si Gallos et Germanos et (pudet dictu) Britannorum plerosque, licet dominationi alienae sanguinem commodent, diutius tamen hostes quam servos, fide et affectu teneri putatis: metus et terror est, infirma vincula caritatis. quae ubi removeris, qui timere desierint, odisse incipient. Omnia victoriae incitamenta pro nobis sunt: nullae Romanos conjuges accendunt; nulli parentes fugam exprobraturi sunt; aut nulla plerisque patria, aut alia est. Paucos numero, trepidos ignorantia, coelum ipsum ac mare et silvas, ignota omnia circumspectantes, clausos quodammodo ac vinctos dii nobis tradiderunt. Ne terreat vanus aspectus et auri fulgor atque argenti, quod neque tegit neque vulnerat. In ipsa hostium acie inveniemus nostras manus: agnoscent Britanni suam causam: recordabuntur Galli priorem libertatem: deserent illos ceteri Germani, tanquam nuper Usipii reliquerunt. Nec quidquam ultra formidinis: vacua castella, senum coloniae, inter male parentes et injuste imperantes aegra municipia et discordantia: hic dux, hic exercitus: ibi tributa et metalla et ceterae servientium poenae: quas in aeternum perferre aut statim ulcisci in hoc campo est. Proinde ituri in aciem et majores vestros et posteros cogitate."

XXXIII. Excepere orationem alacres, ut barbaris

moris, cantu et fremitu clamoribusque dissonis. Jam que agmina, et armorum fulgores audentissimi cujusque procursu: simul instruebantur acies: cum Agricola, quanquam laetum et vix munimentis coercitum militem adhortatus, ita disseruit: "Octavus annus est, commilitones, ex quo virtute et auspiciis imperii Romani fide atque opera vestra Britanniam vicistis: tot expeditionibus, tot proeliis, seu fortitudine adversus hostes seu patientia ac labore paene adversus ipsam rerum naturam opus fuit, neque me militum neque vos ducis poenituit. Ergo egressi, ego veterum legatorum, vos priorum exercituum terminos, finem Britanniae non fama nec rumore, sed castris et armis tenemus. Inventa Britannia et subacta. Equidem saepe in agmine, cum vos paludes montesve et flumina fatigarent, fortissimi cujusque voces audiebam, Quando dabitur hostis, quando acies? Veniunt, e latebris suis extrusi: et vota virtusque in aperto, omniaque prona victoribus, atque eadem victis adversa. Nam, ut superasse tantum itineris, silvas evasisse, transisse aestuaria pulchrum ac decorum in frontem; ita fugientibus periculosissima, quae hodie prosperrima sunt. Neque enim nobis aut locorum eadem notitia aut commeatuum eadem abundantia: sed manus et arma et in his omnia. Quod ad me attinet, jam pridem mihi decretum est, neque exercitus neque ducis terga tuta esse. Proinde et honesta mors turpi vita potior; et incolumitas ac decus eodem loco sita sunt: nec inglorium fuerit, in ipso terrarum ac naturae fine cecidisse."

XXXIV. "Si novae gentes atque ignota acies constitisset, aliorum exercituum exemplis vos hortarer. nunc vestra decora recensete, vestros oculos interrogate. Ii sunt, quos proximo anno, unam legionem furto noctis aggressos, clamore debellastis : ii ceterorum Britannorum fugacissimi, ideoque tam diu superstites. Quomodo silvas saltusque penetrantibus fortissimum quodque animal contra ruere, pavida et inertia ipso agminis sono pelluntur, sic acerrimi Britannorum jam pridem ceciderunt : reliquus est numerus ignavorum et metuentium, quos quod tandem invenistis, non restiterunt, sed deprehensi sunt: novissimae res et extremo metu corpora defixere aciem in his vestigiis, in quibus pulchram et spectabilem victoriam ederetis. Transigite cum expeditionibus : imponite quinquaginta annis magnum diem : approbate reipublicae nunquam exercitui imputari potuisse aut moras belli aut causas rebellandi."

XXXV. Et alloquente adhuc Agricola, militum ardor eminebat, et finem orationis ingens alacritas consecuta est, statimque ad arma discursum. Instinctos ruentesque ita disposuit, ut peditum auxilia, quae octo millia erant, mediam aciem firmarent, equitum tria millia cornibus affunderentur: legiones pro vallo stetere, ingens victoriae decus citra Romanum sanguinem bellanti, et auxilium, si pellerentur. Britannorum acies, in speciem simul ac terrorem, editioribus ocis constiterat ita, ut primum agmen aequo, ceteri per acclive jugum connexi velut insurgerent : media campi covinarius et eques strepitu ac discursu complebat. Tum Agricola superante hostium multitudine veritus, ne simul in frontem, simul et latera suorum pugnaretur, diductis ordinibus, quanquam porrectior acies futura erat et arcessendas plerique legiones admonebant, promptior in spem et firmus adversis, dimisso equo pedes ante vexilla constitit

XXXVI. Ac primo congressu eminus certabatur simul constantia, simul arte Britanni ingentibus gladiis et brevibus cetris missilia nostrorum vitare vel excutere, atque ipsi magnam vim telorum superfundere: donec Agricola Batavorum cohortes ac Tungrorum duas cohortatus est, ut rem ad mucrones ac manus adducerent: quod et ipsis vetustate militiae exercitatum, et hostibus inhabile parva scuta et enormes gladios gerentibus: nam Britannorum gladii sine mucrone complexum armorum et in aperto pugnam non tolerabant. Igitur, ut Batavi miscere ictus, ferire umbonibus, ora foedare, et stratis qui in aequo obstiterant, erigere in colles aciem coepere, ceterae cohortes, aemulatione et impetu commistae, proximos quosque caedere; ac plerique semineces aut integri festinatione victoriae relinquebantur. Interim equitum turmae fugere, covinarii peditum se proelio miscuere: et, quanquam recentem terrorem intu lerant, densis tamen hostium agminibus et inaequalibus locis haerebant: minimeque equestris ea pugnae facies erat, cum aegre diu stantes simul equorum corporibus impellerentur, ac saepe vagi currus, exterriti sine rectoribus equi, ut quemque formido tulerat. transversos aut obvios incursabant.

XXXVII. Et Britanni, qui adhuc pugnae expertes summa collium insederant et paucitatem nostrorum vacui spernebant, degredı paulatim et circumire terga vincentium coeperant: ni id ipsum veritus Agricola, quatuor equitum alas, ad subita belli retentas, venientibus opposuisset, quantoque ferocius accurrerant, tanto acrius pulsos in fugam disjecisset. Ita consilium Britannorum in ipsos versum: transvectaeque praecepto ducis a fronte pugnantium alae, aversam hostium aciem invasere. Tum vero patentibus locis grande et atrox spectaculum: sequi, vulnerare, capere atque eosdem, oblatis aliis, trucidare. Jam hostium, prout cuique ingenium erat, catervae armatorum paucioribus terga praestare, quidam inermes ultro ruere ac se morti offerre; passim arma et corpora et laceri artus et cruenta humus: et aliquando etiam victis ira virtusque; postquam silvis appropinquarunt, collecti primos sequentium incautos et locorum ignaros circumveniebant. Quod ni frequens ubique Agricola validas et expeditas cohortes indaginis modo, et, sicubi arctiora erant, partem equitum dimissis equis, simul rariores silvas equitem persultare jussisset, acceptum aliquod vulnus per nimiam fiduciam foret. Ceterum, ubi compositos firmis ordinibus sequi rursus videre, in fugam versi, non agminibus, ut prius, nec alius alium respectantes, rari et vitabundi invicem, longinqua atque avia petiere. Finis sequendi nox et satietas fuit: caesa hostium ad decem millia: nostrorum trecenti sexaginta cecidere: in quis Aulus Atticus praefectus cohortis, juvenili ardore et ferocia equi hostibus illatus.

XXXVIII. Et nox quidem gaudio praedaque laeta victoribus: Britanni palantes, mixtoque virorum mulierumque ploratu, trahere vulneratos, vocare integros, deserere domos ac per iram ultro incendere: eligere latebras et statim relinquere: miscere invicem consilia aliqua, dein separare: aliquando frangi aspectu pignorum suorum, saepius concitari: satisque constabat, saevisse quosdam in conjuges ac liberos, tanquam misererentur. Proximus dies faciem victoriae latius aperuit: vastum ubique silentium, secreti colles, fumantia procul tecta, nemo exploratoribus obvius: quibus in omnem partem dimissis, ubi incerta fugae vestigia neque usquam conglobari hostes compertum et exacta jam aestate spargi bellum nequibat, in fines Horestorum exercitum deducit. Ibi acceptis obsidibus, praefecto classis circumvehi Britanniam praecepit. Datae ad id vires, et praecesserat terror. Ipse peditem atque equites lento itinere, quo novarum gentium animi ipsa transitus mora terrerentur, in hibernis locavit. Et simul classis secunda tempestate ac fama Trutulensem portum tenuit, unde proximo latere Britanniae lecto omni redierat.

XXXIX. Hunc rerum cursum, quanquam nulla verborum jactantia epistolis Agricolae actum, ut Domitiano moris erat, fronte laetus, pectore anxius excepit. Inerat conscientia derisui fuisse nuper falsum e Germania triumphum, emptis per commercia, quorum habitus et crines in captivorum speciem formarentur: at nunc veram magnamque victoriam, tot millibus hostium caesis, ingenti fama celebrari. Id sibi maxime formidolosum, privati hominis nomen supra principis attolli: frustra studia fori et civilium artium decus in silentium acta, si militarem gloriam alius occuparet: et cetera utcumque facilius dissimulari: ducis boni imperatoriam virtutem esse. Talibus curis exercitus, quodque saevae cogitationis indicium erat, secreto suo satiatus, optimum in praesentia statuit reponere odium, donec impetus famae et favor exercitus languesceret: nam etiam tum Agricola Britanniam obtinebat.

XL. Igitur triumphalia ornamenta et illustris statuae honorem et quidquid pro triumpho datur, multo verborum honore cumulata, decerni in senatu jubet;

addique insuper opinionem, Syriam provinciam Agricolae destinari, vacuam tum morte Atilii Rufi consularis et majoribus reservatam. Credidere plerique libertum ex secretioribus ministeriis missum ad Agricolam codicillos, quibus ei Syria dabatur, tulisse cum praecepto, ut, si in Britannia foret, traderentur: eumque libertum in ipso freto Oceani obvium Agricolae, ne appellato quidem eo, ad Domitianum remeasse: sive verum istud, sive ex ingenio principis fictum ac compositum est. Tradiderat interim Agricola successori suo provinciam quietam tutamque. Ac, ne notabilis celebritate et frequentia occurrentium introitus esset, vitato amicorum officio, noctu in urbem, noctu in palatium, ita ut praeceptum erat, venit: exceptusque brevi osculo et nullo sermone turbae servientium immixtus est. Ceterum, ut militare nomen, grave inter otiosos, aliis virtutibus temperaret, tranquillitatem atque otium penitus auxit, cultu modicus, sermone facilis, uno aut altero amicorum comitatus; adeo ut plerique quibus magnos viros per ambitionem aestimare mos est, viso aspectoque Agricola, quaererent famam, pauci interpretarentur.

XLI. Crebro per eos dies apud Domitianum absens accusatus, absens absolutus est. Causa periculi non crimen ullum aut querela laesi cujusquam, sed infensus virtutibus princeps et gloria viri ac pessimum inimicorum genus, laudantes. Et ea insecuta sunt reipublicae tempora, quae sileri Agricolam non sinerent: tot exercitus in Moesia Daciaque et Germania Pannoniaque, temeritate aut per ignaviam ducum amissi: tot militares viri cum tot cohortibus expugnati et capti: nec jam de limite imperii et ripa, sed de hibernis legionum et possessione dubitatum Ita, cum damna damnis continuarentur atque omnis annus funeribus et cladibus insigniretur, poscebatur ore vulgi dux Agricola: comparantibus cunctis vigorem, constantiam et expertum bellis animum cum inertia et formidine ceterorum. Quibus sermonibus satis constat Domitiani quoque aures verberatas, dum optimus quisque libertorum amore et fide, pessimi malignitate et livore, pronum deterioribus principem exstimulabant. Sic Agricola simul suïs virtutibus, simul vitiis aliorum, in ipsam gloriam praeceps agebatur.

XLII. Aderat jam annus, quo proconsulatum Asiae et Africae sortiretur, et occiso Civica nuper nec Agricolae consilium deerat, nec Domitiano exemplum. Accessere quidam cogitationum principis periti, qui, iturusne esset in provinciam, ultro Agricolam interrogarent: ac primo occultius quietem et otium laudare, mox operam suam in approbanda excusatione offerre: postremo non jam obscuri, suadentes simul terrentesque, pertraxere ad Domitianum; qui paratus simulatione, in arrogantiam compositus, et audiit preces excusantis, et, cum annuisset, agi sibi gratias passus est: nec erubuit beneficii invidia. Salarium tamen, proconsulari solitum offerri et quibusdam a se ipso concessum, Agricolae non dedit: sive offensus non petitum, sive ex conscientia, ne, quod vetuerat, videretur emisse. Proprium humani ingenii est, odisse quem laeseris: Domitiani vero natura praeceps in iram, et quo obscurior, eo irrevocabilior, moderatione tamen prudentiaque Agricolae leniebatur: quia non contumacia neque inani jactatione libertatis famam fatumque provocabat. Sciant.

quibus moris illicita mirari, posse etiam sub malis principibus magnos viros esse: obsequiumque ac modestiam, si industria ac vigor adsint, eo laudis excedere, quo plerique per abrupta, sed in nullum reipublicae usum, ambitiosa morte inclaruerunt.

XLIII. Finis vitae ejus nobis luctuosus, amicis tristis, extraneis etiam ignotisque non sine cura fuit. Vulgus quoque et hic aliud agens populus et ventitavere ad domum, et per fora et circulos locuti sunt: nec quisquam audita morte Agricolae aut laetatus est aut statim oblitus. Augebat miserationem constans rumor, veneno interceptum. Nobis nihil comperti affirmare ausim: ceterum per omnem valetudinem jus, crebrius quam ex more principatus per nuntios visentis, et libertorum primi et medicorum intimi venere: sive cura illud sive inquisitio erat. Supremo quidem die, momenta deficientis per dispositos cursores nuntiata constabat, nullo credente sic accelerari, quae tristis audiret. Speciem tamen doloris animo vultuque prae se tulit, securus jam odii, et qui facilius dissimularet gaudium, quam metum. Satis constabat, lecto testamento Agricolae, quo cohaeredem optimae uxori et piissimae filiae Domitianum scripsit, laetatum eum velut honore judicioque: tam caeca et corrupta mens assiduis adulationibus erat, ut nesciret a bono patre non scribi haeredem, nisi malum principem.

XLIV. Natus erat Agricola, Caio Caesare tertium consule, Idibus Juniis: excessit sexto et quinquagesimo anno, decimo Kalendas Septembris, Collega Priscoque consulibus. Quod si habitum quoque ejus posteri noscere velint, decentior quam sublimior fuit; nihil metus in vultu, gratia oris supererat·

bonum virum facile crederes, magnum libenter. Et ipse quidem, quanquam medio in spatio integrae aetatis ereptus, quantum ad gloriam, longissimum aevum peregit. Quippe et vera bona, quae in virtutibus sita sunt, impleverat, et consulari ac triumphalibus ornamentis praedito, quid aliud adstruere fortuna poterat? Opibus nimiis non gaudebat; speciosae contigerant. Filia atque uxore superstitibus, potest videri etiam beatus; incolumi dignitate, florente fama, salvis affinitatibus et amicitiis, futura effugisse. Nam sicuti durare in hac beatissimi saeculi luce ac principem Trajanum videre, quod augurio votisque apud nostras aures ominabatur, ita festinatae mortis grande solatium tulit, evasisse postremum illud tempus, quo Domitianus non jam per intervalla ac spiramenta temporum, sed continuo et velut uno ictu rempublicam exhausit.

XLV. Non vidit Agricola obsessam curiam, et clausum armis senatum, et eadem strage tot consularium caedes, tot nobilissimarum feminarum exsilia et fugas. Una adhuc victoria Carus Metius censebatur, et intra Albanam arcem sententia Messalini strepebat, et Massa Bebius jam tum reus erat. Mox nostrae duxere Helvidium in carcerem manus: nos Maurici Rusticique visus, nos innocenti sanguine Senecio perfudit. Nero tamen subtraxit oculos jussitque scelera, non spectavit: praecipua sub Domitiano miseriarum pars erat videre et aspici: cum suspiria nostra subscriberentur; cum denotandis tot hominum palloribus sufficeret saevus ille vultus et rubor, quo se contra pudorem muniebat. Tu vero felix, Agricola, non vitae tantum claritate, sed etiam opportunitate mortis, Ut perhibent qui interfuerunt novissimis sermonibus tuis, constans et libens fatum excepisti; tanquam pro virili portione innocentiam principi donares. Sed mihi filiaeque ejus, praeter acerbitatem parentis erepti, auget moestitiam, quod assidere valetudini, fovere deficientem, satiari vultu, complexu, non contigit: excepissemus certe mandata vocesque, quas penitus animo figeremus. Noster hic dolor, nostrum vulnus: nobis tam longae absentiae conditione ante quadriennium amissus est. Omnia sine dubio, optime parentum, assidente amantissima uxore, superfuere honori tuo: paucioribus tamen lacrimis compositus es, et novissima in luce desideravere aliquid oculi tui.

XLVI. Si quis piorum manibus locus, si, ut sapientibus placet, non cum corpore exstinguuntur magnae animae, placide quiescas, nosque, domum tuam, ab infirmo desiderio et muliebribus lamentis ad contemplationem virtutum tuarum voces, quas neque lugeri neque plangi fas est: admiratione te potius, te immortalibus laudibus, et, si natura suppeditet, similitudine decoremus. Is verus honos, ea conjunctissimi cujusque pietas. Id filiae quoque uxorique praeceperim, sic patris, sic mariti memoriam venerari, ut omnia facta dictaque ejus secum revolvant, formamque ac figuram animi magis quam corporis complectantur: non quia intercedendum putem imaginibus, quae marmore aut aere finguntur; sed ut vultus hominum, ita simulacra vultus imbecilla ac mortalia sunt; forma mentis aeterna, quam tenere et exprimere non per alienam materiam et artem, sed tuis ipse moribus possis. Quidquid ex Agricola amavimus, quidquid mirati sumus, manet mansurumque est in animis hominum, in aeternitate temporum, fama rerum. Nam multos veterum, velut inglorios, et ignobiles, oblivio obruet: Agricola posteritati narratus et traditus superstes erit.

TABLE OF ABBREVIATIONS.

Several words, which occur most frequently in the Notes, are abbreviated. Of these the following classes may require explanation. The other abbreviations are either familiar or sufficiently obvious of themselves.

1. Works of Tacitus.

A.	Agricola.
Ann.	Annals.
G.	Germania.
H.	Histories.
T.	Tacitus.

2. Annotators cited as authorities.

Br.	Brotier.
D. or Död.	Döderlein.
Dr.	Dronke.
E.	Ernesti.
Gr.	Gruber.
Gün.	Günther.
K.	Kiessling.
Ky.	Kingsley.
Mur.	Murphy.
Or.	Orelli.
Pass.	Passow.
R.	Roth.
Rhen.	Rhenanus.
Rit.	Ritter.
Rup.	Ruperti.
W.	Walch.
Wr.	Walther.

3. Other Authorities.

H.	Harkness' Latin Grammar.
Beck. Gall.	Becker's Gallus.
Böt. Lex. Tac.	Bötticher's Lexicon Taciteun..
For. and Fac.	Forcellini and Facciolati's Latin Lexicon.
Tur. His. Ang. Sax.	Turner's History of the Anglo-Saxons.
Z.	Zumpt's Latin Grammar.

NOTES.

GERMANIA.

The Treatise De Situ, Moribus et Populis Germaniae, was written (as appears from the treatise itself, see § 37) in the second consulship of the Emperor Trajan, A. U. C. 851, A. D. 98. The design of the author in its publication has boen variously interpreted. From the censure which it frequently passes upon the corruption and degeneracy of the times, it has been considered as a mere satire upon Roman manners, in the age of Tacitus. But to say nothing of the ill adaptation of the whole plan to a satirical work, there are large parts of the treatise, which must have been prepared with great labor, and yet can have no possible bearing on such a design. Satires are not wont to abound in historical notices and geographical details, especially touching a foreign and distant land.

The same objection lies against the *political* ends, which have been imputed to the author, such as the persuading of Trajan to engage, or *not* to engage, in a war with the Germans, as the most potent and dangerous enemy of Rome. For both these aims have been alleged, and we might content ourselves with placing the one as an offset against the other. But aside from the neutralizing force of such contradictions, wherefore such an imposing array of geographical research, of historical lore, of political and moral philosophy, for the accomplishment of so simple a purpose? And why is the purpose so scrupulously concealed, that confessedly it can be gathered only from obscure intimations, and those of ambiguous import? Besides, there are passages whose tendency must have been directly counter to either of these alleged aims (cf. note § 33).

The author does indeed, in the passage just cited, seem to appreciate with almost prophetic accuracy, those dangers to the Roman Empire, which were so fearfully illustrated in its subsequent fall beneath the power of the German Tribes; and he utters, as what true Roman would not in such forebodings, the warnings and the prayers of a patriot sage. But he does this only in episodes, which are so manifestly incidental, and yet arise so naturally out of the narrative or description, that it is truly surprising it should ever have occurred to any reader, to seek in them the key to the whole treatise.

The entire warp and woof of the work is obviously *historical* and *geographical.* The satire, the political maxims, the moral sentiments, and all the rest, are merely incidental, interwoven for the sake of instruction and embellishment, inwrought because a mind so thoughtful and so acute as that of Tacitus, could not leave them out. Tacitus had long been collecting the materials for his Roman Histories. In so doing, his attention was necessarily drawn often and with special interest to a people, who, for two centuries and more, had been the most formidable enemy of the Roman State. In introducing them into his history, he would naturally wish to give some preliminary account of their origin, manners, and institutions, as he does in introducing the Jews in the Fifth Book of his Histories, which happens to be, in part, preserved. Nor would it be strange, if he should, with this view, collect a mass of materials, which he could not incorporate entire into a work of such compass, and which any slight occasion might induce him to publish in a separate form, perhaps as a sort of forerunner to his Histories.* Such an occasion now was furnished in the campaigns and victories of Trajan, who, at the time of his elevation to the imperial power, was at the head of the Roman armies in Germany, where he also remained for a year or more after his accession to the throne, till he had received the submission of the hostile tribes and wiped away the disgrace which the Germans, beyond any other nation of that age, had brought upon the Roman arms. Such a people, at such a time, could not fail to be an object of deep interest at Rome. This was the time when Tacitus published his work on Germany; and such are believed to have been the motives and the circumstances, which led to the undertaking. His grand object was not to point a satire or to compass a

* It has even been argued by highly respectable scholars, that the Germania of Tacitus is itself only such a collection of materials, not published by the Author, and never intended for publication in that form. But it is quite too methodical, too studied, and too finished a work to ad[illegible] of that supposition (cf. Prolegom. of K.).

political end, but as he himself informs us (§27), to treat of the origin and manners, the geography and history, of the German Tribes

The same candor and sincerity, the same correctness and truthfulness, which characterize the Histories, mark also the work on Germany. The author certainly aimed to speak the truth, and nothing but the truth, on the subject of which he treats. Moreover, he had abundant means of knowing the truth, on all the main points, in the character and history of the Germans. It has even been argued from such expression as *vidimus* (§ 8), that Tacitus had himself been in Germany, and could, therefore, write from personal observation. But the argument proceeds on a misinterpretation of his language (cf. note in *loc. cit.*). And the use of *accepimus* (as in § 27), shows that he derived his information from others. But the Romans had been in constant intercourse and connection, civil or military, with the Germans, for two hundred years. Germany furnished a wide theatre for their greatest commanders, and a fruitful theme for their best authors, some of whom, as Julius Cæsar (to whom Tacitus particularly refers, 28), were themselves the chief actors in what they relate. These authors, some of whose contributions to the history of Germany are now lost (e. g. the elder Pliny, who wrote twenty books on the German wars), must have all been in the hands of Tacitus, and were, doubtless, consulted by him; not, however, as a servile copyist, or mere compiler (for he sometimes differs from his authorities, from Caesar even, whom he declares to be the best of them), but as a discriminating and judicious inquirer. The account of German customs and institutions may, therefore, be relied on, from the intrinsic credibility of the author. It receives confirmation, also, from its general accordance with other early accounts of the Germans, and with their better known subsequent history, as well as from its strong analogy to the well-known habits of our American aborigines, and other tribes in a like stage of civilization (cf. note, § 15). The geographical details are composed with all the accuracy which the ever-shifting positions and relations of warring and wandering tribes rendered possible in the nature of the case (cf. note, § 28). In sentiment, the treatise is surpassingly rich and instructive, like all the works of this prince of philosophical historians. In style, it is concise and nervous, yet quite rhetorical, and in parts, even poetical to a fault (see notes passim, cf. also, Monboddo's critique on the style of Tacitus). "The work," says La Bletterie, "is brief without being superficial. Within the compass of a few pages, it comprises more of ethics and politics, more fine delineations of character, more substance and pith (*su*), than can be collected from many a ponderous volume. It is not one of those barely agreeable descriptions, which gradually diffuse their influence over the soul, and leave it in undisturbed tranquillity. It is a picture in strong light, like the subject itself, full of fire, of sentiment, of lightning-flashes, that go at once to the heart. We imagine ourselves in Germany; we become familiar with these so-called barbarians; we pardon their faults, and almost their vices, out of regard to their virtues; and in our moments of enthusiasm, we even wish we were Germans."

The following remarks of Murphy will illustrate the value of the treatise, to modern Europeans and their descendants. "It is a draught of savage manners, delineated by a masterly hand; the more interesting, as the part of the world which it describes was the seminary of the modern European nations, the Vagina Gentium, as historians have emphatically called it. The work is short, but, as Montesquieu observes, it is the work of a man who abridged every thing, because he knew every thing. A thorough knowledge of the transactions of barbarous ages, will throw more light than is generally imagined on the laws of modern times. Wherever the barbarians, who issued from their northern hive, settled in new habitations, they carried with them their native genius, their original manners, and the first rudiments of the political system which has prevailed in different parts of Europe. They established monarchy and liberty, subordination and freedom, the prerogative of the prince and the rights of the subject, all united in so bold a combination, that the fabric, in some places, stands to this hour the wonder of mankind. The British constitution, says Montesquieu, came out of the woods of Germany. What the state of this country (Britain) was before the arrival of our Saxon ancestors, Tacitus has shown in the life of Agricola. If we add to his account of the Germans and Britons, what has been transmitted to us, concerning them, by Julius Caesar, we shall see the origin of the Anglo-Saxon government, the great outline of that Gothic constitution under which the people enjoy their rights and liberties at this hour. Montesquieu, speaking of his own country, declares it impossible to form an adequate notion of the French monarchy, and the changes of their government, without a previous inquiry into the manners, genius, and spirit of the German nations. Much of what was incorporated with the institutions of those fierce invaders, has flowed down in the stream of time, and still mingles with our modern jurisprudence. The subject, it is conceived, is interesting to every Briton. In the manners of the Germans, the reader will see our present frame of government, as it were, in its cradle, *gentis cu nabula nostrae!* in the Germans themselves, a fierce and warlike people, to whom this country owes that spirit of liberty, which, through so many centuries, has preserved our excellent form of government, and raised the glory of the British nation:

> —— Genus unde Latinum,
> Albanique patres, atque altae moenia Romae."

CHAP. I. *Germania* stands first as the emphatic word, and is followed by *omnis* for explanation. *Germania omnis* here does not include Germania Prima and Secunda, which were Roman provinces on the left bank of the Rhine (so called because settled by Germans). It denotes *Germany proper*, as a *whole*, in distinction from the provinces just mentioned and from the several tribes, of which Tacitus treats in the latter part of the work. So Caesar (B. G. 1, 1) uses *Gallia omnis*, as exclusive of the Roman provinces called Gaul and inclusive of the three *parts*, which he proceeds to specify.

Gallis–Pannoniis. People used for the countries. Cf. His. 5, 6: *Phoenices. Gaul*, now France; *Rhaetia*, the country of the Grisons and the Tyrol, with part of Bavaria; *Pannonia*, lower Hungary and part of Austria. Germany was separated from Gaul by the Rhine; from Rhaetia and Pannonia, by the Danube.—*Rheno et Danubio.* Rhine and Rhone are probably different forms of the same root (Rh–n). Danube, in like manner, has the same root as Dnieper (Dn-p); perhaps also the same as Don and Dwina (D-n). Probably each of these roots was originally a generic name for *river, water, stream.* So there are several *Avons* in England and Scotland. Cf. Latham's Germania sub voc.

Sarmatis Dacisque. The Slavonic Tribes were called Sarmatians by the ancients. *Sarmatia* included the country north of the Carpathian Mountains, between the Vistula and the Don in Europe, together with the adjacent part of Asia, without any definite limits towards the north, which was terra incognita to the ancients—in short, Sarmatia was *Russia*, as far as known at that time. *Dacia* lay between the Carpathian mountains on the north, and the Danube on the south, including Upper Hungary, Transylvania, Wallachia, and Moldavia.

Mutuo metu. Rather a poetical boundary! Observe also the

alliteration. At the same time, the words are not a bad description of those wide and solitary wastes, which, as Caesar informs us (B. G. 6, 23), the Germans delighted to interpose between themselves and other nations, so that it might appear that *no one dared to dwell near them*.—*Montibus.* The Carpathian.—*Cetera.* Ceteram Germaniae partem.

Sinus. This word denotes any thing with a curved outline (cf. 29, also A. 23); hence bays, peninsulas, and prominent bends or borders, whether of land or water. Here *peninsulas* (particularly that of Jutland, now Denmark), for it is to the author's purpose here to speak of land rather than water, and the ocean is more properly said to *embrace peninsulas*, than *gulfs* and *bays*. Its association with *islands* here favors the same interpretation. So Passow, Or., Rit. Others, with less propriety, refer it to the *gulfs* and *bays*, which so mark the Baltic and the German Oceans.—*Oceanus* here, includes both the Baltic Sea, and the German Ocean (Oceanus Septentrionalis).

Insularum–spatia. *Islands of vast extent*, viz. Funen, Zealand, &c. Scandinavia also (now Sweden and Norway) was regarded by the ancients as an island, cf. Plin. Nat. His. iv. 27: quarum (insularum) clarissima Scandinavia est, incompertae magnitudinis.

Nuper–regibus. Understand with this clause *ut compertum est*. The above mentioned features of the Northern Ocean had been *discovered* in the prosecution of the late wars, of the Romans, among the tribes and kings previously unknown. *Nuper* is to be taken in a general sense=recentioribus temporibus, cf. *nuper additum*, § 2, where it goes back one hundred and fifty years to the age of Julius Caesar.—*Bellum.* War in general, no particular war. — *Versus.* This word has been considered by some as an adverb, and by others as a preposition. It is better however to regard it as a participle, like *ortus*, with which it is connected, though without a conjunction expressed. Ritter omits *in*.

Molli et clementer edito. *Of gentle slope and moderate elevation* in studied antithesis to *inaccesso ac praecipiti*, *lofty and steep*. In like manner, *jugo*, *ridge*, *summit*, is contrasted with *vertice*, *peak*, *height*, cf. Virg. Ecl. 9, 7: *molli clivo;* Ann. 17, 38: *colles clementer assurgentes.* The *Rhaetian* Alps, now the mountains of the Grisons. *Alp* is a Celtic word=hill. *Albion* has the same root=*hilly country*. *Mons Abnoba* (al. Arnoba) is the northern part of the Schwartzwald, or Black Forest.—*Erumpat*, al. erumpit. But the best MSS. and all the recent editions have *erumpat:* and Tacitus never uses the pres ind. after *donec, until,* cf. Rup. & Rit. in loc. Whenever he uses the present after *donec, until,* he seems to have conceived the relation of the two clauses, which it connects, as that of a means to an end, or a condition to a result, and hence to have used the subj. cf. chap. 20: *separet;* 31: *absolvat;* 35: *sinuetur;* Ann. 2, 6: *misceatur.* The two examples last cited, like this, describe the course of a river and boundary line. For the general rule of the modes after *donec,* see H. 522; Z. 575. See also notes H. 1, 13. 35.—*Septimum.* According to the common understanding, the Danube had *seven* mouths. So Strabo, Mela, Ammian, and Ovid; Pliny makes six. T. reconciles the two accounts. The *enim* inserted after *septimum* in most editions is not found in the best mss. and is unnecessary. Or. & Rit. omit it.

II. *Ipsos* marks the transition from the country to the people= *the Germans themselves.* So A. 13: *Ipsi Britanni.*

Crediderim. Subj. attice. A modest way of expressing his opinion, like our: I should say, I am inclined to think. H. 486, I. 3; Z. 527.

Adventibus et hospitiis. Immigrants and visitors. Adventibus certae sedes, *hospitiis* preregrinationes significantur. Gün. Both abstract for concrete. Död. compares ἔποικοι and μέτοικοι.

Terra–advehebantur. Zeugma for *terra adveniebant,* classibus advehebantur. H. 704, I. 2; Z. 775.

Nec–et. These correlatives connect the members more closely than et–et; as in Greek οὔτε-τέ. The sentiment here advanced touching colonization (as by sea, rather than by land), though true of Carthage, Sicily, and most *Grecian* colonies, is directly the reverse of the general fact; and Germany itself is now known to have received its population by land emigration, from western Asia. The Germans, as we learn from affinities of languages and occasional references of historians and geographers, belonged to the same great stock of the human family with the Goths and Scythians, and may be traced back to that hive of nations, that primitive residence of mankind, the country east and south of the Caspian Sea and in the vicinity of Mount Ararat: cf. Tur. His. Ang. Sax. B. II. C. 1; also Donaldson's New Cratylus, B. I. Chap. 4. Latham's dogmatic skepticism will hardly shake the now established faith on this subject. The science of ethnography was unknown to the ancients. Tacitus had not the remotest idea, that all mankind were sprung from a common ancestry, and diffused themselves over the world from a common centre, a fact asserted in the Scriptures, and daily receiving fresh confirmation from literature and science. Hence he speaks of the Germans as *indigenas*, which he explains below by *editum terra*, sprung from the earth, like the mutum et turpe pecus of Hor. Sat. 1. 3, 100. cf. A. 11.

Mutare quaerebant. Quaerere with inf. is poet. constr., found, however, in later prose writers, and once in Cic. (de Fin. 313: quaeris scire, enclosed in brackets in Tauchnitz's edition), to avoid repetition of *cupio. Cupio* or *volo mutare* would be regular classic prose.

Adversus. That the author here uses *adversus* in some unusual and recondite sense, is intimated by the clause: *ut sic dixerim.* It is understood by some, of a sea *unfriendly to navigation.* But its connexion by *que* with *immensus ultra*, shows that it refers to *position*, and means *lying opposite*, i. e., belonging, as it were, to another hemisphere or world from ours; for so the Romans regarded the Northern Ocean and Britain itself, cf. A 12: ultra *nostri orbis* mensuram; G. 17: *exterior* oceanus. So Cic. (Som. Scip. 6.) says: Homines partim obliquos, partim aversos, partim etiam *adversos*, stare vobis. This interpretation is confirmed by *ab orbe nostra* in the antithesis. On the use of *ut sic dixerim* for *ut sic dicam*, which is peculiar to the silver age, see Z. 528.

Asia, sc. Minor. *Africa*, sc. the Roman Province of that name, comprising the territory of Carthage.—*Peteret.* The question implies a negative answer, cf. Z. 530. The subj. implies a protasis understood: if he could, or the like. H. 502.

Sit. Praesens, ut de re vera. Gün. *Nisi si* is nearly equivalent to *nisi forte: unless perchance;* unless if we may suppose the case. Cf. Wr. note on Ann. 2, 63, and Hand's Tursellinus, 3, 240.

Memoriae et annalium. Properly opposed to each other as *tradition* and *written history*, though we are not to infer that written books existed in Germany in the age of Tacitus.

Carminibus. Songs, ballads (from cano). Songs and rude poetry have been, in all savage countries, the memorials of public transactions, e. g. the runes of the Goths, the bards of the Britons and Celts, the scalds of Scandinavia, &c.

Tuisconem. The god from whom Tuesday takes its name, as Wednesday from Woden, Thursday from Thor, &c., cf. Sharon Turner's His. of Ang. Sax. app. to book 2. chap. 3. Some find in the name of this god the root of the words Teutonic, Dutch (Germ. Deutsche or Teutsche) &c. Al. Tuistonem, Tristonem, &c. More likely it has the same root as the Latin divus, dius, deus, and the Greek θεῖος, δῖος, θεός, cf. Grimm's *Deutsche Mythologie*, sub v.

Terra editum=*indigena* above; and γηγενής and αὐτόχθων in Greek.

Originem=auctores. It is predicate after *Mannum*.

Ut in licentia vetustatis. *As in the license of antiquity*, i. e. since such license is allowed in regard to ancient times.

Ingaevones. "According to some German antiquaries, the *Ingaevones* are die *Einwohner*, those dwelling inwards towards the sea; the *Istaevones* are die *Westwohner*, the inhabitants of the western parts; and the *Hermiones* are the *Herumwohner*, midland inhabitants," Ky. cf. Kiessling in loc. Others, e. g. Zeuss and Grimm, with more probability, find in these names the roots of German words significant of *honor* and *bravery*, assumed by different tribes or confederacies as epithets or titles of distinction. Grimm identifies these three divisions with the Franks, Saxons, and Thuringians of a later age. See further, note chap. 27.

Vocentur. The subj. expresses the opinion of others, not the direct affirmation of the author. H. 529; Z. 549.

Deo=hoc deo, sc. Mannus=Germ. Mann, Eng. Man.

Marsos, Gambrivios. Under the names of Franci and Salii these tribes afterwards became formidable to the Romans. Cf. Prichard's Researches into the Physical History of Mankind, Vol. III. chap. 6, sec. 2.—*Suevos*, cf. note, 38.—*Vandalios*. The Vandals, now so familiar in history.

Additum, sc. esse, depending on *affirmant*.

Nunc Tungri, sc. vocentur, cf. His. 4, 15, 16. In confirmation of the historical accuracy of this passage, Gr. remarks, that Caes. (B. G. 2, 4) does not mention the Tungri, but names four tribes on the left bank of the Rhine, who, he says, are called by the common name of *Germans*; while Pliny (Nat. His. 4, 31), a century later, gives not the names of these four tribes, but calls them by the new name *Tungri*.

Ita-vocarentur. Locus vexatissimus! exclaim all the critics. And so they set themselves to amend the text by conjecture. Some have written *in nomen gentis* instead of *non gentis*. Others have proposed *a victorum metu*, or *a victo ob metum*, or *a victis ob metum*. But these emendations are wholly conjectural and unnecessary. Günther and Walch render *a victore*, *from* the victorious tribe, i. e. *after the name of* that tribe. But *a se ipsis* means *by* themselves; and the antithesis doubtless requires *a* to be understood in the same sense in both clauses. Grüber translates and explains thus: "In this way the name of a single tribe, and not of the whole people, has come into use, so that all, at first by the victor (the Tungri), in order to inspire fear, then by themselves (by the mouth of the whole people), when once the name became known, were called by the name of Germans. That is, the Tungri called all the kindred tribes that dwelt beyond the Rhine, Germans, in order to inspire fear by the wide extension of the name, since they gave themselves out to be a part of so vast a people; but at length all the tribes began to call themselves by this name, probably because they were pleased to see the fear which it excited." This is, on the whole, the most satisfactory explanation of the passage, and meets the essential concurrence of Wr., Or. and Död.—*Germani.* If of German etymology, this word=gehr or wehr (Fr. guerre) and mann, *men of war;* hence the *metus,* which the name carried with it. If it is a Latin word corresponding only in *sense* with the original German, then =*brethren.* It will be seen, that either etymology would accord with Grüber's explanation of the whole passage—in either case, the name would inspire fear. The latter, however, is the more probable, cf. Ritter in loc. A people often bear quite different names abroad from that by which they call themselves at home. Thus the people, whom we call *Germans,* call themselves *Deutsche* (Dutch), and are called by the French *Allemands,* cf. Latham. *Vocarentur* is subj. because it stands in a subordinate clause of the oratio obliqua, cf. H. 531; Z. 603.

Metum. Here taken in an *active* sense; oftener passive, but used in both senses. Quintilian speaks of *metum duplicem,* quem patimur et quem facimus (6, 2, 21). cf. A. 44: nihil metus in vultu, i. e., nothing to inspire fear in his countenance. In like manner admiratio (§ 7) is used for the admiration which one excites, though it usually denotes the admiration which one feels. For *ob,* cf. Ann. 1, 79: *ob moderandas Tiberis exundationes.*

Nationis–gentis. *Gens* is often used by T. as a synonym with *natio.* But in antithesis, *gens* is the whole, of which *nationes* or *populi* are the parts. e. g. G. 4: populos–gentem; § 14: nationes-genti. In like manner, in the civil constitution of Rome, a *gens* included several related *families.*

III. *Herculem.* That is, Romana interpretatione, cf. § 34. The Romans found *their* gods everywhere, and ascribed to Hercules, quidquid ubique magnificum est, cf. note 34: *quicquid–consensimus.* That this is a Roman account of the matter is evident, from the use of *eos*, for if the Germans were the subject of *memorant*, *se* must have been used. On the use of *et* here, cf. note 11.

Primum=ut principem, fortissimum. Gün.

Haec quoque. *Haec* is rendered *such* by Ritter. But it seems rather, as Or. and Död. explain it, to imply nearness and familiarity to the mind of the author and his readers: *these* well known songs. So 20: *in haec corpora, quae miramur*. *Quoque*, like *quidem*, follows the emphatic word in a clause, **H.** 602, III. 1; Z. 355.

Relatu, called *cantus trux*, H. 2, 22. A Tacitean word. Freund. Cf. H. 1, 30.

Baritum. Al. barditum and barritum. But the latter has no ms. authority, and the former seems to have been suggested by the bards of the Gauls, of whose existence among the Germans however there is no evidence. Död. says the root of the word is common to the Greek, Latin, and German languages, viz. *baren*, i. e. *fremere*, a verb still used by the Batavians, and the noun *bar*, i. e. carmen, of frequent occurrence in Saxon poetry to this day.

Terrent trepidantve. *They inspire terror or tremble with fear, according as the line* (the troops drawn up in battle array) *has sounded*, sc. the *baritus* or battle cry. Thus the Batavians perceived, that the *sonitus aciei* on the part of the Romans was more feeble than their own, and pressed on, as to certain triumph. H. 4, 18. So the Highlanders augured victory, if their shouts were louder than those of the enemy. See Murphy in loco.

Repercussu. A post-Augustan word. The earlier Latin authors would have said *repercussa*, or *repercutiendo*. The later Latin, like the English, uses more abstract terms.—*Nec tam–videntur*. *Nor do those carmina seem to be so much voices* (well modulated and harmonized), *as acclamations* (unanimous, but inarticulate and indistinct) *of courage*. So Pliny uses *concentus* of the acclamations of the people. Panegyr. 2. It is often applied by the poets to the concerts of birds, as in Virg. Geor. 1, 422. It is here plural, cf. Or. in loc. The reading *vocis* is without MS. authority.

Ulixem. "The love of fabulous history, which was the passion of ancient times, produced a new Hercules in every country, and made Ulysses wander on every shore. Tacitus mentions it as a romantic tale; but Strabo seems willing to countenance the fiction, and gravely tells us that Ulysses founded a city, called Odyssey, in Spain. Lipsius observes, that Lisbon, in the name of Strabo, had the appellation of Ulysippo, or Olisipo. At this rate, he pleasantly adds, what should hinder us inhabitants of the Low Countries from asserting that Ulysses built the city of Ulyssinga, and Circe founded that of Circzea or Ziriczee?" Murphy.

Fabuloso errore. *Storied, celebrated in song*, cf. fabulosus Hydaspes. Hor. Od. 1, 227. Ulysses having *wandered westward* gave plausibility to alleged traces of him in Gaul, Spain and Germany —*Asciburgium.* Now Asburg.

Quin etiam, cf. notes, 13: *quin etiam*, and 14: *quin immo.*—*Ulixi*, i. e. ab Ulixe, cf. Ann. 15, 41: Aedes statoris Jovis Romulo vota, i. e. by Romulus. This usage is especially frequent in the poets and the later prose writers, cf. H. 388, II. 3; Z. 419; and in T. above all others, cf. Böt. Lex. Tac. sub *Dativus.* Wr. and Rit. understand however an altar (or monument) consecrated to Ulysses, i. e. erected in honor of him by the citizens.

Adjecto. Inscribed with the name of his father, as well as his own, i. e. Λαερτιάδῃ.

Graecis litteris. *Grecian characters*, cf. Caes. B. G. 1, 29: In castris *Helvetiorum*, tabulae repertae sunt *litteris Graecis* confectae; and (6, 14): *Galli* in publicis privatisque rationibus *Graecis utuntur litteris.* T. speaks (Ann. 11, 14) of alphabetic characters, as passing from Phenicia into Greece, and Strabo (4, 1) traces them from the Grecian colony at Marseilles, into Gaul, whence they doubtless passed into Germany, and even into Britain.

IV. *Aliis aliarum.* The Greek and Latin are both fond of a repetition of different cases of the same word, even where one of them is redundant, e. g. οἰόθεν οἶος (Hom. Il. 7, 39), and particularly in the words ἄλλος and *alius.* *Aliis* is not however wholly redundant; but brings out more fully the idea: *no intermarriages, one with one nation, and another with another.* Walch and Ritter omit *aliis*, though it is found in all the MSS.

Infectos. Things are said *infici* and *imbui*, which are so penetrated and permeated by something else, that that something becomes a part of its nature or substance, as inficere colore, sanguine, veneno, animum virtutibus. It does not necessarily imply corruption or degeneracy.

Propriam–similem. Three epithets not essentially different, used for the sake of emphasis=*peculiar, pure, and sui-generis.* *Similis* takes the gen., when it expresses, as here, an internal resemblance in character; otherwise the dat., cf. Z. 411, H. 391, 2. 4.

Habitus. Form and features, external appearance. The physical features of the Germans as described by Tacitus, though still sufficient to distinguish them from the more southern European nations, have proved less permanent than their mental and social characteristics.

Idem omnibus. Cf. Juv. 13, 164:

> *Caerula* quis stupuit *Germani lumina? flavam*
> *Caesariem*, et madido torquentem cornua cirro?
> Nempe quod haec illis natura est *omnibus una.*

Magna corpora. "Sidonius Apollinaris says, that, being in Germany and finding the men so very tall, he could not address verses of six feet to patrons who were seven feet high:

> Spernit senipedem stilum Thalia,
> Ex quo septipedes vidit patronos." Mur.

Skeletons, in the ancient graves of Germany, are found to vary from 5 ft. 10 in. to 6 ft. 10 in. and even 7 ft. Cf. Ukert, Geog. III. 1. p. 197. These skeletons indicate a *strong* and *well formed* body.

Impetum. *Temporary exertion*, as opposed to *persevering toil and effort, laboris atque operum.*

Eadem. Not so much *patientia*, as *ad impetum valida.* See a like elliptical use of *idem* § 23: eadem temperantia; § 10: iisdem nemoribus. Also of totidem § 26.

Minime–assueverunt. "Least of all, are they capable of sustaining thirst and heat; cold and hunger, they are accustomed, by their soil and climate, to endure." Ky. The force of *minime* is confined to the first clause, and the proper antithetic particle is omitted at the beginning of the second. *Tolerare* depends on *assueverunt*, and belongs to both clauses. *Ve* is distributive, referring *coelo* to *frigora* and *solo* to *inediam.* So *vel* in H. 1, 62: strenuis *vel* ignavis spem metumque addere=strenuis spem, ignavis metum addere.

V. *Humidior–ventosior.* *Humidior* refers to *paludibus*, *ventosior* to *silvis;* the mountains (which were exposed to sweeping *winds*) being for the most part covered with forests, and the low grounds with marshes. *Ventosus*=Homeric ἠνεμόεις, windy, i. e. lofty. Il. 3, 305: Ἴλιον ἠνεμόεσσαν.

Satis ferax. *Satis*=*segetibus* poetice. *Ferax* is constructed with abl., vid. Virg. Geor. 2, 222: ferax oleo.

Impatiens. Not to be taken in the absolute sense, cf. § 20, 23, 26, where fruit trees and fruits are spoken of.

Improcera agrees with *pecora* understood.

Armentis. *Pecora*=flocks in general. *Armenta* (from *aro*, *to* plough), larger cattle in particular. It *may* include horses.

Suus honor. Their proper, i. e. usual size and beauty.

Gloria frontis. Poetice for *cornua.* Their horns were small.

Numero. Emphatic: *number,* rather than *quality.* Or, with Ritter, *gaudent* may be taken in the sense of enjoy, possess: *they have a good number of them.* In the same sense he interprets *gaudent* in A. 44: *opibus nimiis non gaudebat.*

Irati, sc. quia *opes* sunt *irritamenta malorum.* Ov. Met. 1, 140.—*Negaverint.* Subj. H. 525; Z. 552.–*Affirmaverim.* cf. note, 2: *crediderim.*

Nullam venam. "Mines of gold and silver have since been discovered in Germany; the former, indeed, inconsiderable, but the latter valuable." Ky. T. himself in his later work (the Annals), speaks of the discovery of a silver mine in Germany. Ann. 11, 20.

Perinde. Not so much as might be expected, or as the *Romans,* and other civilized nations. So Gronovius, Död. and most commentators. See Rup. in loc. Others, as Or. and Rit. allow no ellipsis, and render: *not much.* See Hand's Tursellinus, vol. IV. p 454. We sometimes use *not so much, not so very, not so bad,* &c., for *not very, not much,* and *not bad.* Still the form of expression strictly implies a comparison. And the same is true of *haud perinde,* cf. Böt. Lex. Tac.

Est videre. Est for *licet.* Graece et poetice. Not so used in the earlier Latin prose. See Z. 227.

Non in alia vilitate, i. e. eadem vilitate, aeque vilia, *held in the same low estimation.—Humo.* Abl. of material.

Proximi, sc. ad ripam. Nearest to the Roman border, opposed to *interiores.*

Serratos. Not elsewhere mentioned; probably coins with serrated edges, still found. The word is post-Augustan.

Bigatos. Roman coins stamped with a biga or two-horse chariot. Others were stamped with a quadriga and called quadrigati. The bigati seem to have circulated freely in foreign lands, cf. Ukert's Geog. of Greeks and Romans, III. 1: Trade of Germany, and places cited there. "The serrati and bigati were old coins, of purer silver than those of the Emperors." Ky. Cf. Pliny, H. N. 33, 13.

Sequuntur. Sequi=expetere. So used by Cic., Sal., and the best writers. Compare our word *seek.*

Nulla affectione animi. Not from any partiality for the silver in itself (but for convenience).

Numerus. Greater number and consequently less relative value of the silver coins. On *quia*, cf. note, H. 1, 31.

VI. *Ne — quidem.* *Not even*, i. e. iron is scarce as well as gold and silver. The weapons found in ancient German graves are of *stone*, and bear a striking resemblance to those of the American Indians. Cf. Ukert, p. 216. Ad verba, cf. note, His. 1, 16: *ne–fueris.* The emphatic word always stands between *ne* and *quidem.* H. 602, III. 2; Z. 801.—*Superest.* Is over and above, i. e. *abounds.* So superest ager, § 26.

Vel. Pro *sive*, Ciceroni inauditum. Gün. Cf. note, 17.

Frameas. The word is still found in Spain, as well as Germany. *Lancea* is also a Spanish word, cf. Freund.

Nudi. Cf. § 17, 20, and 24. Also Caes., B. G. 6, 21: magna corporis parte nuda.

Sagulo. Dim. of sago. A small short cloak.—*Leves*=leviter induti. The clause *nudi–leves* is added *here* to show, that their dress is favorable to the use of missiles.

Missilia spargunt. Dictio est Virgiliana. K.

Coloribus. Cf. nigra scuta, § 43. "Hence coats of arms and the origin of heraldry." Mur.

Cultus. Military equipments. Cultus complectitur omnia, quae studio et arte eis, quae natura instituit, adduntur. K.

Cassis aut galea. *Cassis,* properly of metal; *galea* of leather (Gr. γαλέη); though the distinction is not always observed.

Equi–conspicui. Cf. Caes. B. G. 4, 2. 7, 65.

Sed nec variare. *But* (i. e. on the other hand) *they are not even* (for *nec* in this sense see Ritter in loc.) *taught to vary their curves* (i. e. as the antithesis shows, to bend now towards the right and now towards the left in their gyrations), *but they drive them straight forward or by a constant bend towards the right in so connected a circle* (i. e. a complete ring), *that no one is behind* (for the obvious reason, that there is neither beginning nor end to such a ring). Such is on the whole the most satisfactory explanation of this difficult passage, which we can give after a careful examination. A different version was given in the first edition. It refers not to battle, but to equestrian exercises, cf. Gerlach, as cited by Or. in loc.

Aestimanti. Greek idiom. Elliptical dative, nearly equivalent to the abl. abs. (nobis aestimantibus), and called by some the dat abs. In A. 11. the ellipsis is supplied by *credibile est.* Cf. Bötticher's Lex. Tac. sub *Dativus.*

Eoque mixti. *Eo*, causal particle=for that reason. Caesar adopted this arrangement in the battle of Pharsalia. B. C. 3, 84. The Greeks also had πέζοι ἅμιπποι. Xen. Hellen. 7, 5.

Centeni. A hundred is a favorite number with the Germans and their descendants. Witness the hundred *pagi* of the Suevi (Caes. B. G. 4, 1), and of the Semnones (G. 39), the *cantons* of Switzerland, and the *hundreds* of our Saxon ancestors in England. The *centeni* here are a military division. In like manner, Caesar (B. G. 4, 1) speaks of a *thousand* men drafted annually from each *pagus* of the Suevi, for military service abroad.

Idque ipsum. Predicate nominative after a verb of calling, H. 362, 2. 2); Z. 394. The division was called a *hundred*, and each man in it a *hundreder;* and such was the estimation in which this service was held, that to be a hundreder, became an honorable distinction, *nomen et honor*=honorificum nomen.

Cuneos. A body of men arranged in the form of a wedge, i. e. narrow in front and widening towards the rear; hence peculiarly adapted to break the lines of the enemy.

Consilii quam formidinis. Supply *magis.* The conciseness of T. leads him often to omit one of two correlative particles, cf. note on *minime*, 4.

Referunt. *Carry into the rear*, and so secure them for burial.

Etiam in dubiis proeliis. Even while the battle remains undecided. Gün.

Finierunt. In a present or aorist sense, as often in T. So *prohibuerunt*, § 10; *placuit* and *displicuit*, 11. cf. Lex. Tac. Böt.

VII. *Reges*, civil rulers; *duces*, military commanders. *Ex*= secundum. So *ex ingenio*, § 3. The government was elective, yet not without some regard to hereditary distinctions. They *chose* (*sumunt*) their sovereign, but chose him from the royal family, or at least one of noble extraction. They chose also their commander —the king, if he was the bravest and ablest warrior; if not, they were at liberty to choose some one else. And among the Germans, as among their descendants, the Franks, the authority of the commander was quite distinct from, and sometimes (in war) paramount to, that of the king. Here Montesquieu and others find the original of the kings of the first race in the French monarchy, and the *mayors of the palace*, who once had so much power in France. Cf. Sp. of Laws, B. 31, chap. 4.

Nec is correlative to *et.* *The kings on the one hand do not possess unlimited or unrestrained authority, and the commanders on the other*, &c. *Infinita*=sine modo; *libera*=sine vinculo. Wr. *Potestas*=rightful power, authority; *potentia*=power without regard to right, ability, force, cf. note, 42. Ad rem, cf. Caes. B. G. 5, 27 Ambiorix tells Caesar, that though he governed, yet the people made laws for him, and the supreme power was shared equally between him and them.

Exemplo–imperio. "*Dative* after *sunt*=*are to set an example, rather than to give command.*" So Grüber and Död. But Wr. and Rit. with more reason consider them as ablatives of means limiting a verb implied in *duces: commanders* (command) *more by example, than by authority* (official power). See the principle well stated and illustrated in Döderlein's Essay on the style of Tacitus, p. 15, in my edition of the Histories.

Admiratione praesunt. Gain influence, or ascendency, by means of the admiration which they inspire, cf. note on metus, § 2.

Agant. Subj., ut ad judicium admirantium, non mentem scriptoris trahatur. Gün.

Animadvertere=interficere. Cf. H. 1, 46. 68. *None but the priests are allowed to put to death, to place in irons, nor even* (ne quidem) *to scourge.* Thus punishment was clothed with divine authority.

Effigies et signa. Images and standards, i. e. images, which serve for standards. Images of wild beasts are meant, cf. H. 4, 22: depromptae silvis lucisve ferarum imagines.—*Turmam*, cavalry. *Cuneum*, infantry, but sometimes both. *Conglobatio* is found only in writers after the Augustan age and rarely in them. It occurs in Sen. Qu. Nat. 1, 15, cf. Freund.

Familiae is less comprehensive than *propinquitates. Audiri*, sc. solent. Cf. A. 34 *ruere.* Wr. calls it histor. inf., and Rit. pronounces it a gloss.

Pignora. Whatever is most dear, particularly mothers, wives, and children.—*Unde*, adv of place, referring to *in proximo.*

Vulnera ferunt, i. e. on their return from battle.

Exigere. Examine, and compare, to see who has the most and the most honorable, or perhaps to soothe and dress them.—*Cibos et hortamina.* Observe the singular juxtaposition of things so unlike. So 1: *metu aut montibus;* A. 25: *copiis et laetitia;* 37: *nox et satietas;* 38: *gaudio praedaque.*

VIII. *Constantia precum*=*importunate entreaties.*

Objectu pectorum. By opposing their breasts, not to the enemy but to their retreating husbands, praying for death in preference to captivity.

Monstrata-captivitate. Cominus limits *captivitate*, pointing to captivity as just before them.—*Impatientius. Impatienter* and *impatientia* (the adv. and the subst.) are post-Augustan words. The adj. (impatiens) is found earlier. Cf. Freund.

Feminarum-nomine, i. e. propter feminas suas. Gün. So Cic.: tuo nomine et reipublicae=on your account and for the sake of the republic. But it means perhaps more than that here, viz. in the person of. They dreaded captivity more for their women than for themselves. *Adeo=insomuch that.*

Inesse, sc. feminis. *They think, there is in their women something sacred and prophetic.* Cf. Caes. B. G. 1, 50, where Caesar is informed by the prisoners, that Ariovistus had declined an engagement, because the *women* had declared against coming to action before the new moon.—*Consilia, advice* in general; *responsa, inspired answers*, when consulted.

Vidimus. i. e. she lived in our day—under the reign of Vespasian.—*Veledam.* Cf. H. 4, 61. 65.

Auriniam. Aurinia seems to have been a common name in Germany for prophetess or wise woman. Perhaps=Al-runas, women knowing all things. So *Veleda*=wise woman. Cf. Wr. in loc.

Non adulatione, etc. "Not through adulation, nor as if they were raising mortals to the rank of goddesses." Ky. This is one of those oblique censures on Roman customs in which the treatise abounds. The Romans in the excess of their adulation to the imperial family *made* ordinary women goddesses, as Drusilla, sister of Caligula, the infant daughter of Poppaea (Ann. 15, 23), and Poppaea herself (Dio 63, 29). The Germans, on the other hand, really thought some of their wise women to be divine. Cf. His. 4, 62, and my note ibid. Reverence and affection for woman was characteristic of the German Tribes, and from them has diffused itself throughout European society.

IX. *Deorum.* T. here, as elsewhere, applies Roman names, and puts a Roman construction (Romana interpretatione, § 43), upon the gods of other nations, cf. § 3.

Mercurium. So Caes. B. G. 6, 17: Deum maxime Mercurium colunt. Probably the German *Woden*, whose name is preserved in our Wednesday, as that of Mercury is in the French name of the same day, and who with a name slightly modified (Woden, Wuotan,

Odin), was a prominent object of worship among all the nations of Northern Europe. *Mars* is perhaps the German god of war (Tiw, Tiu, Tuisco) whence Tuesday, French Mardi, cf. Tur. His. Ang. Sax. App. to B. 2. chap. 3. *Herculem* is omitted by Ritter on evidence (partly external and partly internal) which is entitled to not a little consideration. Hercules is the god of strength, perhaps Thor.

Certis diebus. Statis diebus. Gün.

Humanis–hostiis. Even *facere* in the sense of *sacrifice* is construed with abl. Virg. Ec. 3, 77. *Quoque*=even. For its position in the sentence, cf. note, 3.

Concessis animalibus. Such as the Romans and other civilized nations offer, in contradistinction to *human* sacrifices, which the author regards as *in*-concessa. The attempt has been made to remove from the Germans the stain of human sacrifices. But it rests on incontrovertible evidence (cf. Tur. His. Ang. Sax., App. to B. 2. cap. 3), and indeed attaches to them only in common with nearly all uncivilized nations. The Gauls and Britons, and the Celtic nations generally, carried the practice to great lengths, cf. Caes. B. G. 6, 15. The neighbors of the Hebrews offered human victims in great numbers to their gods, as we learn from the Scriptures. Nay, the reproach rests also upon the Greeks and Romans in their early history. Pliny informs us, that men were sacrificed as late as the year of Rome 657.

Isidi. The Egyptian Isis in Germany! This shows, how far the Romans went in comparing the gods of different nations. Gr. Ritter identifies this goddess with the Nertha of chap. 40, the Egyptian Isis and Nertha being both equivalent to Mother Earth, the Terra or Tellus of the Romans.

Liburnae. A light galley, so called from the Liburnians, a people of Illyricum, who built and navigated them. The *signum*, here likened to a galley, was more probably a rude crescent, connected with the worship of the moon, cf. Caes. B. G. 6, 21: Germani deorum numero ducunt Solem et *Lunam.*

Cohibere parietibus=aedificiis includere, K. T. elsewhere speaks of temples of German divinities (e. g. 40: templum Nerthi; Ann. 1, 51: templum Tanfanae); but a consecrated grove or any other sacred place was called *templum* by the Romans (templum from τέμνω, cut off, set apart).

Ex magnitudine. Ex=secundum, cf. *ex nobilitate, ex virtute* § 7. *Ex magnitudine* is predicate after *arbitrantur: they deem it unbecoming the greatness*, etc.

Humani–speciem. Images of the gods existed at a later day in Germany (S. Tur. His. of Ang. Sax., App. to B. 2. cap. 3). But this does not prove their existence in the days of T. Even as late as A. D. 240 Gregory Thaumaturgus expressly declares, there were no images among the Goths. No traces of temple-walls or images have been discovered in connection with the numerous sites of ancient altars or places of offering which have been exhumed in *Germany*, though both these are found on the *borders*, both south and west, cf. Ukert, p. 236.

Lucos et nemora. "Lucus (a λύκη, crepusculum) sylva densior, obumbrans; nemus (νέμος) sylva rarior, in quo jumenta et pecora pascuntur." Bredow.

Deorumque–vident. *They invoke under the name of gods that mysterious existence, which they see* (not under any human or other visible form, but) *with the eye of spiritual reverence alone.* So Gr. and K. Others get another idea thus loosely expressed: They give to that sacred recess the name of the divinity that fills the place, which is never profaned by the steps of man.

Sola reverentia, cf. *sola mente* applied by T. to the spiritual religion of the Jews, H. 5, 5. The religion of the Germans and other northern tribes was more spiritual than that of southern nations, when both were Pagan. And after the introduction of Christianity, the Germans were disinclined to the image-worship of the Papists.

X. *Auspicia sortesque. Auspicia* (avis-spicia) properly divination by observing the flight and cry of birds; *sortes,* by drawing lots: but both often used in the general sense of omens, oracles.

Ut qui maxime, sc. *observant.* Ellipsis supplied by repeating *observant*=to the greatest extent, none more.

Simplex. Sine Romana arte, cf. Cic. de Div. 2, 41, K. The Scythians had a similar method of divining, Herod. 4, 67. Indeed, the practice of *divining* by *rods* has hardly ceased to this day, among the descendants of the German Tribes.

Temere, without plan on the part of the diviner.—*Fortuito,* under the direction of chance. Gr.

Si publice consuletur. If the question to be decided is of a public nature. *Consuletur,* fut., because at the time of drawing lots the deliberation and decision are future. Or it may refer to the consultation of the gods (cf. Ann. 14, 30: *consulere deos*): *if it is by the state that the gods are to be consulted.* So Ritter in his last edition.

Ter singulos tollit. A three-fold drawing for the sake of certainty. Thus Ariovistus drew lots three times touching the death of Valerius (Caes. B. G. 1, 53). So also the Romans drew lots three times, Tibul. 1, 3, 10: sortes ter sustulit. Such is the interpretation of these disputed words by Grüber, Ritter and many others, and such is certainly their natural and obvious meaning: *he takes up three times one after another* all the slips he has *scattered* (*spargere* is hardly applicable to *three* only): if the signs are twice or thrice favorable, the thing is permitted; if twice or thrice unfavorable it is prohibited. The language of Caesar (in loc. cit.) is still more explicit: *ter sortibus consultum.* But Or., Wr. and Död. understand simply the taking up of three lots one each time.

Si prohibuerunt sc. sortes=dii. The reading *prohibuerunt* (al. prohibuerint) is favored by the analogy of *si displicuit,* 11, and other passages. *Sin* (=*si–ne*) is particularly frequent in antithesis with *si,* and takes the same construction after it.

Auspiciorum–exigitur. Auspiciorum, here some other omens, than lots; such as the author proceeds to specify. *Adhuc*=ad hoc, praeterea, i. e. in addition to the lots. The sense is: *besides drawing lots, the persuasion produced by auspices is required.*

Etiam hic. In Germany also (as well as at Rome and other well known countries). *Hic* is referred to Rome by some. But it was hardly needful for T. to inform the Romans of that custom at Rome.

Proprium gentis. It is a peculiarity of the German race. It is not, however, exclusively German. Something similar prevailed among the Persians, Herod. 1, 189. 7, 55. Darius Hystaspes was indebted to the neighing of his horse for his elevation to the throne.

Iisdem memoribus, § 9.—*Mortali opere*=hominum opere.—*Contacti.* Notio contaminandi inest, K.—*Pressi curru.* Harnessed to the sacred chariot. More common, pressi jugo. Poetice.

Conscios, sc. deorum. *The priests consider themselves the servants of the gods, the horses the confidants of the same.* So Tibullus speaks of the *conscia* fibra *deorum.* Tibul. 1, 8, 3.

Committunt. Con and mitto, send together=*engage in fight.* A technical expression used of gladiators and champions.

Praejudicio. Sure prognostic. Montesquieu finds in this custom the origin of the duel and of knight-errantry.

XI. *Apud–pertractentur. Are handled,* i. e. discussed, among, i. e. *by the chiefs,* sc. before being referred to the people.

6

Nisi refers not to *coeunt*, but to *certis diebus*.

Fortuitum, casual, unforeseen; *subitum*, requiring immediate action.

Inchoatur–impletur. Ariovistus would not *fight* before the new moon, Caes. B. G. 1, 50.

Numerum–noctium. Of which custom, we have a relic and a proof in our seven-*night* and fort-*night*. So also the Gauls. Caes. B. G. 6, 18.

Constituunt=decree, determine; *condicunt*=proclaim, appoint. The *con* in both implies *concerted* or public action. They are forensic terms.

Nox–videtur. So with the Athenians, Macrob. Saturn. 1, 3.; and the Hebrews, Gen. 1, 5.

Ex libertate, sc. *ortum*, *arising from*. Gün.

Nec ut jussi. *Not precisely at the appointed time*, but a day or two later, if they choose.

Ut turbae placuit. *Ut*=simul ac, as soon as, *when*. It is the *time of commencing their session*, that depends on the will of the multitude; not their sitting *armed*, for that they always did, cf. *frameas concutiunt* at the close of the section; also § 13: nihil neque publicae neque privatae rei nisi armati agunt. To express this latter idea, the order of the words would have been reversed thus: *armati considunt.*

Tum et coercendi. When the session is commenced, *then* (*tum*) the priests have the right not merely to command silence, but *also* (*et*) *to enforce it.* This use of *et* for *etiam* is very rare in Cic., but frequent in Livy, T. and later writers. See note, His. 1, 23.

Imperatur. *Imperare* plus est, quam *jubere.* See the climax in Ter. Eun. 2, 3, 98; jubeo, cogo atque impero. *Impero* is properly military command. K.

Prout refers, not to the order of speaking, but to the degree of influence they have over the people. Gr.—*Aetas.* Our word *alderman* (elderman) is a proof, that office and honor were conferred on *age* by our German ancestors. So *senator* (senex) among the Romans.

Armis laudare, i. e. armis concussis. "Montesquieu is of opinion that in this Treatise on the manners of the Germans, an attentive reader may trace the origin of the British constitution. That beautiful system, he says, was formed in the forests of Germany, Sp. of Laws 11, 6. The *Saxon* Witena-gemot (Parliament) was, beyond all doubt, an improved political institution, grafted on the rights exercised by the people in their own country." Murphy, cf. S. Tur. His. of Ang. Sax. B. 8. cap. 4.

XII. *Accusare–intendere.* *To accuse and impeach for capital crimes.* Minor offences were tried before the courts described at the end of the section.—*Quoque.* In addition to the legislative power spoken of in the previous section, the council exercised *also* certain judicial functions. *Discrimen capitis intendere,* lit. *to endeavor to bring one in danger of losing his life.*

Ignavos–infames. *The sluggish, the cowardly, and the impure;* for so *corpore infames* usually means, and there is no sufficient reason for adopting another sense here. *Infames* foeda Veneris aversae nota. K. Gr. understands those, whose persons were disfigured by dishonorable wounds, or who had mutilated themselves to avoid military duty. Gün. includes both ideas: *quocunque,* non tantum *venereo,* corporis abusu contempti.

Insuper=superne. So 16: multo *insuper* fimo onerant.

Diversitas is a post-Augustan word, cf. Freund, sub v.

Illuc respicit. *Has respect to this principle.* *Scelera*=*crimes; flagitia*=*vices, low and base actions.* *Scelus* poena, *flagitium* contemptu dignum. Gün.

Levioribus delictis. Abl. abs.=*when lighter offences are committed;* or abl. of circum.=*in case of lighter offences.*

Pro modo poenarum. Such is the reading of all the MSS. *Pro modo, poena* is an ingenious *conjecture* of Acidalius. But it is un necessary. Render thus: *in case of lighter offences, the convicted persons are mulcted in a number of horses or cattle, in proportion to the severity of the sentence adjudged to be due.*

Qui vindicatur. *The injured party,* or *plaintiff.* This principle of pecuniary satisfaction was carried to great lengths among the Anglo-Saxons. See Turner, as cited, 21.

Qui reddunt. Whose *business* or *custom* it is to administer justice, etc. E. proposes *reddant.* But it is without authority and would give a less appropriate sense.

Centeni. Cf. note, § 6: centeni ex singulis pagis. "Sunt in quibusdam locis Germaniae, velut Palatinatu, Franconia, etc. Zentgericht (hundred-courts)," cf. Bernegger.

Consilia et auctoritas. Abstract for concrete=*his advisers and the supporters of his dignity.*

XIII. *Nihil nisi armati.* The *Romans* wore arms only in time of war or on a journey.

Moris, sc. est. A favorite expression of T. So 21: concedere moris (est). And in A. 39.

Suffecturum probaverit. On examination has pronounced him competent (sc. to bear arms). Subj. after *antequam.* H. 523, II.; Z. 576.

Ornant. Ornat would have been more common Latin, and would have made better English. But this construction is not unfrequent in T., cf. 11: rex vel princeps audiuntur. Nor is it without precedent in other authors. Cf. Z. 374. Ritter reads *propinqui.* The attentive reader will discover here traces of many subsequent usages of *chivalry.*

Haec toga. This is the badge of manhood among the Germans, as the toga virilis was among the Romans. The Romans assumed the toga at the age of seventeen. The Athenians were reckoned as Ἔφηβοι at the same age, Xen. Cyr. 1, 2, 8. The Germans (in their colder climate) not till the 20th year. Caes. B. G. 6, 21.

Dignationem. Rank, title. It differs from *dignitas* in being more external. Cf. H. 1, 19: *dignatio Caesaris;* 3, 80: *dignatio viri.* Ritter reads *dignitatem.*

Assignant. High birth or great merits of their fathers assign (i. e. mark out, not consign, or fully confer) *the title of chief even to young men.*

Gradus–habet. Observe the emphatic position of *gradus*, and the force of *quin etiam ipse: Gradations of rank, moreover the retinue itself has*, i. e. the retainers are not only distinguished as a body in following such a leader, *but* there are *also distinctions* among *themselves. Quin etiam* seldom occupies the second place. T. is fond of anastrophe. Cf. Böt. Lex. Tac.

Si–emineat. If he (cuique) *stands pre-eminent for the number and valor of his followers. Comitatus* is gen. *Emineat*, subj. pres. H. 504 & 509; Z. 524.

Ceteris–aspici. These noble youth, thus designated to the rank of chieftains, *attach themselves* (for a time, with some followers perhaps) *to the other* chiefs, who are *older and already distinguished, nor are they ashamed to be seen among their attendants.*

Quibus–cui, sc. sit=*who shall have*, etc.

Ipsa fama. Mere reputation or *rumor* without coming to arms.

Profligant=ad finem perducunt. So Kiessling, Bötticher and Freund. Ritter makes it=*propellunt*, frighten away. *Profligare bella, proelia*, &c., is Tacitean. *Profligare hostes*, &c., is the common expression.

XIV. *Jam vero*=porro. Cf. Böt. Lex. Tac. It marks a transi tion to a topic of special importance. Cf. H. 1, 2. See Död. in loc.

Recessisse. All the best Latin writers are accustomed to use the preterite after pudet, taedet, and other words of the like signification. Gün. The cause of shame is prior to the shame.

Infame. "When Chonodomarus, king of the Alemanni, was taken prisoner by the Romans, his military companions, to the number of two hundred, and three of the king's most intimate friends, thinking it a most flagitious crime to live in safety after such an event, surrendered themselves to be loaded with fetters. Ammian. Marcell. 16, 12, 60. There are instances of the same kind in Tacitus." Mur. Cf. also Caes. B. G. 3, 22. 7, 40.

Defendere, to defend him, when attacked; *tueri, to protect him* at all times.

Praecipuum sacramentum. Their most sacred duty, Gün. and K.; *or the chief part of their oath,* Gr.—*Clarescunt–tuentur.* So Ritter after the best MSS. Al. *clarescant–tueantur,* or *tueare.*

Non nisi. In Cic. usually separated by a word or a clause. In T. generally brought together.

Exigunt. They expect.—*Illum–illam.* Angl. *this–that,* cf. *hinc–hinc,* A. 25.—*Bellatorem equum.* Cf. Virg. G. 2, 145.

Incompti–apparatus. Entertainments, though inelegant yet liberal. Apparatus is used in the same way, Suet. Vitel. 10 and 13.—*Cedunt* =iis dantur. Gün.

Nec arare, etc. The whole language of this sentence is poetical, e. g. the use of the inf. after *persuaseris,* of *annum* for annuam mensem, the sense of *vocare* and *mereri,* &c. *Vocare,* i. e. provocare, cf. H. 4, 80, and Virg. Geor. 4, 76. *Mereri, earn, deserve,* i. e. by bravery.

Pigrum et iners. Piger est natura ad laborem tardus; iners, in quo nihil artis et virtutis. K. Render: *a mark of stupidity and incapacity.*

Quin immo. Nay but, nay more. These words connect the clause, though not placed at the beginning, as they are by other writers. They seem to be placed after *pigrum* in order to throw it into an emphatic position. So *gradus quin etiam,* 13, where see note.—*Possis.* You, i. e., any one can. Z. 524. Cf. note H. 1, 10: *laudares.* So *persuaseris* in the preceding sentence. The subj. gives a contingent or potential turn=*can procure,* sc. if you will *would persuade,* sc. if you should try. An indefinite person is always addressed in the subj. in Latin, even when the ind. would be used if a definite person were addressed. Z. 524.

In the chieftains and their retainers, as described in the last two sections, the reader cannot fail to discover the germ of the feudal system. Cf. Montesq. Sp. of Laws, 30, 3, 4; also Robertson's Chas. V.

XV. *Non multum.* The common reading (multum without the negative) is a mere conjecture, and that suggested by a misapprehension of the meaning of T. *Non multum* is to be taken comparatively. Though in time of peace they hunt often, yet they spend *so much more time in eating, drinking, and sleeping,* that the former is comparatively small. Thus understood, this passage of T. is not inconsistent with the declarations of Caesar, B. G. 6, 21: Vita Germanorum omnis in venationibus atque in studiis rei militaris consistit. Caesar leaves out of account their periods of inaction, and speaks only of their active employments, which were war and the chase. It was the special object of Tacitus, on the contrary, to give prominence to that striking feature of the German character which Caesar overlooks; and therein, as Wr. well observes, the later historian shows his more exact acquaintance with the Germans. *Non multum,* as opposed to *plus,* is nearly equivalent to *minus.*

Venatibus, per otium. Enallage for *venatibus, otio,* H. 704, III. This figure is very frequent in T., e. g. § 40: per obsequium, proeliis; A. 9: virtute aut per artem; A. 41: temeritate aut per ignaviam, &c. Seneca, and indeed most Latin authors, prefer a *similar* construction in antithetic clauses; T. seems rather to avoid it. In all such cases however, as the examples just cited show, *per* with the acc. is not precisely equivalent to the abl. The abl. is more active and implies means, agency; the acc. with *per* is more passive and denotes manner or occasion.

Delegata, transferred.

Familiae. Household, properly of servants (from famel, Oscan for servant), as in chapp. 25 and 32: but sometimes the whole family, as here and in chap. 7: *familiae et propinquitates.*

Ipsi. The men of middle life, the heads of the *familiae.*

Diversitate. Contrariety.—Ament. Subj. H. 518, I.; Z. 577.—*Oderint.* Perf. in the sense of the pres. H. 297, I. 2; Z. 221.

Inertiam. Inertiam=idleness, freedom from business and care (from *in* and *ars*); *quietem=tranquillity,* a life of undisturbed repose without action or excitement. Cf. 14: *ingrata genti quies.* In this account of the habits of the Germans, one might easily fancy he was reading a description of the manner of life among our American Indians. It may be remarked here, once for all, that this resemblance may be traced in very many particulars, e. g. in their personal independence, in the military chieftains and their followers, in their extreme fondness for the hardships and dangers of war, in their strange inactivity, gluttony and drunkenness in peace, in their deliberative assemblies and the power of eloquence to sway their counsels, in their half elective, half hereditary form of government, in the spirituality of their conceptions of God, and some other features of their religion (Robertson has drawn out this comparison in his history of Charles V). All tribes in a rude and savage state must have many similar usages and traits of character. And this resemblance between the well-known habits of our wandering savages and those which T. ascribes to the rude tribes of Germany, may impress us with confidence in the truthfulness of his narrative.

Vel armentorum vel frugum. Partitive gen. Supply aliquid.—*Vel–vel=whether—or,* merely distinctive; *aut–aut=either—or,* adversative and exclusive. *Vel–vel* (from *volo*) implies, that one may *choose* between the alternatives or particulars named; *aut–aut* (from αὖ, αὖτις), that if one is affirmed, the other is denied, since both cannot be true at the same time. Cf. note, A. 17: *aut–aut.*—*Pecuniam.* An oblique censure of the Romans for purchasing peace and alliance with the Germans, cf. H. 4, 76. Herodian 6, 7: τούτῳ γὰρ (sc. χρυσίῳ) μάλιστα Γερμανὸι πείθονται, φιλάργυροί τε ὄντες καὶ τὴν εἰρήνην ἀεὶ πρὸς τοὺς Ῥωμαίους χρυσίου καπηλεύοντες. On *et*, cf. note 11.

XVI. *Populis.* Dative of the agent instead of the abl. with *a* or *ab.* Cf. note 3: *Ulixi.*

Ne–quidem. These words are always separated, the word on which the emphasis rests being placed between them. H. 602, III. 2; Z. 801. Here however the emphasis seems to belong to the whole clause.—*Inter se,* sc. *sedes junctas inter se.*

Colunt=in-colunt. Both often used intransitively, or rather with an ellipsis of the object,=*dwell.*

Discreti ac diversi. Separate and scattered in different directions, i. e. without regular streets or highways. See Or. in loc.

Ut fons–placuit. Hence to this day, the names of German towns often end in bach (brook), feld (field), holz (grove), wald (wood), born (spring). On the permanence of names of places, see note H. 1, 53.

Connexis, with some intervening link, such as fences, hedges, and outhouses; *cohaerentibus,* in immediate contact.

Remedium–inscitia. It may be as a remedy, etc.—*or it may be through ignorance,* etc. *Sive–sive* expresses an alternative conditionally, or contingently=it may be thus, or it may be thus. Compare it with *vel–vel,* chap. 15, and with *aut–aut,* A 17. See also Ramshorn's Synonyms, 138. *Remedium* is acc. in app. with the foregoing clause. *Inscitia* is abl. of cause=per inscitiam.

Caementorum. Properly *hewn* stone (from caedo), but in usage any building stone.—*Tegularum.* Tiles, any materials for the *roof* (tego), whether of brick, stone, or wood.

Citra. Properly this side of, hence short of, or *without,* as used by the *later* Latin authors. This word is kindred to *cis,* i. e. *is* with the demonstrative prefix *ce.* Cf. Freund sub v.

Speciem refers more to the *eye, delectationem* to the *mind.* Taken with *citra,* they are equivalent to adjectives, connected to *informi* and limiting *materia* (citra speciem=non speciosa, Gün.). Render: *rude materials, neither beautiful to the eye nor attractive to the taste. Materia* is distinctively wood for building. Fire-wood is *lignum.*

Quaedam loca. Some parts of their houses, e. g. the walls.

Terra ita pura. Probably red earth, such as chalk or gypsum.

Imitetur. Resembles painting and colored outlines or figures.

Aperire. Poetice=*excavate.* Cellars under ground were unknown to the Romans. See Beck. Gal., and Smith's Dict. Ant.

Ignorantur–fallunt. They are not known to exist, or else (though known to exist) *they escape discovery from the very fact that they must be sought* (in order to be found). Gün. calls attention to the multiform enallage in this sentence: 1. in number (*populatur, ignorantur, fallunt*); 2. of the active, passive, and deponent verbs; 3. in the change of cases (*aperta,* acc.; *abdita* and *defossa,* nom.).

XVII. *Sagum.* A short, thick cloak, worn by Roman soldiers and countrymen.

Fibula=figibula, any artificial fastening; *spina*=natural.

Si desit. Observe the difference between this clause, and *si quando advenit* in the preceding chapter. This is a mere supposition without regard to fact; that implies an expectation, that the case will sometimes happen.

Cetera intecti. Uncovered as to the rest of the body, cf. 6: nudi aut sagulo leves.

Totos dies. Acc. of duration of time.—*Agunt*=vivunt. K.

Fluitante. The flowing robe of the southern and eastern nations; *stricta,* the close dress and short clothes of the northern nations.

Artus exprimente. Quae tam arte artus includit, ut emineant, earumque lineamenta et forma appareant, K. K. and Gr. understand this of coat and vest, as well as breeches; Gün. of breeches only.

Proximi ripae. Near the banks of the Rhine and the Danube, so as to have commercial intercourse with the Romans. These having introduced the cloth and dress of the Romans, attached little importance to the manner of wearing their *skins.* But those in the interior, having no other apparel, valued themselves on the nice adjustment of them.

Cultus, artificial refinement. Cf. note, 6.

Maculis pellibusque, for maculatis pellibus or maculis pellium, perhaps to avoid the concurrence of genitives.

Belluarum–gignit. *Oceanus*=terrae, quas Oceanus alluit; and *belluae*=lutrae, mustelae, erminiae, etc., so K. But Gr. says *belluae* cannot mean such small creatures, and agrees with Lipsius, in understanding by it marine animals, seadogs, seals, &c. Freund connects it in derivation with θήρ, fera (bel=ber=ther=fer), but defines it as properly an animal remarkable for size or wildness. *Exterior Oceanus*=Oceanus extra orbem Romanum, further explained by *ignotum mare.* Cf. note, 2: adversus Oceanus.

Habitus, here=vestitus; in § 4.=forma corporis.

Saepius, oftener than the *men,* who also wore linen more or less. Gün.

Purpura. Facta e succo plantis et floribus expresso. Gün.

Nudae–lacertos. Graece et poetice. Brachia a manu ad cubitum; lacerti a cubito ad humeros.

XVIII. *Quanquam*=sed tamen, i. e. notwithstanding the great freedom in the dress of German women, yet the marriage relation is sacred. This use of *quanquam* is not unfrequent in T., and sometimes occurs in Cic., often in Pliny. See Z. 341, N.

Qui ambiuntur. This passage is construed in two ways: *who are surrounded* (ambiuntur=circumdantur, cf. H. 5, 12.) *by many wives not to gratify lust, but to increase their rank and influence* (*ob* in the sense *for the sake of,* cf. ob metum, 2). Or thus: *who* (take many wives) *not to gratify lust, but on account of their rank they are solicited to form many matrimonial alliances.* For *ambio* in this sense and with the same somewhat peculiar construction after it, see H. 4, 51: *tantis sociorum auxiliis ambiri;* also Virg. Aen. 7, 333: connubiis ambire Latinum. The latter is preferable, and is adopted by Wr., K., Gr., &c. The former by Gün. and others. Ariovistus had two wives. Caes. B. G. 1, 53.

Probant, cf. probaverit, 13, note.—*Comatur.* Subj. denoting the intention of the presents *with which she is to be adorned.* H 500, 1; Z. 567.

Frenatum, bridled, *caparisoned=paratus* below.

In haec munera= ἐπὶ τούτοις τοῖς δωροῖς. *In*=upon the basis of, *on condition of.* So Liv. ꞉ in has leges, in easdem leges.

Hoc–vinculum. So, § 13: haec apud illos toga. In both passages the allusion is to Roman customs (for which see Becker's Gallus, Exc. 1. Scene 1). In Germany, *these presents* take the place of the *confarreatio* (see Fiske's Manual, p. 286. 4. ed.), and the various other methods of ratifying the marriage contract at Rome; *these*, of the religious rites in which the parties mutually engaged on the wedding day (see Man., p. 287).—*Conjugales deos.* Certain gods at Rome presided over marriage, e. g. Jupiter, Juno, Venus, Jugatinus, Hymenaeus, Diana, &c.

Extra. Cic. would have said *expertem* or *positum extra.* But T. is fond of the adv. used elliptically.

Auspiciis=initiatory rites.

Denuntiant, proclaim, denote.—*Accipere* depends on *denuntiant* or *admonetur.*

Rursus, quae–referantur. Rhenanus conjectured; rursusque–referant, which has since become the common reading. But *referantur* is the reading of all the MSS., and needs no emendation; and *quae*, with as good authority as *que*, makes the construction more natural and the sense more apposite. The passage, as Gr. well suggests, consists of two parts (*accipere–reddat*, and *quae–accipiant–referantur*), *each* of which includes the *two* ideas of *receiving* and *handing down* to the next generation. Render thus: *she is reminded that she receives gifts, which she is to hand over pure and unsullied to her children; which her daughters-in-law are to receive again* (sc. from her sons, as she did from her husband), *which are to be transmitted by them to her grand-children.*

Referantur. In another writer, we might expect *referant* to correspond in construction and subject with *accipiant.* But Tacitus is fond of varying the construction. Cf. Bötticher's Lex. Tac., and note, 16: *ignorantur.*

XIX. *Septa.* So the MSS. for the most part. Al. *septae.* Meaning: *with chastity guarded*, sc. by the sacredness of marriage and the excellent institutions of the Germans.

Nullis–corruptae. Here, as every where else in this treatise, T. appears as the censor of Roman manners. He has in mind those fruitful sources of corruption at Rome, public shows, (cf. Sen. Epist. 7: *nihil vero est tam damnosum bonis moribus, quam in aliquo spectaculo desidere*), convivial entertainments (cf. Hor. Od. 3, 6, 27), and epistolary correspondence between the two sexes.

Litterarum secreta=litteras secretas, *secret correspondence* between the sexes, for this limitation is obvious from the connexion. —*Praesens. Immediate.*

Maritis permissa, sc. as a *domestic* crime, cf. Caes. B. G. 6, 19: Viri in uxores, sicut in liberos, vitae necisque habent potestatem. Cf. Beck. Gall., Exc. 1. Sc. 1.

Accisis crinibus, as a special mark of *disgrace*, cf. 1 Cor. 11, 6. So in the laws of the Lombards, the punishment of adulteresses was *decalvari et fustigari.*—*Omnem vicum, the whole village*, cf. Germania omnis, § 1.—*Aetate=juventa.*

Non–invenerit. She would not find, could not expect to find. This use of the perf. subj., for a softened fut., occurs in negative sentences oftener than in positive ones. Cf. Arnold's Prose Comp. 417, Note.

Saeculum=indoles et mores saeculi, *the spirit of the age, the fashion.*

Adhuc (=ad–hoc) is generally used by Cicero, and often by Tacitus, in the sense either of *still* (to this day), or *moreover* (in addition to this). From these, it passed naturally, in Quintilian and the writers after him, into the sense of *even more, still more, even*, especially in connection with the comparative degree; where the authors of the Augustan age would have used *etiam.* See Z. 486 · Böttichers Lex. Tac. sub. voce; and Hand's Tursellinus, vol. 1. p 165. *Melius quidem adhuc=still better even.* For a verb, supply *sunt* or *agunt.* Cf. note A. 19: *nihil.*

Eae civitates. Such as the Heruli, among whom the wife was expected to hang herself at once at the grave of her husband, if she would not live in perpetual infamy. At Rome, on the contrary, divorces and marriages might be multiplied to any extent, cf. Mart. 6, 7: *nubit decimo viro;* also Beck. as above cited.

Semel, like ἅπαξ, *once for all.*

Transigitur. Properly a business phrase. The business is *done up, brought to an end.* So A. 34: transigite cum expeditionibus.

Ultra, sc. pirmum maritum. So the ellipsis might be supplied. *Ultra* here is equivalent to *longior* in the next clause, as T. often puts the adverb in place of the adjective, whether qualifying o: predicate.

Ne tanquam–ament, sc. maritum: *that they may not love* a husband *merely as a husband but as* they love *the married state.* See this and similar examples of *brachylogy* well illustrated in Döderlein's Essay on the style of Tacitus, H. p. 14. Since but one marriage was allowed, all their love for the married state must be concentrated in one husband.

Numerum–finire. In any way contrary to nature and by design. Gün. *Quod fiebat etiam abortus procuratione.* K.

Ex agnatis. Agnati hoc loco dicuntur, qui *post familiam constitutam,* ubi haeres jam est, *deinde nascuntur.* Hess. To put such to death was a barbarous custom among the Romans. Cf. Ann. 3, 25; see Beck. Gall. Exc. 2. scene 1.

Alibi. e. g. at Rome.—*Boni mores* vs. *bonae leges.* These words involve a sentiment of great importance, and of universal application. Good habits wherever they exist, and especially in a republic, are of far greater value and efficacy than good laws.

XX. *Nudi.* Cf. 6: nudi aut sagulo leves. Not literally naked, but slightly clad, cf. Sen. de benef. 5, 13: qui *male vestitum* et pannosum vidit, *nudum* se vidisse dicit.

Sordidi. Gün. understands this of personal filth. But this is inconsistent with the daily practice of bathing mentioned, § 22. It doubtless refers to the *dress,* as Gr. and K. understand it: *nudi ac sordidi*=*poorly and meanly clad.* So also Or.

Quae miramur. Cf. 4: *magna corpora.* See also Caes. B. G. 1, 39. 4, 1. On *haec,* see note, 3: *haec quoque.*

Ancillis ac nutricibus. So in the Dial. de Clar. Orat., T. animadverts upon the custom here obliquely censured: nunc natus infans delegatur Graeculae alicui ancillae. In the early ages of Roman History it was not so, see Becker's Gall. Exc. 2. scene 1.—*Delegantur. Delegamus,* quum, quod *ipsi* facere debebamus, id per *alterum* fieri curamus. E.

Separet. For the use of the subj. pres. after *donec,* see note, 1 *erumpat.*—*Agnoscat*=faciat ut agnoscatur. So Död., Gün. and K. But it is better with Gr., to regard the expression as poetical, and *virtus,* as personified: *and valor acknowledge* them, sc. as brave men and therefore by implication free born.

Venus=concubitus.—*Pubertas*=facultas generandi. Gr. Cf.

Caes, B. G. 6, 21: qui diutissime impuberes permanserunt, maximam inter suos ferunt laudem.

Virgines festinantur=nuptiae virginum festinantur, poetice. The words properare, festinare, accelerare are used in both a trans. and intrans. sense, cf. Hist. 2, 82: festinabantur; 3, 37: festinarentur. Among the Romans, boys of fourteen contracted marriage with girls of twelve. Cf. Smith's Dic. Ant.

Eadem, similis, pares. The comparison is between the youth of the two sexes at the time of marriage; they marry at the same age, equal in stature and equal in strength. Marriages unequal in these respects, were frequent at Rome.—*Pares–miscentur.* Plene: pares paribus, validae validis miscentur. On this kind of brachylogy, see further in Död. Essay on style of T., II. p. 15. *Miscentur* has a middle sense, as the passive often has, particularly in Tacitus. Cf. note 21: *obligantur.*

Referunt. Cf. Virg. Aen. 4, 329: parvulus Aeneas, qui te tamen ore *referret.* See note, 39: auguriis.

Ad patrem. Ad is often equivalent to *apud* in the best Latin authors; e. g. Cic. ad Att. 10, 16: ad me fuit=apud me fuit. Rhenanus by conjecture wrote *apud* patrem to correspond with apud avunculum. But Passow restored *ad* with the best reason. For T. prefers *different* words and constructions in antithetic clauses. Perhaps also a different sense is here intended from that which would have been expressed by *apud.* Wr. takes *ad* in the sense, *in respect to: as in respect to a father*, i. e. as they would have, if he were their father.

Exigunt, sc. hunc nexum=sororum filios.

Tanquam. Like Greek ὡς to denote the views of others, not of the writer. Hence followed by the subj. H. 531; Z. 571.

Et in animum. In=quod attinet ad, *in respect to.* The commonly received text has *ii et animum,* which is a mere conjecture of Rhen. According to K., *teneant* has for its subject not *sororum filii*, but the same subject as *exigunt.* Render: *Since, as they suppose, both in respect to the mind* (the affections), *they hold it more strongly, and in respect to the family, more extensively.*

Heredes properly refers to property, *successores* to rank, though the distinction is not always observed.—*Liberi* includes both sons and daughters.

Patrui, paternal uncles; *avunculi,* maternal.

Propinqui, blood relations; *affines,* by marriage.

Orbitatis pretia. Pretia=*proemia. Orbitatis*=*childlessness.*

Those who had no children, were courted at *Rome* for the sake of their property. Vid. Sen. Consol. ad Marc. 19: in civitate nostra, plus gratiae orbitas confert, quam eripit. So Plutarch de Amore Prolis says: the childless are entertained by the rich, courted by the powerful, defended gratuitously by the eloquent: many, who had friends and honors in abundance, have been stripped of both by the birth of a single child.

XXI. *Necesse est.* It is their duty and the law of custom. Gün. —*Nec*=non tamen.—*Homicidium.* A post-Augustan word.

Armentorum ac pecorum. For the distinction between these words, see note, § 5. The high value which they attached to their herds and flocks, as their *solae et gratissimae opes,* may help to explain the law or usage here specified. Moreover, where the individual was so much more prominent than the state, homicide even might be looked upon as a private wrong, and hence to be atoned for by a pecuniary satisfaction, cf. Tur. Hist. Ang. Sax., App. No. 3, chap. 1.

Juxta libertatem, i. e. *simul cum libertate,* or inter liberos homines. The form of expression is characteristic of the later Latin. Cf. Hand's Tursellinus, vol. III. p. 538. Tacitus is particularly partial to this preposition.

Convictibus, refers to the entertainment of countrymen and friends, *hospitiis* to that of strangers.

Pro fortuna. According to his means. So Ann. 4, 23: fortunae inops.

Defecere, sc. epulae. Quum exhausta sint, quae apparata erant, cf. 24: omnia defecerunt.

Hospes. Properly *stranger;* and hence either *guest* or *host.* Here the latter.—*Comes. Guest.* So Gün. and the common editions. But most recent editors place a colon after *comes,* thus making it *predicate,* and referring it to the *host* becoming the guide and *companion* of his guest to another place of entertainment.

Non invitati, i. e. etiam si non invitati essent. Gün.

Nec interest, i. e. whether invited or not.

Jus hospitis. The right of the guest to a hospitable reception. So Cic. Tus. Quaes., 1, 26: jus hominum.

Quantum ad belongs to the silver age. In the golden age they said: *quod attinet ad,* or simply *ad.* Gr. Cicero however has *quantum in,* N. D. 3, 7; and Ovid, *quantum ad,* A. A. 1, 744. Cf. Freund sub voce.

Imputant. Make charge or *account of.* Nearly confined to the later Latin. Frequent in T. in the reckoning both of debt and credit, of praise and blame. Cic. said: *assignare* alicui aliquid.

Obligantur, i. e. obligatos esse putant. Forma passiva ad modum medii verbi Graeci. Gün. Cf. note, 20: *miscentur*.

Victus–comis. The mode of life between host and guest is courteous. For *victus*=manner of life, cf. Cic. Inv. 1, 25, 35.

XXII. *E* is not exactly equivalent here to *a*, nor does it mean simply *after*, but immediately on awaking *out of* sleep.—*Lavantur*, wash themselves, i. e. bathe; like Gr. λούομαι. So aggregantur, 13; *obligantur*, 21, et passim.

Calida, sc. aqua, cf. in Greek, θερμῷ λούεσθαι, Aristoph. Nub. 1040. In like manner Pliny uses *frigida*, Ep. 6, 16: semel iterumque *frigidam* poposcit transitque. Other writers speak of the Germans as bathing in their rivers, doubtless in the summer; but in the winter they use the warm bath, as more agreeable in that cold climate. So in Russia and other cold countries, cf. Mur. in loco.

Separatae–mensa. Contra Romanorum luxuriam, ex more fere *Homerici* aevi. Gün.

Sedes, opposed to the triclinia, on which the Romans used to *recline*, a practice as unknown to the rude Germans, as to the *early* Greeks and Hebrews. See Coler. Stud. of Gr. Poets, p. 71 (Boston, 1842).

Negotia. Plural=*their* various *pursuits.* So Cic. de Or. 2, 6: *forensia negotia. Negotium*=*nec–otium*, C. and G. being originally identical, as they still are almost *in form.*—*Armati.* Cf. note, 11: *ut turbae placuit.*

Continuare, etc. est diem noctemque jungere potando, sive die nocteque perpotationem continuare. K.

Ut, sc. solet fieri, cf. ut in licentia, § 2. The clause limits *crebrae;* it is the *frequent occurrence* of brawls, that is customary among those given to wine.

Transiguntur. See note on transigitur, § 19.

Asciscendis. i. e. assumendis.

Simplices manifestly refers to the *expression* of thought; explained afterwards by *fingere* nesciunt=*frank, ingenuous.* Cf. His. 1, 15: *simplicissime loquimur;* Ann. 1, 69: *simplices curas.*

Astuta–callida. Astutus est natura, *callidus* multarum rerum peritia. Rit. *Astutus*, cunning; *callidus*, worldly wise. Död.

Adhuc. To this day, despite the degeneracy and dishonesty of the age. So Död. and Or. Rit. says: quae adhuc pectore clauserant. Others still make it=*etiam*, *even*. Cf. note, 19.

Retractatur. Reviewed, *reconsidered.*

Salva–ratio est. The proper relation of both times is preserved, or the advantage of both is secured, as more fully explained in the next member, viz. by *discussing when they are incapable of disguise, and deciding, when they are not liable to mistake.* Cf. Or. in loc., and Bötticher, sub v.

Passow well remarks, that almost every German usage, mentioned in this chapter, is in marked contrast with Roman manners and customs.

XXIII. *Potui*=pro potu, or in potum, dat. of the end. So 46: Victui herba, vestitui pelles. T. and Sallust are particularly fond of this construction. Cf. Böt. Lex. Tac., sub *Dativus.*

Hordeo aut frumento. Hordeo=barley; frumento, properly fruit (frugimentum, fruit κατ' ἐξοχὴν, i. e. grain), grain of any kind, here *wheat,* cf. Veget. R. M. 1, 13: et milites pro frumento hordeum cogerentur accipere.

Similitudinem vini. Beer, for which the Greeks and Romans had no name. Hence Herod. (2, 77) speaks of οἶνος ἐκ κριθέων πεποιημένος, among the Egyptians.

Corruptus. Cum Tacitea indignatione dictum, cf. 4: *infectos,* so Gün. But the word is often used to denote mere change, without the idea of being made worse, cf. Virg. Geor. 2, 466: Nec casia liquidi *corrumpitur* usus olivi. Here render *fermented.*

Ripae, sc. of the Rhine and Danube, i. e. the Roman border, as in 22: proximi ripae.

Poma. Fruits of any sort, cf. Pliny, N. H. 17, 26: arborem vidimus omni genere *pomorum* onustum, alio ramo *nucibus,* alio *baccis,* aliunde *vite, ficis, piris,* etc.

Recens fera. Venison, or other game *fresh,* i. e. *recently taken,* in distinction from the tainted, which better suited the luxurious taste of the Romans.

Lac concretum. Called *caseus* by Caes. B. G. 6, 22. But the Germans, though they lived so much on milk, did not understand the art of making cheese, see Pliny, N. H. 11, 96. "De caseo non cogitandum, potius quod nostrates dicunt dickemilch" (i. e. *curdled milk*). Gün.

Apparatu. Luxurious preparation.—Blandimentis. Dainties.

Haud minus facile. Litotes for multo facilius.

Ebrietati. Like the American Aborigines, see note, § 15.

XXIV. *Nudi.* See note, § 20.

Quibus id ludicrum. For whom it is a sport; not whose business it is to furnish the amusement: that would be *quorum est* K. and Gr.

Infestas=porrectas contra saltantes. K.—*Decorem.* Poetic.

Quaestum=quod quaeritur, *gain.*—*Mercedem,* stipulated pay, *wages.*

Quamvis limits *audacis*=*daring as it is* (as you please).

Sobrii inter seria. At Rome gaming was forbidden, except at the Saturnalia, cf. Hor. Od. 3, 24, 58: vetita legibus alea. The remarkable circumstance (*quod mirere*) in Germany was, that they practised it not merely as an amusement at their feasts, but when sober among (*inter*) their ordinary every-day pursuits.

Novissimo. The last in a series. Very frequently in this sense in T., so also in Caes. Properly newest, then latest, *last.* Cf. note, His. 1, 47. *Extremo,* involving the greatest hazard, like our *extreme: last and final* (decisive) *throw.* This excessive love of play, extending even to the sacrifice of personal liberty, is seen also among the American Indians, see Robertson, Hist. of America, vol. 2, pp. 202–3. It is characteristic of barbarous and savage life, cf. Mur. in loco.

De libertate ac de corpore. Hendiadys=*personal liberty.*

Voluntariam. An earlier Latin author would have used *ipse, ultro,* or the like, limiting the subject of the verb, instead of the object. The Latin of the golden age prefers *concrete* words. The later Latin approached nearer to the English, in using more *abstract* terms. Cf. note on *repercussu,* 3.

Juvenior. More youthful, and therefore more vigorous; not merely younger (*junior*). See Död. and Rit. in loc. Forcellini and Freund cite only two other examples of this full form of the comparative (Plin. Ep. 4, 8. and Apul. Met. 8, 21), in which it does not differ in meaning from the common contracted form.

Ea=talis or tanta. *Such* or *so great.* Gr.

Pervicacia. Pervicaces sunt, qui in aliquo certamine *ad vincendum* perseverant, Schol. Hor. Epod. 17, 14.

Pudore. Shame, *disgrace.* So also His. 3, 61; contrary to usage of earlier writers, who use it for sense of shame, *modesty.*

XXV. *Ceteris.* All but those who have gambled away their own liberty, as in § 24.—*In nostrum morem,* &c., with specific duties distributed through the household (the slave-household, cf. note, 15), as explained by the following clause. On the extreme subdivision of office among slaves at *Rome*, see Beck. Gall. Exc. 2 Sc. 2; and Smith's Dic. Antiq. under Servus.

Descripta=dimensa, distributa. Gün.

Familiam. Here the entire *body of servants*, cf. note, § 15.

Quisque. Each *servant* has his own house and home.

Ut colono. Like the *tenant* or *farmer* among the Romans; also the vassal in the middle ages, and the serf in Modern Europe.

Hactenus. *Thus far*, and *no farther*, i. e. if he pays his rent or tax, no more is required of him.

Cetera. The *rest of the duties* (usually performed by a *Roman servant*), viz. those of the *house*, *the wife and children* (sc. of the master) *perform.* Gr. strangely refers *uxor et liberi* to the wife and children of the servant. Passow also refers *domus* to the house of the servant, thus making it identical with the *penates* above, with which it seems rather to be contrasted. With the use of *cetera* here, compare His. 4, 56: *ceterum vulgus*=the rest, viz. the common soldiers, and see the principle well illustrated in Döderlein's Essay, His. p. 17.

Opere. *Hard labor*, which would serve as a punishment. The Romans punished their indolent and refractory domestics, by sending them to labor in the *country*, as well as by heavy chains (*vinculis*) and cruel flagellations (*verberare*). They had also the power of life and death (*occidere*). Beck. Gall. Exc. 2. Sc. 2; Smith's Dic. Ant. as above.

Non disciplina–ira. Hendiadys=non disciplinae severitate, sed irae impetu. Cf. His. 1, 51: *severitate disciplinae.*

Nisi–impune, i. e. without the pecuniary penalty or satisfaction, which was demanded when one put to death an enemy (*inimicum*). Cf. 21.

Liberti–libertini. These words denote the same persons, but with this difference in the idea: *libertus*=the freedman of some particular master, *libertinus*=one in the *condition* of a freedman without reference to any master. At the time of the Decemvirate, and for some time after, liberti=emancipated slaves, libertini=the descendants of such, cf. Suet. Claud. 24.

Quae regnantur. *Governed by kings.* Ex poetarum more dictum, cf. Virg. Aen. 6, 794: regnata per arva. So 43: Gothones regnantur, and 44: Suiones. Gun.

Ingenuos=free born; *nobiles*=high born.

Ascendunt, i. e. ascendere possunt.

Ceteros. By synesis (see Gr.) for ceteras, sc. gentes.

Impares, sc. ingenuis et nobilibus.

Libertatis argumentum, inasmuch as they value liberty and citizenship too much to confer it on freedmen and slaves. This whole topic of freedmen is an oblique censure of Roman custom in the age of the Emperors, whose freedmen were not unfrequently their favorites and prime ministers.

XXVI. *Fenus agitare. To loan money at interest.*

Et in usuras extendere. And to put out that interest again on interest. The other explanation, viz. that it means simply to put money at interest, makes the last clause wholly superfluous.

Servatur. Is secured, sc. abstinence from usury, or the non-existence of usury, which is the essential idea of the preceding clause.

Ideo–vetitum esset, sc. ignoti nulla cupido! Cf. 19: boni mores, vs. bonae leges. Gün. The reader cannot fail to recognize here, as usual, the reference to Rome, where usury was practised to an exorbitant extent. See Fiske's Manual, § 270, 4. and Arnold's His. of Rome, vol. 1. passim.

Universis. Whole clans, in distinction from individual owners.

In vices. By turns. Al vices, vice, vicis. Död. prefers in vicis; Rit. in vicos=for i. e. by villages. But whether we translate by turns or by villages, it comes to the same thing. Cf. Caes. B. G. 6, 22.

Camporum, arva, ager, soli, terrae, &c. These words differ from each other appropriately as follows: *Terra* is opposed to mare et coelum, viz. *earth. Solum* is the substratum of any thing, viz. *solid ground or soil. Campus* is an extensive plain or level surface, whether of land or water, here *fields. Ager* is distinctively the territory that surrounds a city, viz. *the public lands. Arvum* is ager *aratus*, viz. *plough lands.* Bredow.

Superest. There is enough, and more, cf. § 6, note.

Labore contendunt. They do not strive emulously to equal the fertility of the soil by their own industry. Passow.

Imperatur. Just as frumentum, commeatus, obsides, etc., *imperantur, are demanded* or *expected.* Gün.

Totidem, sc. quot Romani, cf. idem, 4, note. Tacitus often omits one member of a comparison, as he does also one of two comparative particles.

Species. Parts. Sometimes the logical divisions of a genus; so used by Cic. and Quin. (§ 6, 58): cum genus dividitur in species.

Intellectum. A word of the silver age, cf. note on voluntariam,

24. Intellectum—habent=*are understood and named.* "Quam distortum dicendi genus!" Gün.

Autumni–ignorantur. Accordingly in English, spring, summer and winter are Saxon words, while autumn is of Latin origin (Auctumnus). See Dübner in loc. Still such words as Härfest, Herpist, Harfst, Herbst, in other Teutonic dialects, apply to the autumnal season, and not, like our word harvest, merely to the fruits of it.

XXVII. *Funera,* proprie de toto apparatu sepulturae. E. Funeral rites were performed with great pomp and extravagance at Rome; cf. Fiske's Man., § 340; see also Mur. in loco, and Beck. Gall. Exc. Sc. 12.

Ambitio. Primarily the solicitation of office by the candidate; then the parade and display that attended it; then *parade* in general, especially in a bad sense.

Certis, i. e. rite statutis. Gün.

Cumulant. Structura est poetica, cf. Virg. Aen. 11, 50: *cumulatque* altaria donis. K.

Equus adjicitur. Herodotus relates the same of the Scythians (4, 71); Caesar, of the Gauls (B. G. 6, 19). Indeed all rude nations bury with the dead those objects which are most dear to them when living, under the notion that they will use and enjoy them in a future state. See Robertson's Amer. B. 4, &c., &c.

Sepulcrum–erigit. Still poetical; literally: *a turf rears the tomb.* Cf. His. 5, 6: Libanum *erigit.*

Ponunt=deponunt. So Cic. Tusc. Qu.: ad ponendum dolorem Cf. A. 20: posuere iram.

Feminis–meminisse. Cf. Sen. Ep.: Vir prudens meminisse perseveret, lugere desinat.

Accepimus. Ut ab aliis tradita audivimus, non ipsi cognovimus. K. See Preliminary Remarks, p. 79.

In commune. Cic. would have said, universe, or de universa origine. Gr. Cic. uses *in commune,* but in a different sense, viz. for the common weal. See Freund, sub voc.

Instituta, political; *ritus,* religious.

Quae nationes. And what tribes, etc.; *quae* for *quaeque* by asyndeton, or perhaps, as Rit. suggests, by mistake of the copyist. —*Commigraverint.* Subj. of the indirect question. Gr. 265, Z. 552.

German critics have expended much labor and research, in defining the locality of the several German tribes with which the remainder of the Treatise is occupied. In so doing, they rely not only on historical data, but also on the traces of ancient names still attached to cities, forests, mountains, and other localities (cf. note, § 16). These we shall sometimes advert to in the notes. But on the whole, these speculations of German antiquarians are not only less interesting to scholars in other countries, but are so unsatisfactory and contradictory among themselves, that, for the most part, we shall pass them over with very little attention. There is manifestly an intrinsic difficulty in defining the ever changing limits of uncivilized and unsettled tribes. Hence the irreconcilable contradictions between *ancient authorities*, as well as modern critiques, on this subject. Tacitus, and the Roman writers generally, betray their want of definite knowledge of Germany by the frequency with which they specify the names of mountains and rivers. The following geographical outline is from Ukert, and must suffice for the *geography* of the remainder of the Treatise: "In the corner between the Rhine and the Danube, are the Decumates Agri, perhaps as far as the Mayne, 29. Northward on the Rhine dwell the Mattiaci, whose neighbors on the east are the Chatti, 30. On the same river farther north are the Usipii and the Tencteri; then the Frisii 32–34. Eastward of the Tencteri dwell the Chamavi and the Angrivarii (earlier the Bructeri), and east or southeast of them the Dulgibini and Chasuarii, 34, and other small tribes. Eastward of the Frisii Germany juts out far towards the north, 35. On the coast of the bay thus formed, dwell the Chauci, east of the Frisii and the above mentioned tribes; on the south, they reach to the Chatti. East of the Chauci and the Chatti are the Cherusci, 36, whose neighbors are the Fosi. The Cherusci perhaps, according to Tacitus, do not reach to the ocean; and in the angle of the above bay, he places the Cimbri, 37. Thus Tacitus represents the western half of Germany. The eastern is of greater dimensions. There are the Suevi, 38. He calls the country Suevia, 41, and enumerates many tribes, which belong there. Eastward of the Cherusci he places the Semnones and Langobardi; north of them are the Reudigni, Aviones, Anglii, Varini, Eudoses, Suardones and Nuithones; and all these he may have regarded as lying in the interior, and as the most unknown tribes, 41. He then mentions the tribes that dwell on the Danube, eastward from the Decumates Agri: the Hermunduri, in whose country the Elbe has its source; the Narisci, Marcomanni and Quadi, 41–42. The Marcomanni hold the country which the Boii formerly possessed; and northward of them and the Quadi, chiefly on the mountains which run through Suevia, are the Marsigni, Gothini, Osi and Burii, 43. Farther north are the Lygii, consisting of many tribes, among which the most distinguished are the Arii, Helvecones, Manimi, Elysii and Naharvali, 43. Still farther north dwell the Gothones, and, at the Ocean, the Rugii and Lemovii. Upon islands in the ocean live the Suiones, 44. Upon the mainland, on the coast, are the tribes of the Aestyi, and near them, perhaps on islands, the Sitones, 45. Perhaps he assigned to them the immense islands to which he refers in his first chapter. Here ends Suevia. Whether the Peucini, Venedi and Fenni are to be reckoned as Germans or Sarmatians, is uncertain, 46. The Hellusii and Oxonae are fabulous."

The following paragraph from Prichard's Researches embodies some of the more general conclusions of *ethnographers*, especially of Zeuss, on whom Prichard, in common with Orelli and many other scholars, places great reliance. "Along the coast of the German Ocean and across the isthmus of the Cimbric peninsula to the shore of the Baltic, were spread the tribes of the Chauci and Frisii, the Anglii, Saxones and the Teutones or Jutes, who spoke the *Low-German* languages, and formed one of the four divisions of the German race, corresponding as it seems with the *Ingaevones* of Tacitus, and Pliny. In the higher and more central parts, the second great division of the race, that of the *Herminones*, was spread, the tribes of which spoke *Upper* or *High-German* dialects. Beginning in the West with the country of the Sigambri on the Rhine, and from that of the Cherusci and Angrivarii near the Weser and the Hartz, this division comprehended, besides those tribes, the Chatti, the Langobardi, the Hermunduri, the Marcomanni and Quadi, the Lugii, and beyond the Vistula the Bastarnae, in the neighborhood of the Carpathian hills. To the eastward and northward of the last mentioned, near the lower course of the Vistula and thence at least as far as the Pregel, were the primitive abodes of the Goths and their cognate tribes, who are perhaps the *Istaevones*." The fourth division of Prichard embraced the Scandinavians, who spoke a language kindred to the Germans and were usually classed with them. Those who would examine this subject more thoroughly, will consult Adelung, Zeuss, Grimm, Ritter, Ukert, Prichard, Latham, &c., who have written expressly on the geography or the ethnography of Germany.

XXVIII. *Summus auctorum*, i. e. omnium scriptorum is, qui plurimum *auctoritatis fideique* habet. K. Cf. Sueton. Caes. 56.

Though T. commends so highly the *authority* o Caesar as a writer, yet he differs from him in not a few matters of fact, as well as opinion; owing chiefly, doubtless, to the increased means of information which he possessed in the age of Trajan.

Divus Julius. *Divus*=deified, *divine;* an epithet applied to the Roman Emperors after their decease.—*Tradit.* Cf. Caes. B. G. 6, 24: fuit antea tempus, cum *Germanos Galli* virtute *superarent,* ultro bella inferrent, propter hominum multitudinem agrique inopiam trans Rhenum colonias mitterent. Livy probably refers to the same events, when he says (Lib. 5, 34), that in the reign of Priscus Tarquinius, two immense bodies of Gauls migrated and took possession, the one of the Hercynian Forest, the other of Upper Italy.

Amnis. The Rhine.—Promiscuas. Unsettled, ill defined.

Quo minus after a verb of hindering is followed by the subj. H. 499; Z. 543.

Nulla–divisas, i. e. *not distributed among different and powerful kings.*

Hercyniam silvam. A series of forests and mountains, stretching from Helvetia to Hungary in a line parallel to the Danube, and described by Caesar (B. G. 6, 25), as nine day's journey in breadth and more than sixty in length. The name seems to be preserved in the modern *Hartz* Forest, which is however far less extensive.

Igitur–Helvetii=igitur *regionem* inter, etc. See note on *colunt,* 16. *Igitur* seldom stands as the first word in a sentence in Cicero. Cf. Z. 357; and Kühner's Cic. Tusc. Qu. 1, 6, 11. Here it introduces a more particular explanation of the general subject mentioned at the close of the previous chapter. So in A. 13. When so used, it sometimes stands first in Cic., always in T. Cf. Freund sub v. Touching the Helvetii, see Caes. B. G. 1, 1; T. His. 1, 67.

Boihemi nomen. Compounded of Boii and heim (home of the Boii), now Bohemia. *Heim*=*ham* in the termination of so many names of towns, e. g. Framing*ham*, Notting*ham*. The Boii were driven from their country by the Marcomanni, 42. The fugitives are supposed to have carried their name into Boioaria, now Bavaria. Cf. Prichard's Physical Researches, Vol. III. Chap. 1, Sec. 6; and Latham's Germany of Tacitus in loco.

Germanorum natione, i. e. German in situation, not in origin, for this he expressly denies or disproves in 43, from the fact that they spoke the Pannonian language, and paid tribute. The doubt expressed here has reference only to their original *location,* not to their original stock, and is therefore in no way inconsistent with the affirmation in chapter 43.

Cum=*since.* Hence followed by subj. H. 518, I.; Z. 577.

Utriusque ripae. Here of the *Danube,* the right or Pannonian bank of which was occupied by the Aravisci, and the left or German bank by the Osi. So elsewhere of the *Rhine,* 37, and of both, 17, and 23.

Treveri. Hence modern *Treves.*

Circa. In respect to. A use foreign to the golden age of Latin composition, but not unfrequent in the silver age. See Ann. 11, 2. 15. His. 1, 43. Cf. Z. 298, and note, H. 1, 13.

Affectationem. Eager desire to pass for native Germans. Ad verbum, cf. note, H. 1, 80.

Ultro. Radically the same with *ultra*=beyond. Properly beyond expectation, beyond necessity, beyond measure, beyond any thing mentioned in the foregoing context. Hence unexpectedly, freely, cheerfully, very much, even more. Here *very, quite.* Gr.

Inertia Gallorum. T., says Gün., is an everlasting persecutor of the Gauls, cf. A. 11.

Haud dubie=haud dubii. It limits Germanorum populi. *Undoubtedly German tribes.*

Meruerint. Not merely deserved, but *earned, attained.* For the subj. after *quanquam,* cf. note, 35.

Agrippinenses. From Agrippina, daughter of Germanicus and wife of Claudius. Ann. 12, 27. Now Cologne.

Conditoris. Conditor with the earlier Latins is an epicene, conditrix being of later date. Here used of Agrippina. Of course *sui* cannot agree with *conditoris.* It is a reflexive pronoun, the objective gen. after *conditoris*=the founder of *themselves,* i. e. of their state, cf. *odium sui,* 33.

Experimento. Abl. *on* trial, not *for;* i. e. in consequence of being found faithful. In reference to the Ubii, cf. His. 4, 28.

XXIX. *Virtute* sc. bellica.

Non multum ex ripa. A small tract on the bank, but chiefly an island in the river. Cf. His. 4, 12: extrema Gallicae orae, simulque insulam, occupavere.

Chattorum quondam. The very name Batavi is thought by some to be a corrupted or modified form of Chatti. See Rit. in loc.

Transgressus. *When* is not known, but Julius Caesar found them already in possession of their new territory. B. G. 4, 10.

Fierent. Subj. after *eas–quibus*=*such that.* H. 500, 2; Z. 556.

Nec–contemnuntur. *Are neither dishonored.* So in His. 4, 17, the Batavians are called *tributorum expertes.*

Oneribus. *The burdens of regular taxation.*—*Collationibus. Extraordinary contributions.*

Tela, offensive; *arma,* defensive armor.

In sua ripa. On the right or eastern bank of the Rhine. *Agunt* is to be taken with *in sua ripa,* as well as with *nobiscum,* which are antithetic to each other. Meaning: in situation Germans, in feeling Romans.

Mente animoque. *In mind and spirit.* *Mens* is properly the understanding, *animus* the feeling part, and both together comprehend the whole soul.

Acrius animantur. *Made more courageous by the influence of their very soil and climate even* (*adhuc,* cf. note, 19).

Numeraverim. Subj. cf. note, 2: *crediderim.*

Decumates–exercent. *Exercent*=colunt. So Virg. tellurem, terram, humum, solum, &c., *exercere.*

Decumates=decumanos. Occurs only here. Tithe-paying lands. For their location, see note, 27.

Dubiae possessionis, i. e. *insecure,* till confirmed by *limite acto promotisque praesidiis,* i. e. *extending the boundary and advancing the garrisons or outposts.*

Sinus. *Extreme bend* or *border.* Cf. note, 1. So Virg. (Geor. 2, 123) calls India extremi *sinus* orbis.

Provinciae. *A* province, not any particular one.

XXX. *Initium inchoant.* Pleonastic. So initio orto, His. 1, 76; initium coeptum, His. 2, 79; perferre toleraverit, Ann. 3, 3. *Ultra* is farther back from the Rhine. Chattorum sedes ubi nunc magnus ducatus et principatus *Hassorum,* quorum nomen a Chattis deductum. Ritter. Chatti=Hessians, as Germ. wasser=Eng. water, and πράσσω=πράττω.

Effusis. *Loca effusa* sunt, quae *latis campis* patent. K. This use belongs to the later Latin, though Horace applies the word with *late* to the sea: effusi late maris. Gr.

Durant siquidem, etc. On the whole, I am constrained to yield to the authority and the arguments of Wr., Or., Död., and Rit., and place the pause before *durant,* instead of after it as in the first edition. *Durant* precedes *siquidem* for the sake of emphasis, just as *quin immo* (chap. 14) and *quin etiam* (13) yield their usual place to the emphatic word. These are all departures from established usage. See notes in loc. cit. *Que* must be understood after *paulatim*: it is inserted in the text by Ritter.

Rarescunt. *Become fewer* and farther apart. So Virg. Aen. 3, 411: *Angusti rarescent claustra Pelori.*

Chattos suos. As if the Chatti were the children of the Forest, and the Forest emphatically their country. Passow.

Prosequitur, deponit. Begins, continues, and ends with the Chatti. Poetical=is coextensive with.

Duriora, sc. solito, or his, cf. Gr. 256, 9.—*Stricti, sinewy, strong,* which has the same root as *stringo.*

Ut inter Germanos, i. e. pro ingenio Germanorum, Gün. So we say elliptically: *for Germans.*

Praeponere, etc. A series of infinitives without connectives, denoting a hasty enumeration of particulars; elsewhere, sometimes, a rapid succession of events. Cf. notes, A. 36, and H. 1, 36. The particulars here enumerated, all refer to *military* proceedings.

Disponere–noctem. *They distribute the day,* sc. as the period of various labors; *they fortify the night,* sc. as the scene of danger. Still highly poetical.

Ratione. *Way, manner.* Al. *Romanae.*

Ferramentis. *Iron tools,* axes, mattocks, &c.—*Copiis.* *Provisions.*

Rari. Predicate of *pugna,* as well as *excursus.*—*Velocitas* applies to cavalry, *cunctatio* to infantry; *juxta*=connected with, allied to, cf. juxta libertatem, 21.

XXXI. *Aliis–populis.* Dat. after *usurpatum,* which with its adjuncts is the subject of *vertit.* See same construction, His. 1, 18: observatum id antiquitus comitiis dirimendis non terruit Galbam, etc., cf. also A. 1.—*Audentia* occurs only thrice in T. (G. 31. 34. Ann. 15, 53), and once in Pliny (Ep. 8, 4). It differs from *audacia* in being a *virtue.*

Vertit. Intrans. Not so found in Cic., but in Liv., Caes., and Sall., not unfrequent. Gr. Cic. however uses *anno vertente.*

In consensum vertit. *Has become the common custom.*

Ut primum. *Just as soon as.* A causal relation is also implied; hence followed by the subj.

Crinem–submittere. We find this custom (*of letting the hair and beard grow long*) later among the Lombards and the Saxons, cf. Turn. His. Ang. Sax., App. to B. 2.

Super–spolia, i. e. *over the bloody spoils* of a slain enemy.

Revelant, i. e. they remove the hair and beard, which have so long *veiled* the face.

Retulisse=*repaid, discharged their obligations to those who gave them birth.*

Squalor. This word primarily denotes roughness; secondarily and usually filth: here the deformity of unshorn hair and beard.

Insuper, i. e. besides the long hair and beard. The proper position of *insuper* is, as here, between the adj. and subs., cf. 34: immensos *insuper* lacus; see also *insuper*, 12.

Absolvat. Subj. after *donec.* So *faciat* below. See note, 1.

Hic–habitus, sc. *ferreum annulum*, cf. 17. *Plurimis*=permultis, Rit.

Placet. Antithetic to *ignominiosum genti.* Very many of the Chatti are *pleased* with that which is esteemed a disgrace by most Germans, and *so* pleased with it as to retain it to old age, and wear it as a badge of distinction (*canent insignes*).

Nova. Al. *torva.* *Strange, unusual.* Placed in the *van* (*prima acies*), because as the author says, § 43: primi in omnibus proeliis *oculi* vincuntur.

Mansuescunt. Primarily said of wild beasts, *accustomed to the hand of man* or *tamed.* So *immanis*, *not* handled, wild, savage. The clause introduced by *nam* illustrates or enforces *visu nova*, and may be rendered thus: *for not even in time of peace do they grow gentle* and put on *a milder aspect.*

Exsanguis. Usually lifeless or pale. Here *languid, feeble.*

XXXII. *Alveo*=quoad alveum. Abl. of respect, H. 429; Z. 457.

Certum. Fixed, well defined, i. e. not divided and diffused, (so as to form of itself no sufficient border or boundary to the Roman Empire) as it was nearer its source among the Chatti. So this disputed word seems to be explained by the author himself in the following clause; *quique terminus esse sufficiat*=*and such that it suffices to be a boundary.* *Qui*=*talis ut;* hence followed by the subj. H. 500, I.; Z. 558. So Mela (3, 2) contrasts *solidus et certo alveo lapsus* with *huc et illuc dispergitur.*

Tencteris=apud Tencteros, by *enallage*, cf. note on *ad patrem*, 20, and other references there. The Tencteri and Usipii seem to have been at length absorbed into the mass of people, who appear under the later name of Alemanni. Cf. Prichard.

Familiam. Servants, cf. note on same word, 15. See also Beck, Gall., Exc. 1. Sc. 1.—*Penates*=our *homestead.*

Jura successionum=*heir looms*, all that goes down by hereditary descent.

Excipit. Here in the unusual sense of *inherits.*—*Cetera*, sc. *jura successionum.*

Bello. Abl. and limits both *ferox* and *melior.* Meaning: *The horses are inherited, not, like the rest of the estate, by the eldest son, but by the bravest.*

XXXIII. *Occurrebant. Met the view, presented themselves.* A. most the sense of the corresponding English word. The structure of *narratur* (as impers.) is very rare in the earlier authors, who would say: *Chamavi narrantur.* Cf. His. 1, 50. 90. The *Chamavi*, &c., were joined afterwards to the Franks. Cf. Prichard. The present town of *Ham* in Westphalia probably preserves the name and gives the *original* locality of the *Chamavi*, the present *Engern* that of the *Angrivarii.* The termination varii or uarii probably= inhabitants of. Thus Angrivarii=inhabitants of Engern Chasuarii =inhabitants of the river Hase. The same element is perhaps contained in the termination of Bruct*eri* and Tenct*eri.* See Latham in loco.

Nos, sc. Romanos. *Erga*=inclined to (cf. vergo), *towards.*

Spectaculo. Ablative. Invidere is constructed by the Latins in the following ways: invidere alicui aliquid, alicui alicujus rei, alicui aliqua re, alicui in aliqua re. Hess. The construction here (with the abl. of the thing, which was the object of envy) belongs to the silver age. Cf. Quint. (Inst. 9, 3, 1) who contrasts it with the usage of Cicero, and considers it as illustrating the fondness of the age for *figurative* language.

Oblectationi oculisque. Hendiadys for ad oblectationem oculorum. The author here exults in the promiscuous slaughter of the German Tribes by each other's arms, as a brilliant spectacle to Roman eyes—a feeling little congenial to the spirit of Christianity, but necessarily nurtured by the gladiatorial shows and bloody amusements of the Romans, to say nothing of the habitual hostility which they waged against all other nations, that did not submit to their dominion.

Quaeso, sc. *deos.* Though *fortune* is spoken of below, as controlling the destiny of nations. This passage shows clearly that

Tacitus, with all his partiality for German manners and morals, still retains the heart of a Roman patriot. He loves his country with all her faults, and bears no good-will to her enemies, however many and great their virtues. The passage is important, as illustrating the spirit and design of the whole Treatise. The work was not written as a blind panegyric on the Germans, or a spleeny satire on the Romans. Neither was it composed for the purpose of stirring up Trajan to war against Germany; to such a purpose, such a clause, as *urgentibus imperii fatis*, were quite adverse. Least of all was it written for the mere pastime and amusement of Roman readers. It breathes the spirit at once of the earnest patriot, and the high-toned moralist.

Odium sui. Cf. note, 28: *conditor. Hatred of themselves;* i. e. of one another. So in Greek, the reflexive pronoun is often used for the reciprocal.

Quando=since; a subjective reason. Cf. note, His. 1, 31; and Z. 346.—*Urgentibus-fatis*, sc. to discord and dissolution, for such were the forebodings of patriotic and sagacious minds ever after the overthrow of the Republic, even under the prosperous reign of Trajan.

XXXIV. *A tergo*, i. e. further back from the Rhine, or towards the East.—*A fronte*, nearer the Rhine or towards the West. Both are to be referred to the Angrivarii and Chamavi, who had the Dulgibini and the Chasuarii in their rear (on the east), and the Frisii on their front (towards the west or northwest).—*Frisii*, the Frieslanders.

Majoribus-virium. They have the name of Greater or Less Frisii, according to the measure of their strength. For this sense of *ex* see note 7. For the case of *majoribus minoribusque* see Z. 421, and H. 387, 1.

Praetexuntur. Are bordered by the Rhine (hemmed, as the toga *praetexta* by the purple); or, as Freund explains, are covered by it, i. e. lie behind it.—*Immensos lacus.* The bays, or arms of the sea, at the mouth of the Rhine (Zuyder Zee, etc.), taken for lakes by T. and Pliny (Ann. 1, 60. 2, 8. N. H. 4, 29). They have been greatly changed by inundations. See Mur. in loco.

Oceanum, sc. Septentrionalem.—*Sua*, sc. parte.—*Tentavimus*, *explored.*

Herculis columnas. "Wherever the land terminated, and it appeared impossible to proceed further, ancient maritime nations feigned pillars of Hercules. Those mentioned in this passage some authors have placed at the extremity of Friesland, and others at the entrance of the Baltic." Ky. cf. note, 3.

Adiit, i. e. vere adiit, *actually* visited that part of the world.

Quicquid–consensimus. This passage is a standard illustration of the *Romana interpretatione* (§ 43), the Roman construction, which the Romans put upon the mythology and theology of other nations. It shows that they were accustomed to apply the names of their gods to the gods of other nations on the ground of some resemblance in character, history, worship, &c. Sometimes perhaps a resemblance in the *names* constituted the ground of identification.

Druso Germanico. Some read Druso *et* Germanico; others Druso, Germanico, as a case of asyndeton (Gr. 323, 1 (1.)); for both Drusus and Germanicus sailed into the Northern Ocean, and it is not known that Germanicus (the son of Drusus and stepson of Tiberius, who is by some supposed to be meant here) is ever called *Drusus Germanicus.* But Drusus, the father of Germanicus, is called Drusus Germanicus in the Histories (5, 19), where he is spoken of as having thrown a mole or dam across the Rhine; and it is not improbable that he is the person here intended. So K., Or. and Wr.

Se, i. e. the Ocean. See H. 449, II.; Z. 604.

Inquiri. Impersonal=*investigation to be made. E.* suggests *inquirenti*, agreeing with *Germanico.* But T., unlike the earlier Latin authors, not unfrequently places an infin. after a verb of hindering.

Credere quam scire. T. perhaps alluded to the precept of the Philosopher, who said: Deum cole, atque crede, sed noli quaerere. Murphy.

XXXV. *In Septentrionem*, etc. *On the North, it falls back*, sc. into the Ocean, *with* an immense *bend* or peninsula. The *flexus* here spoken of is called *sinus* in chap. 37, and describes the Cimbric Chersonesus, or Danish Peninsula. See Död., Or. and Rit. in loc. —*Ac primo statim. And first immediately*, sc. as we begin to trace the northern coast.—*Lateribus*, sc. the eastern.

Quanquam followed by the subj., seldom in Cic., but usually in T., Z. 574, Note. Cf. note, His. 5, 21.—*Sinuetur*, sc. southwards. *Donec–sinuetur.* Cf. note, 1: *erumpat.*

Inter Germanos. Considered among the Germans, *in the estimation of the Germans.*

Quique–tueri. A *clause* connected to an *adj.* (nobilissimus), cf.

certum, quique, 32. *Qui* in both passages=talis, ut. Hence followed by subj. H. 501, I.; Z. 558.

Impotentia, ungoverned passion, ἀκράτεια. *Impotentia* seldom denotes want of power, but usually that unrestrained passion, which results from the want of ability to control one's self.

Ut–agant depends on *assequuntur.* Subj. H. 490; Z. 531, *a.*

Si res poscat. Some copies read: si res poscat *exercitus.* But posco and postulo seldom have the object expressed in such clauses, cf. 44: ut res poscit; 6: prout ratio poscit. So also Cic. and Sall., pass. *Exercitus* is subject nom., *promptus* being understood, as pred.; and *plurimum virorum equorumque* explains or rather enforces *exercitus: and, if the case demand, an army, the greatest abundance of men and horses.*

Quiescentibus, i. e. bellum non gerentibus; *eadem,* i. e. the same, as if engaged in war.

XXXVI. *Cherusci.* It was their chief, Arminius (Germ. Hermann), who, making head against the Romans, was honored as the Deliverer of Germany, and celebrated in ballad songs, which are preserved to this day. See his achievements in Ann. B. 1, and 2. This tribe became afterwards the head of the Saxon confederacy.

Marcentem. Enervating. So *marcentia pocula.* Stat. Silv. 4, 6, 56. It is usually intransitive, and is taken here by some in the sense of languid, enervate (literally withered).—*Illacessiti* is a post-Augustan word. Cf. Freund.

Impotentes. Cf. impotentia, 35.

Falso quiescas. Falleris, dum quiescis. Dilthey. Cf. note, 14: *possis.*

Ubi manu agitur. Where matters are decided by might rather than right. Cf. *manu agens,* A. 9.

Nomina superioris. *Virtues* (only) *of the stronger party,* the conqueror. They are deemed vices in the weaker.

Chattis–cessit: while to the Chatti, who were *victorious, success was imputed for wisdom.* The antithetic particle at the beginning of the clause is omitted. Cf. note, 4: *minime.*

Fuissent. Subj. after *cum* signifying *although.* H. 516, II.

XXXVII. *Sinum. Peninsula,* sc. the Cimbric. Cf. note, 35: *flexu;* 31: *sinus.*

Cimbri. The same with the Cimmerii, a once powerful race, who, migrating from western Asia, that hive of nations, overran a large part of Europe, but their power being broken by the Romans, and themselves being overrun and conquered by the Gothic or German Tribes, they were pushed to the extreme western points of the continent and the British Isles, where, and where alone, distinct traces of their language and literature remain to this day. They have left their name indelibly impressed on different localities in their route, e. g. the Cimmerian Bosphorus, the Cimbric Chersonesus (now Jutland, occupied by the Cimbri in the days of T.), Cumberland (Cumbria, from Cimbri) &c. The ancient name of the Welsh was also Cymri, cf. Tur. His. Ang. Sax. 1. 2.

Gloria is abl. limiting *ingens.*

Castra ac spatia. In apposition with *lata vestigia*=spatiosa castra or castrorum spatia. H. 704, II. 2; Z. 741.

Utraque ripa, sc. of the Rhine, *the* river and river bank by eminence.

Molem manusque. The mass of their population, and the number of their armies. Observe the alliteration, as if he had said: measure the mass and might.

Exitus, i. e. *migrationis.* Often used in this sense, cf. Caes. B. C. 3, 69: Salutem et *exitum* sibi pariebant.—*Fidem, proof.*

Sexcentesimum–annum. T. follows the Catonian Era. According to the Varronian Era, received by the moderns, the date would be A. U. C. 641=A. C. 113.

Alterum–consulatum. The second consulship of Trajan (when he was also Emperor) was, after the reckoning of Tacitus, A. U. C. 850, according to modern computation, 851=A. D. 98. This year doubtless marks the time when this treatise was written, else why selected?

Vincitur. So long is Germany in being conquered. (The work was never completed.) Cf. Liv. 9, 3: quem per annos jam prope *triginta vincimus.*

Medio–spatio. In the intervening period, sc. of 210 years.

Samnis–Galliaeve. The Romans had fought bloody, and sometimes disastrous battles with the Samnites (at the Caudine Forks, Liv. 9, 2.), with the Carthaginians (in the several Punic Wars), with the Spaniards under Viriathus and Sertorius (Florus, Lib. 2.), with the Gauls (Caes. B. G. pass.). But none of these were so sanguinary as their wars with the Germans.

Admonuere, sc. vulneribus, cladibus=castigavere.

Regno–libertas. Liberty and monarchy in studied antithesis. T. means to imply that the former is the stronger principle of the two

Arsacis. The family name of the Parthian kings, as Pharaoh and Ptolemy of the Egyptian, Antiochus of the Syrian, &c.

Amisso et ipse, sc. *oriens;* the East *itself also lost* its prince (Pacorus), in the engagement, as well as the Romans their leader (Crassus).—*Objecerit, reproach us with.* Subj. Cf. n. G. 2: *peteret.*

Ventidium. Commander under Anthony, and conqueror of the Parthians in three battles, A. U. C. 715. He was raised from the lowest rank and the meanest employment, hence perhaps the expression, *dejectus infra, humbled beneath Ventidius.*

Carbone–Manlio. Cneius Papirius Carbo defeated at Noreja, A. U. 641 (Liv. Epit. 63.), L. Cassius Longinus defeated and slain, 647 (Caes. B. G. 1, 7. 12.), M. Aurelius Scaurus defeated and taken captive, 648 (Liv. Epit. 67.), Servilius Caepio and M. Manlius defeated with great slaughter at Tolosa, 649 (Liv. Epit. 67.), Quintilius Varus defeated and slain, 762 (Suet. Oct. 23.)—all these victories over the Romans in their highest strength and glory—either in the time of the *Republic* (*Populo Romano*), or of the *Empire* under Augustus (*Caesari*)—all these attested the courage and military prowess of the Germans; and they were still, for the most part, as free and as powerful as ever.

Caius Marius almost annihilated the Cimbri at Aquae Sextiae, A. U. C. 652.

Drusus. Claudius Drusus invaded Germany four times, 742–3, and finally lost his life by falling from his horse on his return, cf. Dio. Libb. 54. 55.

Nero, commonly known as Tiberius (brother of Drusus and stepson of Augustus), had the command in Germany at three different times, 746–7, 756–9, 764–5, cf. Suet. Tib. 9. seq.

Germanicus, son of Drusus, made four campaigns in Germany, A. D. 14–16, cf. Ann. B. 1. and 2.

C. Caesaris. Caligula, cf. Suet. Calig.; T. His. 4, 15.

Discordiae–armorum. The civil wars after the death of Nero under Galba, Otho, and Vitellius.

Expugnatis–hibernis. By the Batavians under Civilis. His. 4, 12 seq.; A. 41.

Affectavere. *Aspired to the government of,* cf. note on affectationem, 28. After *donec,* T. always expresses a single definite past action by the perf. ind., cf. A. 36: *donec–cohortatus est;* a repeated, or continued past action by the imp. subj. cf. note, A. 19: *donec–peteret;* and a present action, which is in the nature of the case also a continued action, by the pres. subj. cf. note, 1: *separet.*

Triumphati. Poetice, cf. Virg. Aen. 6, 837: Triumphata Corintho; Hor. Od. 3, 3, 43: Triumphati Medi. The reference here is to the ridiculous triumph of Domitian, A. 39, in which slaves, purchased and dressed out for the purpose, were borne as captives through the streets.

XXXVIII. *Suevis.* In the time of T. a powerful confederacy, embracing all the tribes enumerated in 39–45, and covering all the eastern and larger half of Germany. But the confederacy was soon dissolved and seldom appears in subsequent history. We still have a trace of their name in the Modern *Suabia.* The name is supposed by some philologists (e. g. Zeuss) to denote *unsettled wanderers* (Germ. Schweben, to wave, to hover, cf. Caes. B. G. 4, 1: Suevis non longius anno remanere uno in loco, etc.); as that of the Saxons does settlers, or *fixed residents* (Germ. Sassen), and that of the Franks, *freemen.* See Rup. in loc. An ingenious Article in the North American Review (July, 1847), makes the distinction of Suevi and non-Suevi radical and permanent in the religion and the language of the Germans; the Suevi becoming Orthodox Catholics, and the non-Suevi Arians in Ecclesiastical History, and the one High-Dutch and the other Low-Dutch in the development of their language.

Adhuc. Cf. note on it, 19. As to position, cf. *insuper* 31, and 34. The Suevi are *still* (*adhuc*) divided into distinct tribes bearing distinct names, though united in a confederacy. Cf. Hand's Tursellinus, 1, 163. Död. renders *besides*, sc. the general designation of Suevi.

In commune. *In common.* Not used in this sense by Cic., Caes. and Liv., though frequent in T. Gr. Cf. note on the same, 27.

Obliquare. *To turn the hair back, or comb it up* contrary to its natural direction—and then fasten it in a knot on the top of the head (*substringere nodo*); so it seems to be explained by the author himself below: *horrentem capillum retro sequuntur ac in ipso solo vertice religant.* Others translate *obliquare* by *twist.* Many ancient writers speak of this manner of tying the hair among the Germans, cf. Sen. de Ira. 3, 26.; Juv. 13, 164.

A servis separantur. *Separantur*=distinguuntur. Servants among the Suevi seem to have had their hair shorn. So also it was among the Franks at a later date. Vid. Greg. Tur. 3, 8.

Rarum et intra, etc. Enallage, cf. note *certum quique*, 32.

Retro sequuntur, i. e. *follow it back*, as it were, in its growth, and *tie it up on the very crown of the head only*, instead of letting it hang down, as it grows (submittere crinem). So K., Or. and many others. Passow and Död. take sequuntur in the sense of *desire, delight in* (our word *seek*). The word bears that sense, e. g. 5: argentum magis quam aurum *sequuntur*. But then what is *retro* sequuntur? for *retro* must be an adjunct of *sequuntur* both from position, and because there is no other word which it can limit. *Saepe* implies, that sometimes they made a knot elsewhere, but *often they fasten* it there, and there *only*. See Or. in loc. This whole passage illustrates our author's disposition to avoid technical language. Cf. note, H. 2, 21.

Innoxiae. Harmless, unlike the beauty cultivated among the *Romans* to dazzle and seduce.

In altitudinem, etc. *For the sake* of (increased) *height and terror*, i. e. to appear tall and inspire terror. Cf. note, A. 5: *in jactationem;* A. 7: *in suam famam.* The antithetic particle is omitted before this clause as it often is by our author.

Ut hostium oculis, to strike with terror the eyes of the enemy, for primi in omnibus proeliis *oculi* vincuntur, 43.

XXXIX. *Vetustissimos. Oldest. Vetus* is *old*, of long *duration* (ἔτος, aetas). *antiquus, ancient*, belonging to a *preceding* age (ante). *Recens* (fresh, young) is opposed to the former: *novus* (new, modern), to the latter. See Ramshorn and Freund.

Fides antiquitatis. Antiquitatis is objective gen.=*the belief, or persuasion of their antiquity.*

Auguriis-sacram. The commentators all note the hexameter structure of these words, and many regard them as a quotation from some Latin poet. The words themselves are also poetical, e. g. *patrum* for *majorum*, and *formidine* for *religione.* The coloring is Virgilian. Cf. Aen. 7, 172; 8, 598. See Or. in loc. and Preliminary Remarks to the Histories, p. 234.

Legationibus coeunt. Just as we say: *convene by their delegates*, or *representatives.*

Publice=publica auctoritate, cf. same word, 10.

Primordia. Initiatory rites.

Minor, sc. numine. *Inferior to the god.*

Prae se ferens. Expressing in his external appearance, or *bearing in his own person an acknowledgment of the power of the divinity.*

Evolvuntur=se evolvunt, cf. Ann. 1, 13: cum Tiberii genua advolveretur; also *lavantur*, 22.

Eo-tanquam. Has reference to this point, as if, i. e. to this opinion, viz. that thence, etc. Cf. *illuc respicit tanquam*, 12.—*Inde.*

From the grove, or the god of the grove. Cf. 3: *Tuisconem* . . *originem gentis.*

Adjicit auctoritatem, sc. isti superstitioni.

Magno corpore=reipublicae magnitudine. *Corpore*, the body politic. So His. 4, 64: redisse vos in corpus nomenque Germanorum.—*Habitantur.* Al. habitant and habitantium, by conjecture. The subject is the Semnonian *country* implied in *Semnonum*: *the Semnonians inhabit a hundred villages*, is the idea.

XL. *Langobardos.* The Lombards of Mediæval history; so called probably from their long beards (Germ. lang and bart). First mentioned by Velleius, 2, 106: gens etiam Germana feritate ferocior. See also Ann. 2, 45. 46. 62–64.—*Paucitas* here stands opposed to the *magno corpore* of the Semnones in 39.

Per–periclitando. Three different constructions, cf. notes 16. 18.

Reudigni. Perhaps the Jutes, so intimately associated with the Angles in subsequent history. See Or. in loc. In like manner, Zeuss identifies the *Suardones* with the Heruli, and the *Nuithones* with the Teutones. *Suardones* perhaps=*sword*-men.

Anglii. The English reader will here recognize the tribe of Germans that subsequently invaded, peopled, and gave name to England (=*Angl-land*), commonly designated as the Anglo-Saxons. T. does not mention the *Saxons.* They are mentioned by Ptolemy and others, as originally occupying a territory in this same part of Germany. They became at length so powerful, as to give their name to the entire confederacy (including the Angles), which ruled northern Germany, as the Franks (the founders of the French monarchy) did southern. The Angles seem to have dwelt on the right bank of the Elbe, near its mouth, in the time of T.

Nerthum. This is the reading of the MSS. and the old editions. It cannot be doubted that T. speaks of Hertha (see Turn. His. Ang. Sax., App. to B. 2. chap. 3). "But we must take care not to correct our author himself." Passow. Grimm identifies this deity with Niördhr of the Edda, and derives the name from Nord (North).—*Terram matrem.* The Earth is worshipped by almost all heathen nations, as the mother of men and the inferior gods. See Mur. in loco. Cf. 2: Tuisconem Deum, *terra editum*; also note, 9: Isidi.

Insula. Scholars differ as to the Island. Probabilities perhaps are in favor of Rugen, where the *secretus lacus* mentioned below is still shown, still associated with superstitious legends.

Castum. *Polluted by nothing profane.* So Hor: *castis lucis.*

Penetrali, viz. *the sacred vehicle.*

Dignatur. Deems worthy of her visits.

Templo, sc. the sacred grove. Templum, like τέμενος, denotes any place *set apart* (from τέμνω) for sacred purposes, cf. 9.

Numen ipsum. The goddess herself, not an image of her; for the Germans have no images of their gods, 9. *Abluitur*, as if contaminated by intercourse with mortals.

Perituri, etc. *Which can be seen only on penalty of death.*

XLI. *Propior*, sc. to the Romans.—*Hermundurorum.* Ritter identifies the name (*Hermun* being omitted, and *dur* being=*thur*) and the people with the *Thur*ingians. Cf. note 2: *Ingaevones.*

Non in ripa. Not only (or *not so much*) *on the border* (the river-bank), but also within the bounds of the Roman Empire.

Splendidissima–colonia. This flourishing colony had no distinctive name in the age of T.; called afterwards Augusta Vindelicorum, now Augsburg.

Passim. Wherever they chose—*Sine custode.* Not so others. Cf. His. 4, 64: ut inermes ac prope nudi, *sub custode* et pretio coiremus.

Cum–ostendamus. Cum=while, although. Hence the subj.

Non concupiscentibus. Since they were not covetous, Gün. Gr renders: *though they were not equally desirous of it.*

Notum–auditur. The Elbe had been *seen* and *crossed* by Drusus Domitius, and Tiberius. But now it was known only by *hearsay* See a like patriotic complaint at the close of 37.

XLII. *Marcomanni*=men of the marches. See Latham in loc —*Sedes*, sc. Bohemia.—*Pulsis olim Boiis*, cf. 28.

Degenerant, sc. *a reliquorum virtute*, i. e. the Narisci and Quadi *are not unworthy, do not fall short* of the bravery of their neighbors, the Marcomanni.

Peragitur. Al. *protegitur, porrigitur*, &c. Different words are supplied as the subject of *peragitur*, e. g. Passow *iter.*; Rit. *cursus;* K. *frons.* The last is preferable. The meaning is: *This country* (sc. of these tribes) *is the front*, so to speak (i. e. the part *facing the Romans*) *of Germany, so far as it is formed by the Danube*, i. e. so far as the Danube forms the boundary between Germany and the Roman Empire.

Marobodui. Cf. Ann. 2, 62; Suet. Tib. 37.

Externos, sc. reges, viz. the kings of the Hermunduri. Ann. 2, 62.—*Potentia. Power* irrespective of right. *Potestas* is lawful *authority.* See note, 7

Nec minus valent, sc. being aided by our money, than they would be if they were reinforced by our arms. This clause in some copies stands at the beginning of 43.

XLIII. *Retro*. *Back* from the Danube and the Roman border. —*Referunt*. *Resemble*. Poetical, cf. 20.

Et quod patiuntur, sc. proves that they are not of German origin. They paid tribute as *foreigners*. The Gothini were probably a remnant of the expelled Boii. Cf. note, 28, and Prichard, as there cited. Hence their Gallic language.

Quo magis pudeat. They have iron beyond even most of the Germans (cf. 6), but (shame to tell) do not know how to use it in asserting their independence. Subj. H. 497; Z. 536.

Pauca campestrium. Poetical, but not uncommon in the later Latin. So 41: secretiora Germaniae; His. 4, 28: extrema Galliarum. H. 396, III. 2. 3); Z. 435.

Jugum. *A mountain chain*.—*Vertices*. *Distinct summits*.

Insederunt. This word usually takes a dat., or an abl., with *in*. But the poets and later prose writers use it as a transitive verb with the acc.=*have settled, inhabited*. Cf. H. 371, 4; Z. 386; and Freund sub voce. Observe the comparatively unusual form of the perf. 3d plur. in *-erunt* instead of *-ere*. Cf. note, His. 2, 20.

Nomen=gens. So nomen Latinum=Latins. Liv. pass.

Interpretatione Romana. So we are every where to understand Roman accounts of the gods of other nations. They transferred to them the names of their own divinities according to some slight, perhaps fancied resemblance. Cf. note, 34: *quicquid consensimus*.

Ea vis numini, i. e. these gods render the same service to the Germans, as Castor and Pollux to the Romans.

Alcis, dat. pl. Perhaps from the Slavonic word holcy=κοῦρος, Greek for Castor and Pollux. Referable to no German root.

Peregrinae, sc. Greek or Roman.—*Tamen*. Though these gods bear no visible trace of Greek or Roman origin, *yet* they are worshipped as brothers, as youth, like the *Greek* and *Roman Twins*.—*Superstitionis*=religionis. Cf. notes, His. 3, 58; 5, 13.

Lenocinantur. *Cherish*, increase. Used rhetorically; properly, *to pander*.—*Arte*, sc. nigra scuta, &c.—*Tempore*, sc. atras noctes, &c.—*Tincta*=*tattooed*.

Ipsaque formidine, etc. *And by the very frightfulness and shadow of the deathlike army*. *Umbra* may be taken of the literal *shadows* of the men in the night, with Rit., or with Död. and Or., of the general *image* or *aspect* of the army. *Feralis*, as an adj., is found only in poetry and post-Augustan prose. See Freund.

Gothones. Probably the Getae of earlier, and the Goths of later history. See Or. in loc. and Grimm and other authorities as there cited. The *Rugii* have perpetuated their name in an island of the Baltic (Rugen).

Adductius. Lit. with tighter rein, *with more absolute power* cf. His. 3, 7: adductius, quam civili bello, imperitabat. The adv. is used only in the comp.; and the part. adductus is post-Augustan. *Jam* and *nondum* both have reference to the writer's progress in going over the tribes of Germany, those tribes growing less and less free as he advances eastward: *already* under more subjection than the foregoing tribes, but *not yet* in such abject slavery, as some we shall soon reach, sc. in the next chapter, where see note on *jam.*

Supra. So as to *trample down* liberty and destroy it.

Protinus deinde ab, etc. *Next in order, from the ocean*, i. e. with territory beginning from or at the ocean.

XLIV. *Suionum.* *Swedes.* Not mentioned under this name, however, by any other ancient author.

Ipso. The Rugii, &c., mentioned at the close of the previous section, dwelt *by* the ocean (*ab* Oceano); but the *Suiones in* the ocean (*in* Oceano). *Ipso* marks this antithesis.

In Oceano. An island in the Baltic. Sweden was so regarded by the ancients, cf. 1, note.

Utrimque prora. *Naves biprorae.* Such also had the Veneti, Caes. B. G. 3, 13. Such Germanicus constructed, His. 3, 47. So also the canoes of the N. Am. Indians.

Ministrantur, sc. naves = *the ships are not furnished with sails*, cf. His. 4, 12: *viros armaque ministrant.* Or it may be taken in the more literal sense: are served, i. e. worked, managed. Cf. Virg. Aen. 6, 302: velisque ministrat.—*In ordinem. For a row*, i. e. so as to form a row, cf. Z. 314: also Rit. and Död. in loc. The northmen (Danes and Swedes) became afterwards still more famous for navigation and piratical excursions, till at length they settled down in great numbers in France and England.

In quibusdam fluminum. Rivers with steep banks require the oars to be removed in order to approach the bank.

Est–honos. Contrary to the usual fact in Germany, cf. 5.

Exceptionibus. Limitations.—*Jam.* Now, i. e. *here*, opposed to the *foregoing* accounts of *free states* and *limited monarchies.*

Precario. Properly: *obtained by entreaty.* Hence: *dependent on the will of another*, cf. A. 16.—*Parendi.* A gerund with passive sense, lit. *with no precarious right of being obeyed.* So Pass., K., Wr. and Gün.

In promiscuo. The privilege of wearing arms is not conceded to the mass of the people.—*Et quidem*=et eo, *and that too.*

Otiosa–manus. Al. *otiosae* by conjecture. But *manus*, a collective noun sing. takes a pl. verb, cf. H. 461, 1; Z. 366.

Regia utilitas est=regibus utile est.

XLV. *Pigrum.* Cf. A. 10: pigrum et grave. The Northern or Frozen Ocean, of which T. seems to have heard, though some refer it to the northern part of the Baltic. See Ky. in loc.

Hinc. For this reason, viz. *quod extremus*, etc.

In ortus. Till the risings (pl.) *of the sun*, i. e. from day to day successively. It was known in the age of T. that the longest day grew longer towards the north, till at length it became six months (cf. Plin. N. H. 2, 77), though T. supposed it to be thus long at a lower latitude than it really was, cf. A. 12.

Sonum–aspici. The aurora borealis, some suppose.

Persuasio adjicit. The common belief adds, i. e. *it is further believed*, cf. His. 5, 5. 13: persuasio inerat.

Illuc–natura. Tantum is to be connected with *illuc usque. Thus far only nature extends.* So thought the ancients. Cf. A. 33: *in ipso terrarum ac naturae fine. Et vera fama* is parenthetic. The *author* endorses this part of the story.

Ergo marks a return from the above digression.

Suevici maris. The Baltic.

Aestyorum=eastern men, modern Esthonians. Their language was probably neither German nor Briton, but Slavonic.

Matrem Deum. Cybele, as the Romans interpreted it, cf. 43.

Insigne–gestant. Worn, as *amulets.*

Frumenta laborant, i. e. labor *for*, or *to produce*, corn. Cf. Hor. Epod. 5, 60. *Laborare* is transitive only in poetry and post-Augustan prose. *Elaborare* would imply too much art for the author's purpose. See Rit. in loc.

Succinum. Amber, an important article of commerce in early ages, combining some vegetable juice (hence the Latin name, from *succus*) with some mineral ingredients.—*Glesum.* This name was transferred to *glass*, when it came into use. The root is German. Compare χάλαζα. Död.

Nec=non tamen. *Yet it is not*, etc.

Ut barbaris. Cf. ut inter barbaros, A. 11. *Barbaris* is dative in apposition with *iis*, which is understood after *compertum.*

Quae–ratio. *What power or process of nature.*

Donec–dedit. Cf. note, 37: *affectavere.*

Plerumque. *Often;* a limited sense of the word peculiar to post-Augustan Latin. Cf. G. 13: *ipsa plerumque fama bella profligant;* and Freund ad v.

Quae–expressa=quorum *succus* expressus, etc.

In tantum. *To such a degree.* Frequent only in late Latin.

A servitute. They fall short of liberty in not being free, like most of the Germans; and they fall below slavery itself, in that they are slaves to a woman.

XLVI. *Venedorum et Fennorum.* Modern *Vends and Finns,* or Fen-men. Cf. Latham in loc.—*Ac torpor procerum.* *The chief men are lazy and stupid,* besides being filthy, like all the rest.

Foedantur. Cf. infectos, 4.—*Habitum,* here personal appearance, cf. note, 17.—*Ex moribus,* sc. Sarmatarum.

Erigitur. Middle sense. *Raise themselves,* or *rise,* cf. evolvuntur, 39.

Figunt. Have *fixed habitations,* in contrast with the Sarmatians, who lived in carts. Cf. Ann. 13, 54: *fixerant domos Frisii.* Al. *fingunt.*

Sarmatis. The stock of the modern Russians, cf. 1. note.

Cubile. We should expect *cubili* to correspond with *victui* and *vestituti.* But cf. note 18: referantur; 20: ad patrem, &c.

Comitantur, i. e. feminae comitantur viris.

Ingemere–illaborare. *Toil and groan upon houses and lands,* i. e. *in building and tilling them;* though some understand *domibus* and *agris* as the places *in* which they toil.

Versare. *To be constantly employed* in increasing the fortune of themselves and others, agitated meanwhile by hope and fear.

Securi. Because they have nothing to lose.

Illis. Emphatic. *They,* unlike others, have no need, &c. Cf. *apud illos,* 44.

In medium relinquam. Leave for the public, i. e. undecided,

Relinquere in medio is the more common expression. Bötticher in his Lex. Tac. explains it, as equivalent by Zeugma to *in medium vocatum relinquam in medio.* So in Greek, ἐν and εἰς often interchange.

AGRICOLA.

The Biography of Agricola was written early in the reign of Trajan (which commenced A. U. C. 851. A. D. 98), consequently about the same time with the Germania, though perhaps somewhat later (cf. notes on Germania). This date is established by inference from the author's own language in the 3d and the 44th sections (see notes). In the former, he speaks of the dawn of a better day, which opened indeed with the reign of Nerva, but which is now brightening constantly under the auspices of Trajan. The use of the past tense (*miscuerit*) here in respect to Nerva, and of the present (*augeat*) in respect to Trajan, is quite conclusive evidence, that at the time of writing, the reign of Nerva was past, and that of Trajan had already begun.

The other passage is, if possible, still more clearly demonstrative of the same date. Here in drawing the same contrast between past tyranny and present freedom, the author, without mentioning Nerva, records the desire and hope, which his father-in-law expressed in his hearing, that he might live to see Trajan elevated to the imperial throne—language very proper and courtly, if Trajan were already Emperor, but a very awkwara compliment to Nerva, if, as many critics suppose, he were still the reigning prince.

It is objected to this date, that if Nerva were not still living, Tacitus could not have failed to attach to his name (in § 3.) the epithet *Divus*, with which deceased Emperors were usually honored. And from the omission of this epithet in connection with the name of *Nerva*, together with the terms of honor in which *Trajan* is mentioned, it is inferred that the piece was written in that brief period of three months, which intervened between the adoption of Trajan by Nerva, and Nerva's death (see Brotier and many others). But the application of the epithet in question, was not a matter of necessity or of universal practice. Its omission in this case might have been accidental, or might have proceeded from unknown reasons. And the bare absence of a single word surely cannot be entitled to much weight, in comparison with the obvious and almost necessary import of the passages just cited.

The primary object of the work is sufficiently obvious. It was to honor the memory of the writer's excellent father-in-law, Agricola (cf. § 3: honori Agricolae, mei soceri, destinatus). So far from apologizing for writing the life of so near a friend, he feels assured that his motives will be appreciated and his design approved, however imperfect may be its execution; and he deems an apology necessary for having so long delayed the performance of that filial duty. After an introduction of singular beauty and appropriateness (cf. notes), he sketches a brief outline of the parentage, education, and early life of Agricola, but draws out more at length the history of his consulship and command in Britain, of which the following summary, from Hume's History of England, may not be unprofitable to the student in anticipation: "Agricola was the general, who finally established the dominion of the Romans in this island. He governed it in the reigns of Vespasian, Titus, and Domitian. He carried his victorious arms northward; defeated the Britons in every encounter, pierced into the forests and the mountains of Caledonia, reduced every state to subjection in the southern parts of the island, and chased before him all the men of fiercer and more intractable spirits, who deemed war and death itself less intolerable than servitude under the victors. He defeated them in a decisive action which they fought under Galgacus; and having fixed a chain of garrisons between the friths of Clyde and Forth, he cut off the ruder and more barren parts of the island and secured the Roman province from the incursions of the more barbarous inhabitants. During these military enterprises, he neglected not the arts of peace. He introduced laws and civility among the Britons; taught them to desire and raise all the conveniences of life; reconciled them to the Roman language and manners; instructed them in letters and science; and employed every expedient to render those chains which he had forged both easy and agreeable to them." (His. of Eng. vol. 1.)

The history of Agricola during this period is of course the history of Britain. Accordingly the author prefaces it with an outline of the geographical features, the situation, soil, climate, productions and, so far as known to the Romans, the past history of the island. Tacitus possessed peculiar advantages for being the historian of the early Britons. His father-in-law was the first to subject the whole island to the sway of Rome. He traversed the country from south to north at the head of his armies, explored it with his own eyes, and reported what he saw to our author with his own lips. He saw the Britons too, in their native nobleness, in their primitive love of liberty and virtue; before they had become the slaves of Roman arms, the dupes of Roman arts, or the victims of Roman vices. A few paragraphs in the concise and nervous style of Tacitus, have made us quite acquainted with the Britons, as Agricola found them; and on the whole, we have no reason to be ashamed of the primæval inhabitants of the land of our ancestry. They knew their rights, they prized them, they fought for them bravely and died for them nobly. More harmony among themselves might have delayed, but could not have prevented the final catastrophe. Rome in the age of Trajan was irresistible; and Britain became a Roman province. This portion of the Agricola of Tacitus, and the Germania of the same author, entitle him to the peculiar affection and lasting gratitude of those, whose veins flow with Briton and Anglo-Saxon blood, as the historian, and the contemporary historian too, of their early fathers. It is a notable providence for us, nay it is a kind providence for mankind, that has thus preserved from the pen of the most sagacious and reflecting of all historians an account, too brief though it be, of the origin and antiquities of the people that of all others now exert the widest dominion whether in the political or the moral world, and that have made those countries which were in his day shrouded in darkness, the radiant points for the moral and spiritual illumination of our race. "The child is father to the man," and if we would at this day investigate the elements of English law, we have it on the authority of Sir William Blackstone, that we must trace them back to their founders in the customs of the Britons and Germans, as recorded by Caesar and Tacitus.

With the retirement of Agricola from the command in Britain, the author falls back more into the province of biography. The few occasional strokes, however, in which the pencil of Tacitus has sketched the character of Domitian in the back ground of the picture of Agricola are the more to be prized, because his history of that reign is lost.

In narrating the closing scenes of Agricola's life, Tacitus breathes the very spirit of an affectionate son, without sacrificing the impartiality and gravity of the historian, and combines all a mourner's simplicity and sincerity with all the orator's dignity and eloquence.

How tenderly he dwells on the wisdom and goodness of his departed father; how artlessly he intersperses his own sympathies and regrets, even as if he were breathing out his sorrows amid a circle of sympathizing friends! At the same time, how instructive are his reflections, how noble his sentiments, and how weighty his words, as if he were pronouncing an eulogium in the hearing of the world and of posterity! The sad experience of the writer in the very troubles through which he follows Agricola, conspires with the affectionate remembrance of his own loss in the death of such a father, to give a tinge of melancholy to the whole biography; and we should not know where to look for the composition, in which so perfect a work of art is animated by so warm a heart. In both these respects, it is decidedly superior to the Germania. It is marked by the same depth of thought and conciseness in diction, but it is a higher effort of the writer, while, at the same time, it gives us more insight into the character of the man. It has less of satire and more of sentiment. Or if it is not richer in refined sentiments and beautiful reflections, they are interwoven with the narrative in a manner more easy and natural. The sentiments seem to be only the language of Agricola's virtuous heart, and the reflections, we feel, could not fail to occur to such a mind in the contemplation of such a character. There is also more ease and flow in the language; for concise as it still is and studied as it may appear, it seems to be the very style which is best suited to the subject and most natural to the author. In another writer we might call it labored and ambitious. But we cannot feel that it cost Tacitus very much effort. Still less can we charge him with an attempt at display. In short, an air of confidence in the dignity of the subject, and in the powers of the author, pervades the entire structure of this fine specimen of biography. And the reader will not deem that confidence ill-grounded. He cannot fail to regard this, as among the noblest, if not the very noblest monument ever reared to the memory of any individual.

"We find in it the flower of all the beauties, which T. has scattered through his other works. It is a chef-d'œuvre, which satisfies at once the judgment and the fancy, the imagination and the heart. It is justly proposed as a model of historical eulogy. The praises bestowed have in them nothing vague or far-fetched, they rise from the simple facts of the narrative. Every thing produces attachment every thing conveys instruction. The reader loves Agricola, admires him, conceives a passion for him, accompanies him in his campaigns, shares in his disgrace and profits by his example. The interest goes on growing to the last. And when it seems incapable of further increase, passages pathetic and sublime transport the soul out of itself, and leave it the power of feeling only to detest the tyrant, and to melt into tenderness without weakness over the destiny of the hero." (La Bletterie.)

I. *Usitatum.* A participle in the acc. agreeing with the preceding clause, and forming with that clause the object of the verb omisit.—*Ne–quidem.* Cf. G. 6, note.

Incuriosa suorum. So Ann. 2, 88: dum vetera extollimus, recentium incuriosi. *Incuriosus* is post-Augustan.

Virtus vicit–vitium. Alliteration, which is not unfrequent in T. as also homœoteleuta, words ending with like sounds. Dr.

Ignorantiam–invidiam. The gen. *recti* limits both subs., which properly denote different faults, but since they are usually associated, they are here spoken of as one (*vitium*).

In aperto. Literally, *in the open* field or way; hence, *free from obstructions.* Sal. (Jug. 5) uses it for *in open* day, or clear light. But that sense would be inappropriate here. *Easy.* Not essentially different from *pronum*, which properly means *inclined*, and hence *easy.* These two words are brought together in like manner in other passages of our author, cf. 33: vota virtusque *in aperto*, omniaque *prona* victoribus. An inelegant imitation may be thus expressed in English: down-hill and open-ground work.

Sine gratia aut ambitione. Without courting favor or seeking preferment. Gratia properly refers more to the present, *ambitio* to the future. Cf. Ann. 6, 46: Tiberio non perinde gratia praesentium, quam in posteros ambitio. *Ambitio* is here used in a bad sense (as it is sometimes in Cic.) For still another bad sense of the word, cf. G. 27.

Celeberrimus quisque. Such men as Pliny the elder, Claudius Pollio, and Julius Secundus, wrote biographies. Also Rusticus and Senecio. See chap. 2.

Plerique. Not most persons, but *many*, or *very many*. Cf. His. 1, 86, and 4, 84, where it denotes a less number than *plures* and *plurimi*, to which it is allied in its root (ple, ple-us, plus, plerus. See Freund ad v.)

Suam ipsi vitam. Autobiography. Cic. in his Epist. to Lucceius says: If I cannot obtain this favor from you, I shall perhaps be compelled to write my own biography, *multorum exemplo et clarorum virorum.* When *ipse* is joined to a possessive pronoun in a reflexive clause, it takes the case of the subject of the clause. Cf. Z. 696, Note; H. 452, 1.

Fiduciam morum. A mark of conscious integrity; literally confidence of, i. e. in their morals. *Morum* is objective gen. For the two accusatives (one of which however is the clause *suam–narrare*) after *arbitrati sunt*, see Z. 394; H. 373. A gen. may take the place of the latter acc., *esse* being understood, Z. 448.

Rutilio. Rutilius Rufus, consul A. U. C. 649, whom Cic. (Brut. 30, 114.) names as a profound scholar in Greek literature and philosophy, and Velleius (2, 13, 2.) calls the best man, not merely of his own, but of any age. He wrote a Roman history in Greek. Plut. Mar. 28. His autobiography is mentioned only by Tacitus.

Scauro. M. Aemilius Scaurus, consul A. U. C. 639, who wrote an autobiography, which Cic. (Brut. 29, 112.) compares favorably with the Cyropaedia of Xenophon.

Citra fidem. Cf. note G. 16.—*Aut obtrectationi.* Enallage, cf. note, G. 15. Render: *This in the case of Rutilius and Scaurus did not impair* (public) *confidence or incur* (public) *censure.*

Adeo. To such a degree, or *so true it is. Adeo* conclusiva, et in initio sententiae collocata, ad *mediam* latinitatem pertinet. Dr. Livy uses *adeo* in this way often; Cic. uses *tantum.*

At nunc, etc. *But now* (in our age so different from those better days) *in undertaking to write* (i. e. if I had undertaken to write) *the life of a man at the time of his death, I should have needed permission; which I would not have asked*, since in that case *I should have fallen on times so cruel and hostile to virtue.* The reference is particularly to the time of Domitian, whose jealousy perhaps occasioned the death of Agricola, and would have been offended by the very asking of permission to write his biography. Accordingly the historian proceeds in the next chapter to illustrate the treat ment, which the biographers of eminent men met with from that cruel tyrant. *Opus fuit* stands instead of *opus fuisset*. Cf. His. 1, 16: *dignus eram;* 3, 22: *ratio fuit;* and Z. 518, 519. The concise mode of using the future participles *narraturo* and *incursaturus* (in place of the verb in the proper mood and with the proper conjunctions, if, when, since) belongs to the silver age, and is foreign to the language of Cicero. Such is the interpretation, which after a thorough reinvestigation, I am now inclined to apply to this much disputed passage. It is that of Ritter. It will be seen that the text also differs slightly from that of the first edition (*in-cursaturus* instead of *ni cursaturus*). Besides the authority of Rit., Död., Freund and others, I have been influenced by a regard to the usage of Tacitus, which lends no sanction to a transitive sense of *cursare*. Cf. Ann. 15, 50; His. 5, 20. In many editions, *mihi* stands before *nunc narraturo*. But *nunc* is the emphatic word, and should stand first, as it does in the best MSS.

II. *Legimus.* Quis? Tacitus ejusdemque aetatis homines alii. Ubi? In actis diurnis. Wr. These *journals* (Fiske's Man. p. 626., 4. ed.) published such events (cf. Dio. 67, 11), and were read through the empire (Ann. 16, 22). T. was absent from Rome when the events here referred to took place (cf. 45: longae absentiae). Hence the propriety of his saying *legimus*, rather than *vidimus* or *meminimus*, which have been proposed as corrections.

Aruleno Rustico. Put to death by Domitian for writing a memoir or penegyric on Paetus Thrasea, cf. Suet. Dom. 10.

Paetus Thrasea. Cf. Ann. 16, 21: Trucidatis tot insignibus viris, ad postremum Nero *virtutem ipsam* exscindere concupivit, interfecto Thrasea Paeto.

Herennio Senecioni. Cf. Plin. (Epist. 7, 19), where Senecio is said to have written the life of Helvidius at the request of Fannia, wife of Helvidius, who was also banished, as accessory to the crime, but who bore into exile the very books which had been the cause of her exile. For the dat. cf. note, G. 3: *Ulixi.*

Priscus Helvidius, son-in-law of Thrasea and friend of the younger Pliny, was put to death by Vespasian. Suet. Vesp. 15; His. 4, 5; Juv. Sat. 5, 36.

Laudati essent. The imp. and plup. subj. are used in narration after *cum*, even when it denotes time merely. Here however a causal connection is also intended. H. 518, II.; Z. 577, 578.

Triumviris. The Triumviri at Rome, like the Undecimviri (of ἕνδεκα) at Athens, had charge of the prisons and executions, for which purpose they had eight lictors at their command.

Comitio ac foro. The comitium was a *part* of the forum. Yet the words are often used together (cf. Suet. Caes. 10). The *comitium* was the proper place for the punishment of criminals, and the word *forum* suggests the further idea of the publicity of the book-burning in the presence of the assembled people.

Conscientiam, etc. *The consciousness,* i. e. *common knowledge of mankind;* for *conscientia* denotes what one knows in common with others, as well as what he is conscious of in himself. Cf. His. 1, 25: *conscientiam facinoris;* Cic. Cat. 1. 1: *omnium horum conscientia.* In his Annals (4, 35), T. ridicules the stupidity of those who expect by any *present* power, to extinguish the memory also of the *next* generation. The sentiment of both passages is just and fine.

Sapientiae professoribus. Philosophers, who were banished by Domitian, A. D. 94, on the occasion of Rusticus's panegyric on Thrasea. T. not unfrequently introduces an *additional circumstance* by the abl. abs., as here.

Ne occurreret. Ne with the subj. expresses a negative intention; *ut non* a negative result. H. 490; Z. 532.

Inquisitiones. A system of espionage, sc. by the Emperor's tools and informers.—*Et*=etiam, *even.* Cf. note, 11. Al. *etiam.*

Memoriam–perdidissemus, i. e. we should not have *dared* to remember, if we could have helped it.

III. *Et quanquam. Et* pro *sed.* So Dr. But *nunc demum animus redit* implies, that confidence is hardly restored yet; and the reason for so slow a recovery is given in the following clause. Hence *et* is used in its proper copulative or explicative sense. So Wr. *Demum* is a lengthened form of the demonstrative *dem.* Cf. i-*dem,* tan-*dem,* δή. *Nunc demum*=νῦν δή. Freund.

Primo statim. Statim gives emphasis: *at the very commencement,* etc.; cf. note, 20.—*Dissociabiles, incompatible.*

Augeatque–Trajanus. This marks the date of the composition early in the reign of Trajan, cf. G. 37; also p. 139 supra.

Securitas publica. "*And public security has assumed not only hopes and wishes, but has seen those wishes arise to confidence and stability. Securitas publica* was a current expression and wish, and was frequently inscribed on medals." Ky.

Assumpserit. This word properly belongs only to *fiduciam ac robur. Spem ac votum* would require rather *conceperit.* Zeugma.

Subit. *Steals in,* lit. creeps under. Cf. note, H. 1, 13.

Invisa primo–amatur. The original perhaps of Pope's lines Vice is a monster, &c.

Quindecim annos. The reign of Domitian from A. D. 81, to A. D. 96.

Fortuitis casibus. Natural and ordinary death, as opposed to death by violence, *saevitia principis.* — *Promptissimus quisque. The ablest,* or *all the ablest.* *Quisque* with a superlative, whether singular or plural, is in general equivalent to *omnes* with the positive, with the additional idea however of a reciprocal comparison among the persons denoted by *quisque.* Z. 710, 6.

Ut ita dixerim. An apology for the strong expression *nostri superstites: survivors not of others only, but so to speak, of ourselves also;* for we can hardly be said to have *lived* under the tyranny of Dom., and our present happy life is, as it were, a renewed existence, after being buried for fifteen years. A beautiful conception! The use of *dixerim* in preference to *dicam* in this formula is characteristic of the later Latin. Cf. Z. 528. The *et* before this clause is omitted by some editors. But it is susceptible of an explanation, which adds spirit to the passage: A few of us survive, *and that* not merely ourselves, but so to speak, others also. In the Augustan age *superstes* was, for the most part, followed by the dative.

Tamen. Notwithstanding the unfavorable circumstances in which I write, after so long a period of deathlike silence, in which we have almost lost the gift of speech, *yet* I shall not regret to have composed *even in rude and inelegant language,* etc. For the construction of *pigebit,* cf. Z. 441, and H. 410, 6.

Memoriam–composuisse. Supposed to refer to his forthcoming history, written, or planned and announced, but not yet published. Some understand it of the present treatise. But then *interim* would have no meaning; nor indeed is the language applicable to his *Agricola.*

Interim, sc. *editus* or vulgatus, *published meanwhile,* i. e. while preparing the history.

The reader cannot but be struck with the beauty of this introduction. It is modest, and at the same time replete with the dignity of conscious worth. It is drawn out to considerable length, yet it is all so pertinent and tasteful, that we would not spare a sentence or a word. With all the thoughtful and sententious brevity of the exordiums of Sallust, it has far more of natural ease and the beauty of appropriateness.

IV. *Cnaeus Julius Agricola.* Every Roman had at least three names: the nomen or name of the gens, which always ended in *ius* (Julius); the praenomen or individual name ending in *us* (Cnaeus); and the cognomen or family name (Agricola). See a brief account of A. in Dion Cassius 66, 20. Mentioned only by Dion and T. Al. Gnaeus, C. and G. being originally identical.

Forojuliensium colonia. Now *Frejus.* A walled town of Gallia Narbonensis, built by Julius Caesar, and used as a *naval station* by Augustus (cf. His. 3, 43: *claustra maris*). Augustus sent thither the beaked ships captured in the battle of Actium, Ann. 4, 5. Hence perhaps called *illustris.*

Procuratorem Caesarum. Collector of imperial revenues in the Roman Provinces.

Quae equestris–est, i. e. the procurator was, as we say, ex officio, a Roman knight. The office was not conferred on senators.

Julius Graecinus. Cf. Sen. de Benef. 2, 21: Si exemplo magni animi opus est, utemur *Graecini Julii,* viri egregii, quem C. Caesar occidit ob hoc unum, quod melior vir esset, quam esse quemquam tyranno expediret.

Senatorii ordinis. Pred. after *fuit* understood, with ellipsis of *vir.* H. 402, III.; Z. 426.

Sapientiae. *Philosophy,* cf. 1.—*Caii Caesaris.* Known in English histories by the name of Caligula.

Marcum Silanum. Father-in-law of Caligula, cf. Suet. Calig. 23: Silanum item *socerum* ad necem, secandasque novacula fauces compulit.

Jussus. Supply *est.* T. often omits *est* in the first of two passive verbs, cf. 9: detentus ac statim . . . revocatus est. In Hand's Tursellinus (2,474) however, jussus is explained as a participle, and *quia abnuerat* as equivalent to another participle=*having been commanded and having refused.*

Abnuerat, lit. *had* refused, because the refusal was prior to the slaying. We, with less accuracy, say *refused.* Z. 505.

Rarae castitatis. Ellipsis of *mulier.* H. 402, III.; Z. 426.

In–indulgentiaque. *Brought up in her bosom and tender love. Indulgentia* is more frequently used to denote excessive tenderness.

Arcebat has for its subject the clause, *quod statim,* etc. He was guarded against the allurements of vice by the wholesome influences thrown around him in the place of his early education.

Massiliam. Now Marseilles. It was settled by a colony of Phocaeans. Hence *Graeca comitate.* Cf. also Cicero's account of the high culture and refinement of Massilia (Cic. pro Flacco, 26).—*Provinciali parsimonia.* *Parsimonia* in a good sense; *economy*, as opposed to the luxury and extravagance of Italy and the City.

Locum–mixtum. Enallage for *locus*, in quo mixta erant, etc. H. 704, III., cf. 25: mixti copiis et laetitia.—*Bene compositum* denotes *a happy combination* of the elements, of which *mixtum* expresses only the *co-existence.*

Acrius, sc. aequo=too eagerly. H. 444, 1, and Z. 104, 1. note.

Concessum–senatori. Military and civil studies were deemed more appropriate to noble Roman youth, than literature and philosophy. *Senatori* must of course refer, not to the office of A., but to his rank by birth, cf. *senatorii ordinis* above.

Hausisse, ni–coercuisset. An analysis of this sentence shows, that there is an ellipsis of *hausurum* fuisse: *he imbibed*, and would have continued to imbibe, *had not*, &c. In such sentences, which abound in T. but are rarely found in Cic., *ni* is more readily translated by *but.* Cf. Z. 519. *b*; and note, His. 3, 28. For the application of *haurire* to the eager study of philosophy, cf. Hor. Sat. 2, 4, 95: *haurire vitae praecepta beatae*, and note, His. 1, 51: *hauserunt animo.*

Prudentia matris. So Nero's mother deterred him from the study of philosophy. Suet. Ner. 52.

Pulchritudinem ac speciem. *The beautiful image*, or beau ideal, by hendiadys. Cf. Cic. Or. 2: *species pulchritudinis.* See Rit. in loc.

Vehementius quam caute. For *vehementius quam cautius*, which is the regular Latin construction. T. uses both. Cf. Z. 690, and note, His. 1, 83.

Mox. In T. subsequently, not presently. R.

Retinuitque–modum. *And, what is most difficult, he retained from philosophy moderation*—moderation in all things, but especially in devotion to philosophy itself, where moderation is difficult in proportion to the excellence of the pursuit, as was shown by the extravagance of the Stoics and some other Grecian sects. As to the sense of *modum*, cf. Hor. Sat. 1, 1, 106: *est modus in rebus;* and for the sentiment, Hor. Ep. 1, 6, 15: *Insani sapiens nomen ferat, aequus iniqui, ultra quam satis est virtutem si petat ipsam.*

V. *Castrorum.* This word is used to express whatever pertains to *military* life, education, &c., as the context may require. Every Roman youth who aspired to civil office, must have a military education.

Diligenti ac moderato. Careful and prudent, cf. our author's character of the same commander, His. 2, 25: *cunctator natura,* etc.

Approbavit=fecit, ut ei probarentur. Dr. It is a constructio praegnans. He obtained the first rudiments of a military education under Paullinus, and he gained his approbation.

Electus–aestimaret. Having been chosen as one whom he would estimate (i. e. test his merit) *by tenting together,* i. e. by making him his companion and aid. Young men of rank and promise were thus associated with Roman commanders. Cf. Suet., Caes. 2. T., as usual, avoids the technical way of expressing the relation. Ad verbum, *contubernium,* cf. note, His. 1, 43. Others make *aestimaret* =*dignum aestimaret,* and *contubernio* abl. of price. Cf. Död. and Dr.

Licenter–segniter, sc. agens. *Licenter* refers to *voluptates, segniter* to *commeatus.*—*Commeatus*=*furloughs, absence from duty.*—*Inscitiam,* sc. tribunatus=*ignorance of his official duty* or *inexperience in war.*—*Retulit. Referre ad* is used very much like the corresponding English, viz. to *refer to* an object, or devote to an end. Sense: *He did not take advantage of his official standing and his military inexperience, to give up his time to ease and pleasure.* Wr. takes *retulit* in the more ordinary sense of brought back, thus: A. did not bring back (to Rome) the empty name of Tribune and no military experience, there to give himself up to leisure and pleasure. The former version accords better with the language of the whole passage. Wr. questions the authority for such a use of *referre.* But it may be found, e. g. Plin. Epist. 1, 22: nihil *ad* ostentationem, omnia *ad* conscientiam *refert.*

Noscere–nosci, etc. T. is fond of such a series of inf. depending on some *one* finite verb understood, and hence closely connected with each other, cf. G. 30: *praeponere,* etc. *note.* Here supply from *retulit* in the preceding number the idea: *he made it his business or aim to know,* etc. The author's fondness for antithesis is very observable in the several successive pairs here: *noscere–nosci; discere–sequi; appetere–recusare; anxius–intentus.*

In jactationem. Al. jactatione. *In* denoting the object or purpose, Z. 314: *he coveted no appointment for the sake of display; he declined none through fear.*

Anxius and *intentus* qualify *agere* like adverbs cf. R. Exc. 23, 1. *He conducted himself both with prudence and with energy.*

Exercitatior=agitatior. So Cic. Som. Scip. 4: agitatus et exercitatus animus; and Hor. Epod. 9, 31: Syrtes Noto exercitatas.

Incensae coloniae. Camalodunum, Londinium and Verulamium. Cf. Ann. 14, 33, where however the historian does not expressly say, the last two were *burned.*

In ambiguo=ambigua, in a critical state. R.

Alterius, sc. ducis.—*Artem et usum.* Military *science and experience.*

Summa . . . cessit. *The general management* (cf. notes, H. 1, 87. 2, 16. 33) *and the glory of recovering the province went to the general* (to his credit). The primary meaning of *cedere* is *to go.* See Freund sub v.—*Juveni,* sc. A.

Tum, sc. while veterani trucidarentur, etc.—*Mox,* sc. when Paullinus and A. came to the rescue.

Nec minus, etc. A remark worthy of notice and too often true.

VI. *Magistratus.* The regular *course* of offices and honors at Rome.

Per–anteponendo. Enallage, cf. G. 15, note. *Per* here denotes manner, rather than means (cf. *per lamenta,* 28); and *anteponendo* likewise=anteponentes. R. Render: *mutually loving and preferring one another.*—*Nisi quod*=*but.* Cf. *ni,* 4. There is an ellipsis before *nisi quod,* which R. would supply thus: greatly to the credit of both parties—*but more praise belongs to the good wife,* etc. *Major* sc. quam in bono viro. So, after *plus* supply quam in malo viro: *But more praise belongs to a good wife,* than to a good husband, *by as much as more blame attaches to a bad wife,* than to a bad husband.

Sors quaesturae. The Quaestors drew *lots* for their respective provinces. Their number increased with the increase of the empire, till from two they became twenty or more. As at first a Quaestor accompanied each Consul at the head of an army, so afterwards each Proconsul, or Governor of a province, had his Quaestor to collect and disburse the revenues of the province. The Quaestorship was the first in the course of Roman honors. It might be entered upon at the age of twenty-four.

Salvium Titianum. Brother of the Emperor Otho. See His. B. 1 and 2. pass. For the office of Proconsul, &c., see note, His. 1, 49.

Parata peccantibus. *Ready for wicked* rulers, i. e. affording great facilities for extortion in its corrupt and servile population. *Paratus* with a dat. of the thing, for which there is a preparation, is peculiar to poetry and post-Augustan prose. Cf. Freund ad v. Ad rem. cf. Cic. Epist. ad Quint. 1, 1, 6: tam corruptrice provincia, sa Asia; and pro Mur. 9.

Quantalibet facilitate. Any indulgence (license) however great.

Redempturus esset. Subj. in the apodosis answering to a protasis understood, sc. if A. would have entered into the plot. Cf. H. 502. Observe the use of *esset* rather than *fuisset* to denote what the proconsul would have been ready to do *at any time* during their *continuance* in office. Cf. Wr. in loc.

—*Dissimulationem.* Concealment (of what is true); simulatio, on the other hand, is an allegation of what is false.

Auctus est filia. So Cic. ad Att. 1, 2: filiolo me auctum scito.

Ante sublatum. *Previously born.* For this use of *sublatum,* see Lexicon. —*Brevi amisit, he lost shortly after;* though R. takes *amisit* as perf. for plup. and renders lost a short time before.

Mox inter, etc., sc. *annum* inter, supplied from *etiam ipsum... annum* below.

Tenor et silentium. Hendiadys for continuum silentium, or tenorem silentem. R.

Jurisdictio. *For the administration of justice in private cases had not fallen to his lot.* Only two of the twelve or fifteen Praetors, viz. the Praetor Urbanus (see note H. 1, 47) and the Praetor Peregrinus (who judged between foreigners and citizens) were said to exercise *jurisdictio.* The adjudication of criminal causes was called *quaestio,* which was now for the most part in the hands of the senate (Ann. 4, 6), from whom it might be transferred by appeal to the Praefect of the City or the Emperor himself. The Praetors received the *jurisdictio* or the *quaestio* by lot; and in case the former did not fall to them, the office was almost a sinecure; except that they continued to preside over the public games. See further, on the name and office of Praetor, His. 1, 47, note. For the plup. in *obvenerat,* see note, 4: *abnuerat.*

Et=et omnino. *The games and in general the pageantry of office* (*inania honoris*) expected of the Praetor. Observe the use of the neuter plural of the adj. for the subst., of which, especially before a gen., T. is peculiarly fond.

Medio rationis. The text is doubtful. The MSS. vacillate between *medio ratinois* and *modo rationis;* and the recent editions, for the most part, follow a third but wholly conjectural reading, viz. *moderationis.* The sense is the same with either reading: *He conducted the games and the empty pageantry of office in a happy mean* (partaking at once) *of prudence and plenty.* See Freund ad *duco.*

Uti–propior. As far from luxury, so (in the same proportion) *nearer to glory,* i. e. the farther from luxury, the nearer to glory Cf. Freund ad *uti.*

Longe–propior. Enallage of the adv. and adj. cf. G. 18: *extra.*

Ne sensisset. Would not have felt, etc., i. e. he recovered all the plundered offerings of the temple, but those which had been sacrilegiously taken away by *Nero* for the supply of his vicious pleasures. This explanation supposes a protasis understood, or rather implied in *quam Neronis.* Cf H. 503, 2. 2). The plup. subj. admits perhaps of another explanation, the subj. denoting the end with a view to which *Agricola labored* (H. 531 ; Z. 549), and the plup. covering all the past down to the time of his labors: he labored that the republic might not have experienced, and *he* virtually *effected that it had not experienced,* since he restored everything to its former state, the plunder of Nero alone excepted. See Wr. and Or. in loc. Perhaps this would not be an unexampled *praegnantia* for Tacitus. For *sentire* in the sense of *experiencing* especially *evil,* see Hor. Od. 2, 7, 10, and other examples in Freund sub v.

VII. *Classis Othoniana.* Ad rem. cf. His. 2, 12, seqq.—*Licenter vaga. Roaming in quest of plunder.*—*Intemelios.* Cf. note, 2, 13. —*In praediis suis. On her own estates. Praedia* includes both lands and buildings.

Ad solemnia pietatis. To perform the last offices of filial affection.

Nuntio deprehensus. Supply *est,* cf. 4: jussus. *Was overtaken unexpectedly by the news of Vespasian's claim (nomination) to the throne.*—*Affectati.* Cf. note, G. 28.—*In partes,* to his (Vesp.) *party.*

Principatus, sc. Vespasiani.—*Mucianus regebat.* Vesp. was detained in Egypt for some time after his troops had entered Rome under Mucianus; meanwhile Mucianus exercised all the imperial power, cf. His. 4, 11. 39: vis penes Mucianum erat.

Juvene–usurpante. Dom. was now eighteen years old, cf. His. 4, 2: nondum ad curas intentus, sed *stupris et adulteriis filium principis agebat.*

Is, sc. Mucianus.—*Vicesimae legioni.* One of three legions, at that time stationed in *Britain,* which submitted to the government of Vesp. *tarde* and *non sine motu* (His. 3, 44).

Decessor. Predecessor. It was Roscius Coelius. His. 1, 60.

Legatis–consularibus. Governors or Proconsuls. The provinces were goverened by men who had been consuls (*consulares*), and as *lėgatus* meant any commissioned officer, these were distinguished as *legati consulares.* With reference to this consular authority, the same were called *proconsules.* Cf. note, H. 1, 49. Trebellius Maximus and Vettius Bolanus are here intended. Cf. 16. and His. 1, 60. 2, 65. *Nimia*=justo potentior. Dr.

Legatus praetorius=*legatus legionis, commander of the legion* Cf. note, His. 1, 7. Here the same person as *decessor.*

Invenisse quam fecisse, etc., involves a maxim of policy worth noting.

VIII. *Placidius. With less energy.* See more of Bolanus at close of 16.

Dignum est. A general remark, applicable to any such province. Hence the present, for which some would substitute *erat* or *esset.*

Ne incresceret, sc. ipse: *lest he should become too great*, i. e. rise above his superior and so excite his jealousy. Referred by W. to *ardorem* for its subject. But then *ne incresceret* would be superfluous.

Consularem, sc. Legatum=Governor, cf. 7, note.

Petilius Cerialis. Cf. 17. Ann. 14, 32. His. 4, 68.

Habuerunt–exemplorum. Had room for exertion and so for *setting a good example*, cf. Ann. 13, 8: videbaturque locus virtutibus patefactus. The position of *habuerunt* is emphatic, as if he had said: *then had virtues*, etc. See Rit. in loc.

Communicabat, sc. cum A.—*Ex eventu*, from *the event*, i. e. *in consequence of his success.*

In suam famam. Cf. in jactationem, 5, note.

Extra gloriam is sometimes put for *sine gloria*, especially by the late writers. His. 1, 49: *extra vitia.* Hand's Turs. 2, 679.

IX. *Revertentem*, etc. Returning from his command in Britain. —*Divus.* Cf. notes, G. 28; His. 2, 33.

Vesp.–ascivit. By virtue of his office as Censor, the Emperor claimed the right of elevating and degrading the rank of the citizens. Inasmuch as the families of the aristocracy always incline to run out and become extinct, there was a necessity for an occasional re-supply of the patrician from the plebeian ranks, e. g. by Julius Caesar, Augustus and Claudius (Ann. 11, 25), as well as by Vespasian (Aur. Vic. Caes. 9. Suet. 9.)—*Provinciae–praeposuit.* Aquitania was one of seven provinces, into which Augustus distributed Gaul, and which with the exception of Narbonne Gaul, were all subject to the immediate disposal and control of the Emperor himself. It was the south-western part of Gaul, being enclosed by the Rhone, the Loire, the Pyrenees and the Atlantic.

Splendidae–destinarat. *A province of the first importance both in its government* (in itself considered), *and the prospect of the consulship, to which he* (Vesp.) *had destined him* (A.), sc. as soon as his office should have expired.

Subtilitatem = calliditatem, nice discernment, *discrimination.*—*Exerceat.* Observe the subj. to express the views of others, not of the author. H. 531; Z. 571.

Secura–agens. *Requiring less anxious thought and mental acumen,* and *proceeding more by physical force.* *Secura*=minus anxia. Dr. Cf. note, His. 1, 1. *Obtusior*=minus acuta.

Togatos. *Civilians* in distinction from military men, like A. The *toga* was the dress of civil life to some extent in the *provinces* (cf. 21, His. 2, 20), though originally worn only in *Rome.* (Beck. Gall., Exc. Sc. 8.)

Remissionumque. The Greeks and Romans both used the pl. of many abstracts, of which we use only the sing. For examples see R. Exc. 4. For the principle cf. Z. 92.

Curarum–divisi. This clause means not merely, that his time was divided between business and relaxation; but that there was a broad line of demarcation between them, as he proceeds to explain. *Divisa*=diversa inter se. Dr. So Virg. Georg. 2, 116: divisae arboribus patriae=countries are *distinguished from* each other by their trees. *Jam vero.* Cf. note, G. 14.

Conventus, sc. juridici=*courts.* The word designates also the districts in which the courts were held, and into which each province was divided. Cf. Smith's Dict. of Ant.: Conventus. So Pliny (N. H. 3, 3.) speaks of juridici conventus. Tacitus, as usual, avoids the technical designation.

Ultra. Adv. for adj., cf. *longe,* 6.—*Persona.* 1. A mask (*per* and *sono*). 2. Outward show, as here.

Tristitiam–exuerat. Some connect this clause by zeugma with the foregoing. But with a misapprehension of the meaning of *exuerat,* which=*was entirely free from;* lit. had divested himself of. Thus understood, the clause is a *general* remark touching the character of A., in implied contrast with other men or magistrates with whom those vices were so common. So in Ann. 6, 25, Agrippina is said to have divested herself of vices (*vitia exuerat*) which were common among women, but which never attached to her.

Facilitas. Opposed to *severitas*=kindness, indulgence.

Abstinentiam. This word, though sometimes denoting temperance in food and drink, more properly refers to the desire and use of money. *Abstinentia* is opposed to *avarice; continentia* to *sensual pleasure.* Cf. Plin. Epis. 6, 8: alieni abstinentissimus. Here render honesty, integrity.

Cui–indulgent. See the same sentiment, His. 4, 6: quando etiam sapientibus cupido gloriae novissima exuitur.

Ostentanda–artem, cf. 6: *per–anteponendo;* also G. 15, note.

Collegas. The governors of other provinces. The word means *chosen together;* hence either those chosen at the same election or those chosen to the same office. Cf. H. 1, 10.

Procuratores. There was but one at a time in each province. There may have been several however in succession, while A. was Proconsul. Or we may understand both this clause and the preceding, not of his government in Aquitania in particular, but as a general fact in the life of A. So E. For the office, see note, 4; and for an instance of a quarrel between the Proconsul and the Procurator, Ann. 14, 38.

Atteri=vinci as the antithesis shows, though with more of the implication of dignity *impaired* (worn off) by conflict with inferiors.

Minus triennium. *Quam* omitted. See H. 417, 3; Z. 485.

Comitante opinione. *A general expectation attending him,* as it were, on his return.

Nullis sermonibus. Ablative of *cause.*

Elegit. Perf. to denote what *has in fact* taken place.

X. *In comparationem.* Cf. in suam famam, 8, note.

Perdomita est. *Completely subdued.*

Rerum fide=*faithfully and truly;* lit. with fidelity to facts.

Britannia. It has generally been supposed (though Gesenius denies it in his Phenician Palœography) that Britain was known to the Phenicians, those bold navigators and enterprising merchants of antiquity, under the name of the *Cassiterides,* or Tin Islands. Greek authors make early mention of Albion (plural of Alp?) and Ierne (Erin) as British Islands. Bochart derives the name (Britain) from the Phenician or Hebrew Baratanac, "the Land of Tin;" others from the Gallic *Britti,* Painted, in allusion to the custom among the inhabitants of painting their bodies. But according to the Welsh Triads, Britain derived its name from Prydain, a king, who early reigned in the island. Cf. Turner's His. Ang. Sax. 1, 2, seqq. The geographical description, which follows, cannot be exonerated from the charge of verbiage and grandiloquence. T. wanted the art of saying a plain thing plainly.

Spatio ac coelo. Brit. not only stretches out or lies over against these several countries in *situation*, but it approaches them also in *climate:* a circumctance which illustrates the great size of the island (cf. *maxima*, above) and prepares the way for the description of both below.

Germaniae and *Hispaniae* are dat. after *obtenditur.* The mistaken notion of the relative position of Spain and Britain is shared with T. by Caesar (B. G. 13), Dion (39, 50), and indeed by the ancients in general. It is so represented in maps as late as Richard of Cirencester. Cf. Prichard, III. 3, 9.

Etiam inspicitur. It is even *seen* by the Gauls, implying nearer approach to Gaul, than to Germany or Spain.

Nullis terris. Abl. abs., *contra* taking the place of the part., or rather limiting a part. understood.

Livius. In his 105th Book; now lost, except in the Epitome.

Fabius Rusticus. A friend of Seneca, and writer of history in the age of Claudius and Nero.

Oblongae scutulae. Geometrically a trapezium.

Et est ea facies. And such is the form, exclusive of Caledonia, whence the account has been extended also to the whole Island.

Sed–tenuatur. But a vast and irregular extent of lands jutting out here (*jam*, cf. note, G. 44) *on this remotest shore* (i. e. widening out again where they seemed already to have come to an end), *is narrowed down as it were into a wedge.* The author likens Caledonia to a wedge with its apex at the Friths of Clyde and Forth, and its base widening out on either side into the ocean beyond. *Enormis* is a post-Augustan word. *Novissimi*=extreme, remotest. G. 24, note.

Affirmavit. *Established* the fact, hitherto supposed, but not fully ascertained. This was done in Agricola's last campaign in Britain, cf. 38.

Orcadas. The Orkneys. Their name occurs earlier than this, but they were little known.

Dispecta est. Was seen through the mist, as it were; discovered in the distance and obscurity. Cf. note, H. 4, 55: dispecturas Gallias, etc.

Thule. Al. Thyle. What island T. meant, is uncertain. It has been referred by different critics, to the Shetland, the Hebrides, and even to Iceland. The account of the island, like that of the surrounding ocean, is obviously drawn from the imagination.

Nam hactenus, etc. *For their orders were* to proceed *thus far* only, *and* (besides) *winter was approaching*. Cf. *hactenus*, G. 25, and *appetere*, Ann. 4, 51: *appetente jam luce*. The editions generally have *nix* instead of *jussum*. But Rit. and Or. with reason follow the oldest and best MSS. in the reading *jussum*, which with the slight and obvious amendment of *nam* for *quam* by Rit. renders this obscure and vexed passage at length easy and clear.

Pigrum et grave. See a similar description of the Northern Ocean, G. 25: pigrum ac prope immotum. The modern reader need not be informed, that this is an entire mistake, as to the matter of fact; those seas about Britain are never frozen; though the navigators in this voyage might easily have magnified the perils and hardships of their enterprise, by transferring to these waters what they had heard of those further north.

Perinde. Al. *proinde*. These two forms are written indiscriminately in the old MSS. The meaning of *ne perinde* here is *not so much*, sc. as other seas. Cf. note, G. 5.

Ne ventis–attolli. Directly the reverse of the truth. Those seas, are in fact, remarkably tempestuous.

Quod–impellitur. False philosophy to explain a fictitious phenomenon, as is too often the case with the philosophy of the ancients, who little understood natural science, cf. the *astronomy* of T. in 12.

Neque–ac. Correlatives. The author assigns two reasons why he does not discuss the subject of the *tides*: 1. It does not suit the design of his work; 2. The subject has been treated by many others, e. g. Strab. 3, 5, 11; Plin. N. H. 2, 99, &c.

Multum fluminum. *Multum* is the object of *ferre*, of which *mare* is the subject, as it is also of all the infinitives in the sentence. *Fluminum* is not rivers but currents among the islands along the shore.

Nec littore tenus, etc. "*The ebbings and flowings of the tide are not confined to the shore, but the sea penetrates into the heart of the country, and works its way among the hills and mountains, as in its native bed.*" Ky. A description very appropriate to a coast so cut up by aestuaries, and highly poetical, but wanting in simplicity.

Jugis etiam ac montibus. *Jugis*, cf. G. 43. *Ac*. *Atque* in the common editions. But *ac*, besides being more frequent before a consonant, is found in the best MSS.

XI. *Indigenae an advecti.* Cf. *note*, G. 2: indigenas.

Ut inter barbaros, sc. fieri solet. Cf. ut in licentia, G. 2; and ut inter Germanos, G. 30.

Rutilae–asseverant. Cf. the description of the Germans, G. 4. The inhabitants of Caledonia are of the same stock as the other Britons. The conclusion, to which our author inclines below, viz. that the Britons proceeded from Gaul, is sustained by the authority of modern ethnologists. The original inhabitants of Britain are found, both by philological and historical evidence, to have belonged to the Celtic or Cimmerian stock, which once overspread nearly the whole of central Europe, but were overrun and pushed off the stage by the Gothic or German Tribes, and now have their distinct representatives only in the Welsh, the Irish, the Highland Scotch, and a few similar remnants of a once powerful race in the extreme west of the continent and the islands of the sea. Cf. note on the Cimbri, G. 37.

Silurum. The people of Wales.

Colorati vultus. *Dark complexion.* So with the poets, colorati Indi, Seres, Etrusci, &c.

Hispania. Nom. subject of *faciunt*, with *crines*, &c.

Iberos. Properly a people on the Iberus (Ebro), who gave their name to the whole Spanish Peninsula. They belonged to a different race from the Celtic, or the Teutonic, which seems once to have inhabited Italy and Sicily, as well as parts of Gaul and Spain. A dialect is still spoken in the mountainous regions about the Bay of Biscay, and called the Basque or Biscayan, which differs from any other dialect in Europe. Cf. Prichard's Physical Researches, vol. III. chap. 2.

Proximi Gallis. Cf. Caes. B. G. 5, 14: Ex his omnibus longe sunt humanissimi, qui Cantium (Kent) incolunt, quae regio est maritima omnis, *neque multum a Gallica differunt consuetudine.* *Et* =*also*: *those nearest the Gauls are also like them.*

Durante vi. *Either because the influence of a common origin still continues*, etc.

Procurrentibus–terris. *Or because their territories running out towards one another*, literally, *in opposite directions*, Britain towards the south and Gaul towards the north, so as to approach each other. See Rit., Död. in loc., and Freund ad *diversus.*

Positio–dedit. The idea of similarity being already expressed in *similes*, is understood here: their situation in the same climate (*coelo*) has given them the *same* personal appearance.

Aestimanti. Indef. dat. after *credibile est*, cf. note, G. 6.

Eorum refers to the Gauls. You (indef. subject, cf. quiescas, G. 36) may discover the religion of the Gauls (among the Britons) in their full belief of the same superstitions. So Caes. B. G. 6, 13: disciplina in Britannia reperta atque inde in Galliam translata esse existimatur; and he adds, that those who wished to gain a more perfect knowledge of the Druidical system still went from Gaul to Britain to learn. Sharon Turner thinks, the system must have been introduced into Britain from the East (perhaps India) by the Phenicians, and thence propagated in Gaul. His. Ang. Sax., B. 1, chap. 5.

Persuasione. See the same use of the word, His. 5, 5: eademque de infernis persuasio.

In-periculis. The same sentiment is expressed by Caesar (B. G. 3, 19).

Ferociae. In a good sense, courage, cf. 31: virtus ac ferocia.

Praeferunt=prae se ferunt, i. e. *exhibit.*

Ut quos. *Ut qui*, like *qui* alone, is followed by the subj. to express a reason for what precedes. It may be rendered by *because* or *since* with the demonstrative. So *quippe cui placuisset*, 18. Cf. Z. 565 and H. 519, 3.

Gallos floruisse. Cf. G. 28.

Otio. Opposed to *bellis*, *peace.*—*Amissa virtute.* Abl. abs. denoting an additional circumstance. Cf. 2: *expulsis-professoribus*, note.—*Olim* limits *victis.*

XII. *Honestior.* *The more honorable* (i. e. the man of rank) *is the charioteer, his dependents fight* (on the chariot). The reverse was true in the Trojan War.

Factionibus trahuntur=distrahuntur in factiones. Dr., and Or. T. is fond of using simple for compound verbs. See note, 22; also numerous examples in the Index to Notes on the Histories.

Civitatibus. Dat. for Gen.—*Pro nobis.* Abl. with prep. for dat. Enallage. R.—*Conventus.* *Convention*, meeting.

Coelum-foedum. The fog and rain of the British Isles are still proverbial.—*Dierum spatia*, etc. Cf. Caes. 513.

Quod si = *and if.* From the tendency to connect sentences by relatives arose the use of *quod* before certain conjunctions, particularly *si*, merely as a copulative. Cf. Z. 807:

also Freund sub v. The fact alleged in this sentence is as false as the philosophy by which it is explained in the next, cf. G. 45: in ortus, note.

Scilicet-cadit. This explanation proceeds on the assumption that night is caused by the shadow of mountains, behind which the sun sets; and since these do not exist in that level extremity of the earth, the sun has nothing to set behind, and so there is no night. The astronomy of T. is about of a piece with his natural philosophy, cf. 10. — *Extrema-terrarum.* Cf. note, 6: *inania honoris.*

Non erigunt, lit. do not elevate the darkness, i. e. do not cast their shadow so high (*infraque-cadit*), as the sky and the stars; hence they are bright (*clara*) through the night!! Pliny also supposed the heavens (above the moon) to be of themselves perpetually luminous, but darkened at night by the shadow of the earth. N. H. 2, 7.

Praeter. *Beyond.* Hence either *besides* or *except.* Here the latter.—*Fecundum.* More than *patiens, fruitful even.*—*Proveniunt.* Ang. *come forward.*

Fert-aurum, etc. This is also affirmed by Strabo, 4, 5, 2, but denied by Cic. ad Att. 4, 16, 7, and ad Div., 7, 7. The moderns decide in favor of T. and Strabo, though it is only in inconsiderable quantities that gold and silver have ever been found in Britain.

Margarita. The neuter form of this word is seldom used, never by Cicero. See Freund sub v.

Rubro mari. The *Red Sea* of the Greeks and Romans embraced both the Arabian and the Persian Gulfs; and it was in the latter especially, that pearls were found, as they are to this day. Cf. Plin. N. H. 9, 54: praecipue laudantur (margaritae) in *Persico sinu maris rubri.* For an explanation of the name (Red Sea), see Anthon's Classical Dictionary.

Expulsa sint. *Cast out,* i. e. *ashore, by the waves.* Subj. in a subordinate clause of the oratio obliqua. H. 531; Z. 603.

Naturam-avaritiam. A very characteristic sentence, both for its antithesis and its satire.

XIII. *Ipsi Britanni.* *Ipsi* marks the transition from the country to the people, cf. ipsos Germanos, G. 2.

Obeunt properly applies only to *munera,* not to *tributa* and *delec-*

tum, which would require *tolerant* or some kindred verb. Zeugma, H. 704, I. 2; Z. 775.

Igitur=*now.* In the first sentence of the section the author has indicated his purpose to speak of the *people* of Britain. And *now in pursuance of that design*, he goes back to the commencement of their history, as related to and known by the Romans. Cf. note, G. 28.

Divus. Cf. note, G. 28: D. Julius. For Julius Caesar's campaigns in Britain, see Caes. B. G. 4, 21. seq.; 5, 5. seq.; Strabo, Lib. 4, &c.

Consilium. His *advice* (to his successor). See Ann. 1, 11.—*Praeceptum.* A *command* (of Augustus, which Tib. affected to hold sacred). Ann. 1, 77; 4, 37.

C. Caesarem. Caligula, cf. 4, note.—*Agitasse*, etc. cf. 39. His. 4, 15; Suet. Calig. 44.

Ni-fuissent. Cf. *Ni*, 4, note. The ellipsis may be supplied thus: he meditated an invasion of Brit. and *would have invaded it*, had he not been *velox ingenio*, etc. But in idiomatic Eng. *ni*=but. Of course *fuisset* is to be supplied with *velox ingenio* and *mobilis poenitentiae*. Al. poenitentia. But contrary to the MSS. *Mobilis* agrees with *poenitentiae* (cf. Liv. 31, 32: celerem poenitentiam), which is a qualifying gen. Gr. 211. R. 6. Lit. *of repentance easy to be moved.* Render: *fickle of purpose.*

Auctor operis. Auctor fuit rei adversus Britannos gerendae et feliciter gestae. Dr. See on the same subject Suet. Claud. 17.—*Assumpto Vespasiano*, cf. Suet Vesp. 4. H. 3, 44.

Quod-fuit. Vespasian's participation in the war against Brit. was the commencement of his subsequent brilliant fortunes.

Monstratus fatis, i. e. a fatis, *by the fates.* The expression is borrowed perhaps from Virg. Aen. 6, 870: *Ostendent* terris hunc tantum *fata.*

XIV. *Consularium.* Cf. note on it, 8.—*Aulus Plautius.* Ann. 13, 32; Dio. 60, 19.—*Ostorius Scapula.* Ann. 12, 31–39.—*Proxima*, sc. Romae.

Veteranorum colonia. Camolodunum. Ann. 12, 32. Now Colchester. Dr.—*Et reges. Kings also*, i. e. besides other means.—*Ut vetere*, etc. So in the MSS. and earliest editions. Rhenanus transferred *ut* to the place before *haberet* which it occupies in the common editions. But no change is necessary. Render: *that in accordance with their established custom, the Roman people might have kings also as the instruments of reducing* (the Britons) *to slavery.*

Didius Gallus. Cf. Ann. 12, 40: arcere hostem satis habebat.—*Parta a prioribus. The acquisitions* (*conquests*) *of his predecessors.*

Aucti officii. Of enlarging the boundaries of his government. Officium is used in a like sense, Caes. B. C. 3, 5: Toti officio maritimo praepositus, etc. So Wr.; Or. and Död. understand by it *going beyond* the mere performance of his *duty.* It was his duty to protect his province: he enlarged it.—*Quaereretur.* Subj. in a relative clause denoting a purpose. H. 500; Z. 567.

Veranius. Ann. 14, 29.—*Paullinus.* Ann. 14, 29–30.

Monam insulam. Now Anglesey. But the *Mona* of *Caesar* is the Isle of Man, called by Pliny *Monapia.* The Mona of T. was the chief seat of the Druids, hence *ministrantem vires rebellibus,* for the Druids animated and led on the Briton troops to battle. T. has given (Ann. 14, 30) a very graphic sketch of the mixed multitude of armed men, women like furies, and priests with hands uplifted in prayer, that met Paullinus on his landing, and, for a time, well nigh paralyzed his soldiers with dismay. In the same connexion, he speaks also of the human sacrifices and other barbarous rites, which were practised by our Briton Fathers in honor of their gods.

XV. *Interpretando. By putting their own,* i. e. *the worst construction upon them.*

Ex facili=facile. A frequent form of expression in T., ad Graecorum consuetudinem. Dr. See R. Exc. 24.

Singulos–binos. Distributives=*one for each tribe—two for each tribe.*

Aeque–aeque. Like Greek correlatives; alike fatal to their subjects in *either case.* So ὁμοίως μέν and ὁμοίως δέ, Xen. Mem. 1, 6, 13; Plat. Symp. 181. C.

Alterius manus centuriones, alterius servos. This is the reading of the latest editions (Dr. Wr. Or. and R.), and the best MSS., though the MSS. differ somewhat: *Centurions, the hands* (instruments) *of the one, and servants,* the hands *of the other, added insult to injury.* For the use of *manus* in the above sense, reference is made to Cic. in Ver. 2, 10, 27: Comites illi tui delecti *manus* erant tuae. So the *centurions* of the *legate* and the *servants* of the *procurator* are said by our author to have robbed the Briton king Prasutagus of his kingdom and his palace, Ann. 14, 31, which is the best commentary on the passage before us.

Ab ignavis. By the feeble and cowardly. Antithetic to *fortiorem. In battle, it is the braver that plunders us; but now* (it is a special aggravation of our sufferings, that) *by the feeble and cowardly,* &c. So in contempt, they call the veterans, cf. 14: *veteranorum colonia;* 32: *senum colonia.*

Tantum limits *pro patria;* as if it was for their *country* only they knew not how to die.

Si sese, etc., i. e. in *comparison* with their own numbers.

Patriam–parentes, sc. *causas belli esse.*

Recessisset. Observe the subj. in the subordinate clauses of the oratio obliqua throughout this chapter. H. 531; Z. 603.

Neve–pavescerant. This verb would have been an imperative in the oratio recta, Z. 603, c. *Neve* is appropriate either to the imp. or the subj.

XVI. *Instincti,* i. e. furore quodam afflati. Dr. For a fuller account of this revolt, see Ann. 14, 31–38; Dio. 62, 1–13.

Boudicea. Wife of Prasutagus, king of the Iceni. When conquered, she ended her life by poison, Ann. 14, 37.

Expugnatis praesidiis. Having stormed the fortresses. The force of *ex* in this word is seen in that it denotes the *actual carrying* of a place by assault, whereas *oppugnatus* only denotes the assault itself. So ἐκ-πολιορκηθείς=*taken* in a siege, πολιορκηθείς =besieged.

Ipsam coloniam. Cf. note 14: veteranorum colonia.

In barbaris=qualis inter barbaros esse solet. R. Exc. 25.

Ira et victoria. Hendiadys. Render: *Nor did they in the excitement of victory omit,* etc. So Dr. R. and Wr. *Ira* may, however, refer to their *long cherished resentment. Ira* causam, *victoria* facultatem explendae saevitiae denotat. Rit.—*Quod nisi. And had not,* etc. Cf. note, 12: *quod si.*

Patientiae. Most Latin authors would have said: ad patientiam. R. *Patientia* here=*submission.*

Tenentibus–plerisque. Though many still retained, i. e. did not lay down *their arms.*

Propius. Al. *proprius.* But that is purely conjectural. Adv. for adj., cf. ultra, 8; longe, 6=propior, like the *propior cura* of Ovid. Metamor. 13, 578. Render: *a more urgent fear.* Some would connect *propius* with *agitabat* notwithstanding its remote position.

Suae quoque. His own also, sc. as well as that of the Empire.

Durius, sc. aequo. H. 444, 1. cf. 4: *acrius*, note.

Delictis–novus. A stranger to their faults. Cf. Sil. Ital. 6, 254: novusque dolori. Wr. Cf. Böt. Lex. Tac. *Dativus.*

Poenitentiae mitior, i. e. mitior erga poenitentiam, or facilior erga poenitentes. *Poenitentiae* dat. of object.

Compositis prioribus. Having restored things to their former quiet state.

Nullis–experimentis. Undertaking no military expeditions. Or. —*Castrorum.* Cf. 5, note.

Comitate–tenuit. "*Retained the province by a popular manner of administering the government.*" Ky.—*Curandi.* Note, H. 1, 52.

Ignoscere. Properly *not to notice*, hence *to view with indulgence, to indulge in.*

Vitiis blandientibus. The reference is to the *luxurious and vicious pleasures* of the Romans, which enervated the Britons, cf. 21, at close, where the idea is brought out more fully.

Cum–lasciviret. Cum=since. Hence the subj.

Precario. Cf. note, G. 44.—*Mox*, cf. note 4.

Velut pacti implies a *tacit* compact. It was understood between them, that the army were to enjoy their liberty; the general, his life. Supply *sunt* with *pacti.* Död. and Wr. supply *essent;* but they read *haec* for *et* before *seditio* contrary to the best MSS.

Et seditio. Et=and so. Al. haec seditio.

Stetit. Not stopped, but stood, as in our phrase: stood them in so much. So Ovid: Multo *sanguine*—victoria *stetit.* And T. His. 3, 53: Majore *damno*—veteres civium discordias reipublicae *stetisse.* Render: *cost no blood.* Dr.

Petulantia. Insubordination.—*Nisi quod*, but, cf. 6.

Bolanus. If the reader wishes to know more of the officers named in this chapter, for Turpilianus, see Ann. 14, 39. His. 1, 6; Trebellius, His. 1, 60; Bolanus, Ann. 15, 3. His. 2, 65. 79.

Caritatem—auctoritatis. "*Had conciliated affection as a substitute for authority.*" Ky.

XVII. *Recuperavit.* Al. *reciperavit.* The two forms are written indiscriminately in the MSS. The word may express either the recovery of what was lost, or the restoration to health of what was diseased. Either would make a good sense here. Cf. chap. 5; also Cic. Phil. 14, 13: *republica recuperata.* Or. renders *acquired again*, sc. what had previously belonged, as it were, to him, rather than to the bad emperors who had preceded him.

Petilius Cerialis. Cf. note, 8.—*Brigantum.* Cf. H. 3, 45; Ann. 12, 32. Their territory embraced Cumberland, Westmoreland, Lancashire, Durham and Yorkshire.

Aut victoria aut bello, i. e. *either received their submission after the victory, or involved them in the calamities of war. Aut–aut* generally adversative=either—or on the contrary. *Vel–vel* only disjunctive=whether—or. Cf. note on vel–vel, G. 15.

Alterius. Another, than Julius Frontinus, i. e. by implication, one *different* from him, *less brave and great.* Cf. His. 2, 90: tanquam apud alterius civitatis senatum; 3, 13, note. *Alius* is the word usually appropriated to express this idea. *Alter* generally implies a *resemblance* between contrasted objects. See Freund, ad v.

Obruisset–sustinuit. These words primarily refer to physical energies, and are exactly counterpart=*crushed–sustained.*

Quantum licebat limits *vir magnus: as great a man, as it was permitted* him to be, restricted as he was in his resources, perhaps by the parsimony of the Emperor. On Julius Frontinus, cf. H. 4, 39. He was the friend of Pliny the Younger (Plin. Ep. 9, 19) and therefore probably of Tacitus. His books on Stratagems, and on the Aqueducts of Rome are still extant.—*Super,* over and above, i. e. *besides.*

XVIII. *Agentem,* sc. excubias or stationem=stationed in, cf. His. 1, 47: copias, quae Lugduni agebant. *Ala.* Cf. note, H. 1, 54.

Ordovicum civitas. Situated over against the Island Mona, north of the Silures, i. e. in the northern part of what is now Wales.

Ad–verterentur. Were turning themselves (middle sense) *towards,* i. e. *looking to or for. Occasionem. An opportunity,* sc. to attack the Romans in their security. Al. *uterentur.*

Quibus–erat. They who wished for war. Greek idiom for qui bellum volebant. See Kühner's Greek Gram. 284, 10, c., cf. His. 3, 43: volentibus fuit, etc., and note, ibid. In Latin, the idiom occurs chiefly in Sallust and T. See Z. 420, and H. 387, 3.

Ac–opperiri. Al. *aut* by conjecture. But *ac=ac tamen, and yet.* Cf. Ann. 1, 36: *exauctorari—ac retineri sub vexillo.*

Transvecta. Al. transacta. Cf. His. 2, 76: abiit et *transvectum est tempus.* Only T. uses the word in reference to time.

Numeri=cohortes or manipuli, cf. His. 1, 6: multi numeri. This use of the word is post-Augustan. Cf. note, His. 1, 6.

Tarda et contraria. In appos. with the foregoing clauses=

circumstances calculated to retard and oppose him in commencing war.

Plerisque, sc. of the inferior officers. They thought it best that those parts of the country, whose fidelity was questionable (*suspecta)* should be secured by garrisons (*custodiri*). *Potius* is an adj. and goes with *videbatur=it seemed preferable.*

Legionum vexillis. Some understand this of veteran soldiers, who had served out their time (twenty years), but were still *sub vexillis* (not dismissed). So R. and W. Others of parts of the legions detached for a season sub vexillis (under separate standards) So Gronovius. The word seems to be used in both senses. See note, H. 1, 31.

In aequum. Into the plain. Aequus, prim. level, hence aequor, sea.

Erexit aciem. Led his troops up the steep. So His. 3, 71: eri gunt aciem per adversum collem.

Ac–ceteris. And that according as the first enterprises *went* (cf. note, 5: *cessit*), *would be the terror in the rest* of his engagements. Cf. H. 2, 20: *gnarus, ut initia belli provenissent, famam in cetera fore.* Al. *fore universa.*

Possessione. Taking possession, cf. 14. A *possīdĕre*, i. e. occupare, non a *possĭdēre*, quod est occupatum tenere. Rit. For the abl. without *a*, cf. H. 2, 79: *Syria remeans.*

Ut in dubiis consiliis, sc. fieri solet. Generals are not apt to be prepared beforehand for enterprises, not contemplated at all in their original plans.

Qui–expectabant. Who were looking out for (*ex* and *specto*) *a fleet, for ships*, in a word *for the sea*, i. e. naval preparations in general, instead of an attack by land. The language is highly rhetorical.—*Crediderint.* Livy, Nepos and Tacitus use the *perf.* subj. after *ut*, denoting a consequence, when a single, specific past act is expressed; when a repeated or continued action, the *imp.* subj. Most writers use the imp. in both cases. See H. 482, 2, and 480; Z. 516; also Z. 504, Note, and note H. 1, 24: *dederit.*

Officiorum ambitum. "*Compliments of office.*" Ky.

Placuisset. Subj. cf. note, 11: *ut quos.*

Expeditionem–continuisse. He did not call it a campaign or a victory to have kept the conquered in subjection.

Laureatis sc. litteris. It was customary to communicate the news of victory to the Emperor and Senate, by letters bound with bay leaves, cf. Liv. 5, 28: *litterae* a Postumio *laureatae* sequuntur.

Without *litterae*, it occurs only here. Or. So in H. 3, 77. T avoids the technical expression and employs the word *laurea*, seldom used in this sense.

Dissimulatione. Cf. note, 6. — *Aestimantibus*, cf. aestimanti, 11. The aspiring, and especially the vain, may learn from this passage a lesson of great practical value. Compare also § 8, at the close.

XIX. *Aliena experimenta. The experience of others.*

Nihil. Ellipsis of *agere* (which is inserted without MS. authority in the common editions). So Cic. Phil. 1, 2: Nihil per senatum, etc. Cf. G. 19: *adhuc*, note.

Ascire, al. accire. *To receive into regular service.* The reference is to the transfer of soldiers from the raw recruits to the legions. So W. followed by Dr. R. and W. The next clause implies, that he took care to receive into the service none but the best men (*optimum quemque*), whom he deemed *trustworthy* (*fidissimum*) just in *proportion* as they were *good.* This use of two superlatives mutually related to each other, the former with *quisque*, is frequent in Latin and resembles the English use of two comparatives: the better, the more trustworthy. Cf. Z. 710, b.; also note, 3: *promptissmus quisque.*

Exsequi=punire. A sense peculiar to the later Latin. Cic. and Caes. use *persequi.* For a similar use of the word in the expression of a similar sentiment, see Suet. Jul. 67: Delicta neque observabat omnia neque pro modo exsequebatur. Compare our word *execute.* And mark the sentiment, as a maxim in the science of government.

Severitatem commodare. W. with Dr. and R. make this an example of zeugma. And in its ordinary acceptation (i. e. in the sense *to give*) the word *commodare* certainly applies only to *veniam*, and not to *severitatem.* But *commodare* in its primary signification means to *adapt;* and in this sense, it suits both of its adjuncts: *He adapted* (awarded) *pardon to small offences, severe punishment to great ones.* So Wr. For the series of infinitives, cf. notes, 5: *nosci*, etc.; G. 30: *praeponere*, etc.

Nec poena—contentus esse. Nor was he always content with punishment, but oftener with repentance. Mere punishment without reformation did not satisfy him; reformation without punishment satisfied him better. See Död. in loc. Here too some have called in the aid of zeugma.

Auctionem. Al. exactionem. The former is the reading of the greater part of the MSS. and the later German editions. *Auctionem tributorum* refers to the increased tribute exacted by Vesp. cf. Sueton. Vesp. 16: *auxisse* tributa provinciis, nonnullis et *duplicasse.*

Munerum. Duties, burdens.—Circumcisis. Cf. note, 2: expulsis, etc., and 11: amissa virtute.

Namque–cogebantur. The best version we can give of this obscure passage is as follows: *For they were compelled in mockery to sit by the closed granaries and to buy corn needlessly* (beyond what was necessary, cf. note on *ultro*, G. 28, when they had enough of their own) *and to sell it at a fixed price* (prescribed by the purchasers). It has been made a question, whether the granaries of the Britons, or those of the Romans are here meant. Död., Dr. and R. advocate the former opinion; Walch, Wr., Or., and Rit. the latter According to the former view, the Britons were often obliged to buy corn of the Romans, because they were forbidden to use their own, to supply themselves and their families; according to the latter, because they were required (as explained below) to carry their contributions to a quarter so distant from their own granaries, that they were fain to buy the corn rather at some nearer warehouse of the Romans. The *selling at a fixed price* is equally intelligible on either supposition. Or. following the best MSS. reads *ludere pretio,* which Rit. has amended into *colludere pretio. Ultro* may well enough be rendered *moreover* or *even,* thus giving emphasis to *emere.*

Devortia itinerum. Bye roads, explained by *avia,* as *longinquïtas* is by *remota.* The object of requiring the people to convey their contributions to such distant and inconvenient points, was to compel them to buy of the Romans, or to pay almost any sum of *money* to avoid compliance. The reader of Cic. will remember in illustration of this whole passage, the various arts to which Verres is said to have had recourse to enrich himself, at the expense of the people of his province (Cic. in Ver. 3, 72, and 82), such as refusing to accept the contributions they brought, obliging them to buy of him at his own price, requiring them to carry supplies to points most distant and difficult of access, *ut vecturae difficultate ad quam vellent aestimationem pervenirent.*

Omnibus, sc. et incolis et militibus; *paucis,* sc. praefectis aut publicanis. Dr.

Donec–fieret. The subj. here denotes a purpose or object in view, and therefore follows *donec* according to the rule. H. 522, II.; Z. 575. Tacitus however always expresses a repeated past action after *donec* by the imp. subj. Cf. note, 37: affectavere; H. 1, 13. 35.

XX. *Statim.* Emphatic, like εὐθύς. Cf. Thucyd. 2, 47: τοῦ θέρους εὐθὺς ἀρχομένου: at the *very* beginning of summer. So in § 3.

Intolerantia, al. tolerantia, but without MS. authority. *Incuria* is *negligence. Intolerantia* is *insufferable arrogance, severity*, in a word *intolerance.* So Cic.: superbia atque intolerantia.

Quae–timebatur. And no wonder, since *ubi solitudinem* faciunt, *pacem* appellant, 30.

Multus, al. militum. *Multus* in the recent editions. *Multus*= frequens, cf. Sal. Jug. 84: multus ac ferox instare.—*Modestiam–disjectos.* These words are antithetic, though one is abstract and the other concrete. The whole clause may be literally rendered thus: *ever present in the line of march, he commended good order* (*discipline*), *the disorderly he restrained.*

Popularetur, sc. A. *Quominus*, that not=*but: but he ravaged their country by unexpected invasions.*

Irritamenta. Inducements.—*Pacis.* Ang. *to* or *for peace.*

Ex aequo egerant, lit. had acted (lived) on an equality, i. e. *had maintained their independence*, cf. His. 4, 64: aut ex aequo agetis aut aliis imperitabitis.

Iram posuere. Cf. Hor. Ars Poet.: et *iram* colligit ac *ponit* temere. See also G. 27: ponunt dolorem, etc.

Ut–transierit. The clause is obscure. The best that can be made of it is this: *they were encompassed by forts and garrisons with so much skill and care that no part of Britain hitherto new went over* (to the enemy) *with impunity* (literally unattacked). For the meaning of *nova*, cf. 22. For *transierit*, cf. *transitio*, H. 2, 99; 3, 61; and Freund, sub v. This is Walther's interpretation. If, with Ernesti, Dr. and some others, we might suppose a *sic, ita* or *tam* to be understood with *illacessita*, we might obtain perhaps a better sense, viz. *came over* (to the Romans) *with so little annoyance* (from the enemy). In the last edition a meaning was attached to *transierit* (*remained*, sc. unattacked), for which I now find no sufficient authority. Among the many amendments, which have been suggested, the easiest and best is that of Susius, followed by Wexius, Dübner, Or. and Rit., viz. placing *Illacessita transiit* at the beginning of the next chapter. But this does violence not only to MS.

authority, but to Latin usage in making the adverb *ut, so as, as,* follow *tanta.* In such a connection, *ut* must be a conjunction= *so that, that.* See Freund sub v. For the *perf.* subj. cf. note, 18: *crediderint.*

Praesidiis castellisque. Gordon, in his Itinerarium Septentrionale, found more remains of Roman works in that part of Britain here referred to, than in any other portion of the Island.

XXI. *Ut–assuescerent. In order that they might become habituated,* etc.—*In bella faciles. Easily inclined to wars.* Cf. Ann. 14, 4: *facili ad gaudia.* Al. *in bello, bello,* and *in bellum.*—*Otio.* See note, 11: otio.—*Privatim. As a private individual; publice, by public authority, and of course from the public treasury,* cf. note G. 39: publice.—*Jam vero. Moreover,* cf. G. 14, note.

Anteferre. Wr. takes this word in its primary sense=bear before, i. e. carry beyond: *he carried (advanced) the native talents of the Britons beyond the learning of the Gauls.* But there is no authority for such a use of the word, when followed by the acc. and dat. It is doubtless used in its more ordinary sense; and the *preference* which A. expressed for the genius of the Britons over the learning of the Gauls, *stimulated* them to greater exertions. It is somewhat curious to observe thus early that mutual emulation and jealousy, which has marked the whole history of Britain and France. The national vanity of La Bletterie is sorely wounded by this remark of T. See his note in loco, also Murphy's.—*Toga.* Cf. note on *togatos,* 9.

Ut–concupiscerent. Ut=so that, denoting a consequence. The verb here denotes a continued or habitual state of mind. Hence the *imp.* subj. Cf. note, 18: *crediderit.*

Discessum, sc. a patrum moribus ad vitia varia. Dr.

Delenimenta=illa, quibus animi *leniuntur.* Dr. *Charms, blandishments.* Cf. H. 1, 77. The word is not found in Cic. or Caes.

Humanitas. Civilization, refinement. Compare the professorships of *humanity* in European Universities.

Pars servitutis. For the sentiment, cf. His. 4, 64: voluptatibus, quibus Romani plus adversus subjectos, quam armis valent. *Cum =while, although.* Hence the subj.

XXII. *Tertius–annus. Third campaign.*

Taum. The Frith of Tay.—*Nationibus.* Here synonymous with *gentes;* sometimes less comprehensive, cf. note, G. 2.

Pactione ac fuga. Al. *aut* fuga, but without authority. There are but *two* distinct clauses marked by *aut–aut: either taken by assault or abandoned by capitulation and flight.*

Nam–firmabantur. This clause assigns a reason, why the Romans were *able* to make frequent sorties (*crebrae eruptiones*), viz. supplies of provision so abundant, as to be proof against blockade.

Moras obsidionis. A protracted siege, or *blockade.*

Annuis copiis. Supplies for a year. This is the *primary* signification of *annuus;* that of our word *annual* is *secondary.*

Intrepida–praesidio=hiberna quieta ac tuta ab hostibus. Fac. and For.—*Irritis, baffled.* Seldom applied to *persons* by prose writers. Cf. H. 4, 32.

Pensare. R. remarks a peculiar fondness in T. for the use of the simple verb instead of the compound, e. g. missa for omissa, sistens for resistens, flammare for inflammare, etc. So here *pensare* =*compensare.* Cf. 12: *trahuntur,* note.

Avidus, sc. laudis=per aviditatem laudis et gloriae. E.: A. never in his eagerness for glory arrogated to himself the honor of the achievements of others.—*Seu–seu. Every one, whether centurion or praefect* (commander of a legion, cf. note, H. 1, 82.), *was sure to have in him an impartial witness to his deeds.*

Acerbior, cf. note on *durius,* 16.—*Apud quosdam*=a quibusdam.

Secretum et silentium. Reserve and silence. So W. and Ky. But R. and Dr.: *private interviews* (to be summoned to which by some commanders was alarming), *and neglect of the usual salutations in public* (which was also often a token of displeasure on the part of a superior officer). The former is the more simple and obvious, though it must be confessed that the latter is favored by the usus loquendi of T., in regard especially to *secretum,* cf. 39; Ann. 3, 8, where *secreto* is opposed to *palam;* and His. 4, 49: incertum, quoniam *secreto eorum* nemo *adfuit.*

XXIII. *Obtinendis. Securing possession of.* —*Pateretur,* sc. terminum inveniri.—*In ipsa Brit.* In the very *nature* or structure of the island, as described in the sequel. See Or. in loc.

Clota et Bodotria. Frith of Clyde and Frith of Forth.

Revectae, i. e. the natural current being driven back by the tide from the sea on either side. *Angusto–spatio.* It is now cut across by a ship canal.

Propior sinus=peninsula on the south side of the Friths, cf. note on sinus G. 1, and 29. *Sinus* refers particularly to the *curved border* on *this side* the aestuaries. This border (wherever the friths were so narrow as to require it), as well as the narrow isthmus, was occupied and secured (*tenebatur*) by garrisons.

XXIV. *Nave prima. The first Roman ship that ever visited those shores.* So Br., Dr., etc. *The foremost ship,* sc., A. himself, followed by others in a line. So Ritter. Wr., and some others understand it of a voyage from *Rome,* where they suppose him to have passed the winter, and whence he crossed over to Britain by the *earliest* vessel in the spring. W. and R. make *prima* equivalent to an adv. and render: crossing over *for the first time* by ship. Or. also makes *prima=tum primum.*

Copiis. Here troops with their equipments=*forces*, cf. 8: majoribus copiis.—*Medio sita* lying between, not midway between. E. —*In spem-formidinem.* More with the hope of invading Ireland, than through fear of invasion by the Irish.—*Valentissimam partem,* viz. Gaul, Spain and Britain.

Miscuerit. The subj. here denotes the aim or purpose of the projector: it would have done so *in his view.*

Invicem=an adj. *mutual.*—*Nostri maris.* The Mediterranean.

Differunt: in melius. The authorities differ greatly as to the reading, the pointing and the interpretation of this passage. Some copies omit *in.* Others insert *nec* before it. Some place the pause before *in melius,* others after. Some read *differt,* others *differunt. Nec in melius* would perhaps give the better sense. But the reading is purely conjectural. I have given that, which, on the whole, seems to rest on the best authority, and to make the best sense. The sense is: *the soil, climate, &c., do not differ much from those of Britain. But that the harbors and entrances to the country are better* (lit. *differ for the better, differre in melius*), *is ascertained through the medium of the merchants, who resort thither for trade* (for Ireland had not yet, like Britain, been explored by a Roman *army*). So Wr. and Död. On *in melius,* see note H. 1, 18. Or. and Rit. make the comparison thus: the harbors and entrances are better known, than the soil, climate, &c. The common interpretation is: the harbors, &c., of Ireland are better known, than those of Britain. But neither of these interpretations accounts for the position of *melius;* and the last is in itself utterly incredible.

Ex eo, sc. A. Pass. and Dr. understand it of the Irish chief, and infer that T. had been in Brit. But A. is the subject of the next sentence without the repetition of his name, as it would have been repeated, if this sentence referred to another.

XXV. *Amplexus.* Some supply *bello,* as in 17: bello amplexus. But better: embracing *in his plan of operations,* i. e. *extending his operations to those tribes.*

Hostilis exercitus. Al. hostili exercitu. But *hostilis exercitus* in the MSS. and earliest editions.—*Infesta* is here active: *hostile inroads of the enemy's forces.*

In partem virium. *For,* i. e. *as a part of his force.*

Impelleretur, was borne on with rapid and resistless power.

Profunda–adversa. Cf. note, 6: *inania honoris.*

Mixti copiis et laetitia. *Uniting their stores and their pleasures,* i. e. their respective means of entertainment. For *mixti,* cf. 4: locum-mixtum. For *copiis* in this sense, 22: annuis copiis. For the other sense, viz. forces, 24: copiis, note.

Hinc–hinc=*on this side—on that.* Cf. note G. 14: *illum–illam.* —*Victus.* Al. *auctus.*

Ad manus et arma. Ang. *to arms.*

Oppugnasse depends on *fama.* Their preparations were great. Rumor as usual (*uti mos,* etc.) represented them still greater; for the rumor went abroad, that the Caledonians had *commenced offensive operations* (*oppugnasse ultro*).—*Castella adorti* is the means by which they *metum addiderant,* i. e. *had inspired additional fear.*

Pluribus agminibus. *In several divisions.* Accordingly it is added: *diviso et ipse,* A. *himself also,* i. e. as well as the Britons, *having divided,* etc.

Agmen (from ago), properly a body of men on the march.—*Exercitus,* under military drill (exerceo.)

XXVI. *Quod ubi,* etc. *When this was known,* etc. Latin writers, as well as Greek, generally link their sentences, chapters, &c., more closely together, than English. Hence we are often obliged to render their relative by our demonstrative. See Z. 803. *Ubi,* here adv. of *time,* as in 20, 38, et passim.

Certabant. Not *fought* with the enemy, but *vied* with each other. So below: utroque–certante. Hence followed by *de* gloria, not *pro* gloria, which some would substitute for it: *secure for* (in regard to) *safety, they vied with each other in respect to* (or *in*) *glory.* With *pro salute,* cf. His. 4, 58: pro me securior.

Erupere. *Sallied forth,* sc. from the camp.

Utroque exercitu. Each of the two *Roman* armies.

Quod. Cf. 12, note.—*Debellatum,* lit. the war would have been fought *out,* i. e. *ended.*

XXVII. *Cujus* refers to *victoria* in the previous section (cf. *quod* 26, note): *inspirited by the consciousness and the glory of this victory.*

Modo cauti. Compare the sentiment with 25: specie prudentium, etc.

Arte–rati, al. arte *usos* rati by conjecture. But T. is fond of such ellipses: *The Britons, thinking it was not by superior bravery, but by favoring circumstances* (on the part of the Romans) *and the skill of their commander* (sc. that they had been defeated). Rit. reads *superati.*

Utrimque. Both the Romans and the Britons; the Romans excited by their victory, the Britons by their coetibus ac sacrificiis.

Discessum. *They separated,* viz. after the battle and at the close of the campaign.

XXVIII. *Cohors Usipiorum.* See same story, Dio Cass. 66, 20.

Adactis. *Forced on board.*—*Remigante*=gubernante, to avoid sameness, with *gubernatoribus,* Br. R. supposes that having but one pilot left, only the vessel on which he sailed was *rowed,* while the others were towed by it; and this rowing *under his direction* is ascribed to *him.* Some MSS. and many editions read *remigrante,* which some translate: *making his escape,* and others connect with *interfectis,* and suppose that he also was slain in trying to *bring back* his boat to shore. Whether we read *remigante* or *remigrante,* the signification of either is unusual.

Praevehebantur. Sailed along the coast (in sight of land).

Inopiae is governed by *eo,* which is the old dat.=*to such a degree.*—*Ad extremum*=*at last.*

Vescerentur followed by the acc. H. 419, 4. 1); Z. 466. For the imp. subj. cf. note 21: *ut–concupiscerent.*

Amissis–navibus. This is regarded by some as proof that *all* the steersmen were slain or escaped. Dr. answers, that it may refer only to the *two* ships that were without steersmen.

Suevis. A people of Northern Germany (G. 38, seq.) whither, after having circumnavigated Britain, the Usipii came.—*Mox, subsequently,* some having escaped the Suevi.

Per commercia. *In trade,* cf. same in 39.

Nostram ripam. The Gallic bank of the Rhine, which was the border of the Roman Empire, cf. G. passim.

Quos–indicium–illustravit. Whom the account of so wonderful an adventure rendered illustrious. The rule would require the subj. H. 501, I. 2; Z. 561

XXIX. *Initio aestatis*, i. e. in the beginning of the *next* summer (the 7th campaign, cf. 25: *aestate, qua sextum*, etc.), as the whole history shows. See especially *proximo anno*, 34. Hence the propriety of commencing a new section here. The common editions begin it below: *Igitur*, etc.

Plerique. Cf. note on it, 1.—*Fortium virorum. Military men.*

Ambitiose, with affected fortitude, stoically.—*Rursus*=contra, *on the contrary*, showing the antith. be ween *ambitiose* and *per lamenta.* —*Per lamenta*, cf. 6: per caritatem.—*Igitur*, cf. 13, note.

Quae–faceret=ut ea faceret. H. 500; Z. 567.

Incertum is explained by *pluribus locis.* Render: *general alarm.* —*Expedito*=sine impedimentis, armis solis instructo. Fac. and For. —*Montem Grampium.* Now *Grampian hills.*

Cruda–senectus. Cf. Virg. Aen. 6, 304: sed cruda deo viridisque senectus. *Crudus* is rarely found in this sense except in the poets. *Crudus* properly=bloody (*cruor, cruidus*); hence the successive significations, raw, unripe, fresh, vigorous.—*Sua decora*=praemia ob virtutem bellicam accepta. E. Any and all *badges of distinction*, especially in *arms.* Wr., Or. and Död.

XXX. *Causas belli.* Explained by *universi servitutis expertes* below, to be the defence of their liberties. In like manner, *nostram necessitatem* is explained by *nullae ultra terrae:* there is no retreat for us, etc.—*Animus. Confidence.*

Proelium–arma. T. has a passion for *pairs* of words, especially nouns, of *kindred signification.* See examples in Index to Histories; and in this chapter, *spem ac subsidium; recessus ac sinus; obsequium ac modestiam.*

Priores pugnae, sc. in which the Caledonians took no part.—*Pugnae* is here, by a figure put for the *combatants* themselves, who are represented as looking to the Caledonians, as a kind of corps de reserve, or last resource.

Eo. For that reason. The best things are always kept guarded and concealed in the *penetralia.* There may also be a reference to a *fact* stated by Caesar (B. G. 5, 12), that the inhabitants of the interior were aborigines, while those on the coast were immigrants.

Terrarum–extremos. The remotest of men and last of freemen. —*Recessus–famae. Our very remoteness and obscurity.* This is the most common and perhaps the most simple translation, making *sinus famae*=seclusion in respect to fame. Perhaps, however, it accords as well with the usual signification of the words, and better with the connexion and spirit of the speech, to take *sinus famae* in the sense, *retreat of glory*, or *glorious retreat*. So Wr. His interpretation of the passage and its connexion is as follows: *our very remoteness and our glorious retreat have guarded us till this day. But now the furthest extremity of Brit. is laid open* (i. e. our retreat is no longer a safeguard); *and every thing unknown is esteemed great* (i. e. this safeguard also is removed—the Romans in our midst no longer magnify our strength). Rit. encloses the clause in brackets, as a gloss. He renders *sinus famae*, *bosom of fame*, fame being personified as a goddess. R., Dr., Or. make *famae* dative after *defendit* =has *kept back from fame*.

Sed nulla jam, etc. But now all the above grounds of confidence—our remoteness, our glory, our greatness magnified by the imagination of our enemies, from the very fact that we were unknown to them—all these are removed; we have none behind us to fall back upon, as our countrymen in former battles have leaned upon us—and we are reduced to the necessity of self-defence and self-reliance. The *sed* seems to be antithetic to the whole as far back as *priores pugnae;* whereas *nunc* is opposed only to the clause which immediately precedes it, and constitutes an antithesis within an antithesis.

Infestiores, sc. quam fluctus et saxa.

Effugeris. Cf. note G. 19: *non invenerit;* also *satiaverit* just below.

Et mare. Et=also. Cf. note, G. 11.

Opes atque inopiam. Abs. for conc.=rich and poor nations.

Falsis nominibus is by some connected with *rapere.* But better with *appellant. They call things by false names*, viz. *plunder, empire; and desolation, peace.*

XXXI. *Annos*=annonam, *yearly produce*, cf. G. 14: expectare annum. So often in the Poets.—*In frumentum. For supplies.* The reading of this clause is much disputed. The text follows that of W. and R. and is approved by Freund. For the meaning of *egerunt*, cf. *praedam egesserunt*, H. 3, 33.

Silvis–emuniendis=viis per silvas et paludes muniendis. E.

Semel. Once for all, G. 19.— *Emit*, sc. tributis pendendis; *pascit*, sc. frumento praebendo. E.

Portus, quibus exercendis. W. and Dr. explain this of collecting revenue at the ports (i. e. farming them), a thing unknown to the early Britons; Wr. of rowing, servile labor. Why not refer it to the *construction* or *improvement* of harbors? By rendering *exercen-*

dis, working, improving, we make it applicable alike to harbors mines and fields.—*Reservemur.* Subj. in a relative clause denoting a purpose. H. 500; Z. 567.

Potuere. Observe the ind., where we use the potential. It is especially frequent with *possum, debeo,* &c. Z. 518 and 519.

Nonne implies an affirmative answer. Z. 352, and H. 346, II. 1. 2).

In poenitentiam, al. in praesentiam. The general idea is essentially the same with either reading. *Non in praesentiam=not to obtain our freedom for the present merely. Non in poenitentiam=not about to obtain our freedom merely to regret it,* i. e. in such a manner as the Brigantes, who forthwith lost it by their *socordia.*

XXXII. *Nisi si*=nisi forte, cf. note, G. 2: nisi si patria.

Pudet dictu. The supine after *pudet* is found only here. Quintilian however has *pudendum dictu.* Cf. Or. in loc.; and Z. 441. 443.

Commendent, etc. *Although they give up their blood to* (i. e. *shed it in support of*) *a foreign tyrant.*—*Tamen* is antithetic to *licet: although* they give, *yet longer enemies, than slaves* (of Rome).

Metus-est. It is fear and terror (sc. that keep them in subjection), *weak bonds of affection.*

Removeris-desierint. Fut. perf. Cf. note, G. 23: *indulseris.*

Nulla-aut alia. Some of the Roman soldiers had lost all attachment to country and could not be said to have any country; others had one, but it was not Britain, it was far away.

Ne terreat. The third person of the imperative is for the most part avoided in ordinary language; and the pres. subj. is used in its stead. Z. 529, Note.

Nostras manus, i. e. those ready to join us and aid our arms, viz. (as he goes on to say), the Gauls and Germans, as well as the Britons now in the Roman ranks.—*Tamquam=just as* (*tam-quam*). Död. renders, *just as certainly as.*

Vacua.—*Destitute of soldiers.*—*Senum,* sc. veterani et emeriti. Cf. note, 15. *Aegra=disaffected.* Cf. H. 2, 86.

Hic dux, etc. *Here a general, here an army* (sc. the Roman, awaits you); *there tributes, mines,* &c. (and you must conquer the former or endure the latter—these are your only alternatives).

In hoc campo est. Depends on this battle field.—T. has laid out all his strength on this speech. It can hardly be matched for martial force and sententious brevity. It breathes, as it should in the mouth of a Briton, an indomitable spirit of liberty, and reminds us, in many features, of the concentrated and fiery eloquence, which has so often roused our American Indians to defend their altars and revenge their wrongs.

XXXIII. *Ut barbaris moris.* Al. et barbari moris. But compare 39: ut Domitiano moris erat; His. 1, 15: ut moris est. Supply *est* here: *as is the custom of* (lit. *to*) *barbarians.* Z. 448, & H. 402, I.

Agmina, sc. conspiciebantur.—*Procursu* is the means by which the gleam of armor was brought into view.

Acies, sc. Britannorum. The *Roman* army was still within the camp, cf. *munimentis coercitum*, below

Coercitum = qui coerceri potest. The part. used in the sense of a verbal. So *monstratus*, G. 31, which, Freund says, is Tacitean. The perf. part. pass. with negative prefix *in* often takes this sense. Z. 328. Cf. note, His. 5, 7: *inexhaustum.*

Octavus annus. This was Agricola's *seventh summer* in Britain. See note 29: *initio aestatis.* But it being now later in the season, than when he entered Britain, he was now entering on his *eighth year.* Cf. Rit. in loc.

Virtute–Romani. By the valor and favoring auspices of the Roman Empire. War was formerly carried on auspiciis *Populi* Rom. But after Augustus, auspiciis *Imperatoris* or *Imperii* Rom.

Expeditionibus–proeliis. These words denote the *time* of *poenituit* (*in* or *during* so many, etc.)—*Patientia* and *labore* are abl. after *opus.*

Terminos. Acc. after *egressi* (H. 371, 4): *having transcended the limits.* Cf. Z. 387.

Fama, rumore. Synonyms. Also *castris, armis.* Cf. note, 30.

Vota–aperto. Your vows and your valor now have free scope (are in the open field), cf. note 1: *in aperto.*

In frontem. Antith. to *fugientibus.* Hence = progredientibus.

Hodie. To-day, i. e. *in our present circumstances of prosperity.* Wr.

Nec–fuerit. Nor will it have been inglorious, sc. when the thing shall have been *done* and men shall look *back* upon our achievements. The fut. perf. is appropriate to such a conception.

Naturae fine. Cf. note, G. 45: *illuc usque natura.*

XXXIV. *Hortarer.* Literally, *I would be exhorting you.* The use of the imperf. subj. in hypothetical sentences, where we should use a plup. (I would have exhorted you), is frequent both in Greek and Latin, even when it denotes a *complete* past action, cf. Z. 525.

When the action is not complete, as here, the Latin form is at once more lively and more exact than the English. —*Proximo anno* This same expression may signify either the next year, or the last year. Here of course: *the last year*, referring to the battle described in 26, cf. also note 29: *Initio aestatis.*

Furto noctis. Cf. Virg. Aen. 9, 397: fraude noctis.

Contra ruere. *Rush forth to meet*, *penetrantibus*, etc. R. and Wr. take *ruere* for perf. 3d pl. instead of *ruerunt*, since T. uses the form in *ere* much more than that in *erunt.* Rit. makes it inf. after *solet* understood, or rather implied in *pelluntur*, which=*pelli solent.*

Quos–quod. *Whom, as to the fact that you have at length found* (*it is not because*) *they have taken a stand, but they have been overtaken.* Cf. Wr. and Or. in loc. On *deprehensi*, cf. note, 7. On *quod*=*as to this, that*, see examples in Freund, or in any Lexicon.

Novissimae–vestigiis. *The extremity of their circumstances, and their bodies* (motionless) *with terror have brought them to a stand for battle on this spot*, etc. One MS. reads *novissime* and omits *aciem*, which reading is followed in the common editions.

Extremo metu is to be closely connected with *corpora.* For the sense of *defixere*, cf. Ann. 13, 5: pavore defixis.

Ederetis. Subj. cf. H. 500, 2; Z. 556, a.

Transigite cum expeditionibus=finite expeditiones. Dr. Cf. G. 19: cum spe–transigitur, note.

Quinquaginta annis. So many years, it might be said to be in *round numbers*, though actually somewhat *less* than fifty years, since the dominion of Rome was first established in Britain under the Emperor Claudius. Cf. 13, supra.—The speech of A. is not equal to that of Galgacus. He had not so good a cause. He could not appeal to the sacred principles of justice and liberty, to the love of home and household gods. But he makes the best of a bad cause. The speech is worthy of a Roman commander, and touches with masterly skill all those chords in a Roman soldier's breast, that were never touched in vain.

XXXV. *Et*=*both.* Both while he was speaking and after he had ceased, the soldiers manifested their ardor, etc.

Instinctos. Cf. note 16: instincti.

Aciem firmarent=aciem firmam facerent, of which use there are examples not only in T., but in Liv. Dr. The auxiliary foot *formed* or *made up* (not merely strengthened) *the centre.*—*Affunderentur*

Were attached to.—*Pro vallo. On the rampart;* properly on the fore part of it. Cf. note, H. 1, 29.

Ingens–decus. In app. with *legiones–stetere.*

Bellanti, sc. Agricolae. Al. bellandi.

In speciem. Cf. in suam famam, 8, and in jactationem, 5.

Aequo. Supply consisteret to correspond with *insurgeret.* Zeugma. Cf. note, 18: in aequum.

Media campi. The intervening parts of the plain, sc. between the two armies.—*Covinarius* is found only in T. *Covinarii*=the essedarii of Caesar. Covinus erat currus Belgarum, a quibus eum Britanni acceperant. Dr.

Pedes. Nom. sing. in app. with subject of *constitit.*

XXXVI. *Ingentibus gladiis,* etc. So below: *parva scuta,* etc. The small shield and broad sword of the Highlanders.

Donec–cohortatus est. Cf. note, G. 37: *affectavere.*—*Batavorum cohortes.* Al. *tres–cohortes.* But the number is not specified in the best MSS. In the Histories, eight cohorts of Batavians are often mentioned as constituting the auxiliaries of the 14th legion, which was now in Britain. See Rit. in loc.

Ad mucrones. The Britons were accustomed to fight with the edge of the sword, and cut and hew the enemy. The Romans, on the contrary, made use of the *point.* Of course in a close engagement, they would have greatly the advantage. Br.—*Ad manus.* The opposite of *eminus,* i. e. *a close engagement.* The same thing is expressed below by *complexum armorum.*

In aperto pugnam. Literally a fight in the open field, i. e. a *regular* pitched *battle,* which with its compact masses would be less favorable to the large swords of the Britons, than a battle on ground uncleared of thickets and forests. Al. *in arto.*

Miscere, ferire, etc. A series of inf. denoting a rapid succession of events, cf. note, 5: noscere–nosci; G. 30: praeponere.

Equitum turmae, sc. Britannorum. The word *turmae* is applicable to such a cavalry as theirs, cf. Ann. 14, 34: *Britannorum* copiae passim per catervas et *turmas* exsultabant. Br. Ky. and others here understand it of the Roman cavalry. But R. Dr. and Wr. apply it to the Britons, and with reason, as we shall see below, and as we might infer indeed from its close connexion with *covinarii,* for the *covinarii* were certainly Britons.

Peditum proelio, hostium agminibus. These also both refer to the *Britons.* The covinarii were interspersed among their own infantry, and, as the Romans advanced, became entangled with them. This is disputed. But the small number of Romans slain in the whole battle is alone enough to show, that *their* cavalry was not routed, nor *their* infantry broken in upon by the chariots of the enemy. Moreover, how could T. properly use the word *hostium* of his own countrymen?

Minimeque, etc. This is one passage, among a few in T., which is so manifestly corrupt that no sense can be made of it, as it stands in the MSS. The reading given in the text is the simplest of all the conjectural readings that have been proposed. It is that of Br. and E., and is followed by the common editions. Cavalry took a large part in the battle. But the battle wore little the aspect of an equestrian fight; for the Britons, after maintaining their position with difficulty for some time, were at length swept away by the bodies (the *mere uncontrolled bodies*) of the horses—in short, the riders had no control over horses or chariots, which rushed on without drivers obliquely athwart, or directly through the lines, as their fears severally impelled them; all which was in marked contrast to a Roman's idea of a regular battle of cavalry.

XXXVII. *Vacui. Free from apprehension.*

Ni. Cf. note 4: ni.—*Subita belli. Unexpected emergencies* arising in the course of the battle. Cf. 6: *inania honoris.*

Grande et atrox spectaculum, etc. See a similar description in Sal. Jug. 101. The series of infinitives and the omission of the connectives (*asyndeton*) make the succession of events very rapid and animated. Compare the famous *veni, vidi, vici*, of Caesar.

Prout–erat. According to their different natural disposition, i. e. *the timid, though armed, turned their backs before inferior numbers; while the brave, though unarmed, met death in the face.*

Praestare terga is an expression found only in T.

Et aliquando, etc. *Et=ac tamen. And* yet (notwithstanding the flight of crowds and the passive death of some as above) *sometimes to the conquered also* there was *anger and bravery.* The language is Virgilian, cf. Aen. 2, 367.

Quod. Cf. note 12.—*Ni frequens–fiduciam foret.* "Had not A., who was everywhere present, caused some strong and lightly equipped cohorts to encompass the ground, while part of the cavalry having dismounted, made their way through the thickets, and part on horseback scoured the open woods, some disaster would have proceeded from this excess of confidence." Ky.

XXXVIII. *Gaudio praedaque laeta.* Cf. note, G. 7: *cibos et hortamina.* Observe also the juxtaposition of *tempestate* and *fama* in this same chapter.

Separare, sc. consilia, i. e. *they sometimes act in concert, sometimes provide only for their individual safety.*

Pignorum. Cf. note G. 7: pignora — *Saevisse. Laid violent hands.* "This picture of rage and despair, of tenderness, fury, and the tumult of contending passions, has all the fine touches of a master who has studied human nature." Mur.—*Secreti*= deserti.

Ubi. When, cf. 26. Its direct influence extends to *nequibat,* and with its clause, it expresses the *reason* why A. drew off his forces into the country of the Horesti.—*Spargi bellum* = diversis locis, vel diviso exercitu, vel vagando bellum geri. E.

Secunda-fama. favored by the weather and the glory of their past achievements (lit. the weather and fame *following* them, *secunda* =*sequunda.*)

Trutulensem portum. Some port, now unknown, probably near the mouth of the Tay or the Forth. *Unde* qualifies *lecto.* E. With *redierat* a corresponding adv. denoting *whither,* is to be supplied: whence it had set sail, and whither, after having surveyed all the nearest coast of Britain, it had now returned. *Had* returned, i. e. prior to *entering* the port; the action of *redierat,* was prior to that of *tenuit.* Hence plup. *Proximo, nearest,* sc. to the scene of Agricola's operations, i. e. the whole northern coast from the Forth to the Clyde and back again. This was all that was necessary to prove Britain to be an island (cf. chap. 10), the southern coast having been previously explored.

XXXIX. *Actum.* Al. auctum, a conjecture of Lipsius. *Actum* =*treated of, reported.*—*Moris erat.* H. 402, I.; Z. 448, N. 1. N. 1.

Falsum-triumphum. He had returned without so much as seeing the enemy (Dio Cass. 67, 4); and yet he bought slaves, dressed them in German style, had their hair stained red (G. 4: *rutilae comae*) and left long, so as to resemble Germans, and then marched in triumph into Rome with his train of pretended captives! Caligula had done the same before him. Suet. Calig. 47.

Formarentur. Subj. in a relative clause denoting a purpose (*quorum*=*ut eorum*). H. 500; Z. 567.

Studia-acta. Lawyers and politicians, all public men, had been gagged and silenced by Domitian.

Alius. Another than the Emperor.—*Occuparet*=*pre-occupy*, so as to rob him of it.

Utcumque. Somehow, possibly, perhaps. *Other things perhaps were more easily concealed; but the merit of a good commander was an imperial prerogative.*

Quodque–satiatus. And what was a proof of some cruel purpose, wholly absorbed in his retirement (where he never plotted any thing but mischief, and where in early life he is said to have amused himself with killing flies, Suet. Dom. 3). Cf. Plin. Panegyr. 48: nec unquam ex solitudine sua prodeuntem, nisi ut solitudinem faceret. The whole passage in Pliny is a graphic picture of the same tyrant, the workings of whose heart are here so laid bare by the pen of Pliny's friend Tacitus. *Secreto–satiatus* may also be translated: *satisfied with his own secret,* i. e. keeping to himself his cherished hatred and jealousy.—*Languesceret.* Subj. after *donec.* Cf. note, G. 37: *affectavere.*

Reponere odium. See lexicon under *repono* for this phrase.

Impetus–exercitus. Until the freshness of his glory, and his popularity with the army should gradually decline.

Etiam tum obtinebat, i. e. he was still in *possession of the government,* and of course in command of the army, in Britain.

XL. *Triumphalia ornamenta.* Not a real triumph, which from the reign of Augustus was conceded only to the Emperor or the princes of the Imperial Family; but triumphal insignia, such as the *corona, laurea, toga praetexta, tunica palmata, sella curulis,* &c. Dr.

Illustris statuae. Called *laureata,* Ann. 4, 23; *triumphalis,* His. 1, 79.

Quidquid datur. Besides the *ornamenta* above mentioned, sacrifices and thanksgivings were offered in the name of the victorious commander. Dr.

Addique. Al. additque. *Addique* is the reading of the MSS. and old editions. And it suits better the genius of Dom.; he did not express the *opinionem* himself, for it was not his real intention, but he *ordered* some one to put it in circulation as if from him, that he might have the credit of it and yet not be bound by it.—*Destinari,* sc. by Domitian.

Majoribus reservatam. Majoribus = illustrioribus. Syria was the richest province in the Empire, and the praefectship of it the most honorable office.

Ex secretioribus ministeriis. *One of his private secretaries*, or *confidential agents.*

Codicillos. Under the Emperors this word is used to denote an imperial letter or diploma. Properly a billet, diminutive of *codex*, tablet (=*caudex*, trunk of a tree).

Syria dabatur. Syria was one of the Provinces, that were at the disposal of the Emperor.

Ex ingenio principis. *In accordance with* (cf. *ex*, G. 7) *the* (dissimulating) *genius or policy of Domitian.* The design, if not real, at least imputed to him, was to withdraw Agricola from his province and his troops at all events, by the offer of the best province in the Empire if need be; but that object having been secured by Agricola's voluntary retirement, the offer, and even the ordinary civilities of life, especially official life, were deemed unnecessary. Compare this with the concluding sentence of the preceding chapter.

Celebritate et frequentia. Hendiadys: *By the number of distinguished men who might go out to meet him* (and escort him into the city).

Officio=salutatione. Dr.—*Brevi osculo*, lit. *a hasty kiss*=*cold and formal salutation.* The kiss was a common mode of salutation among the Romans, in the age of the Emperors. See Becker's Gallus, p. 54.

Turbae servientium. The usual and characteristic associates, as well as attendants of Domitian. A severe cut, though quite incidental and very concise.

Otiosos. Antith. to *militare.* *Men in civil life*, cf. note on *otio*, 11.

Otium auxit. Augere otium=sequi altissimum otium. Dr.

Penitus=inwardly, i. e. sincerely, *zealously.* So R. But Dr.= prorsus, omnino, valde.—*Cultu modicus.* *Simple in dress*, cf. note on *cultus*, G. 6.—*Comitatus*, passive, so used by Cic also.—*Uno aut altero.* *One or two.*

Per ambitionem=ex vitae splendore et numeroso comitatu. Br. cf. note on *ambitio*, G. 27.

Quaererent–interpretarentur. *Many inquired* (with wonder) *into the reputation* (of a man so unassuming), *and few explained* or *understood* (the true reason of his humble manner of life). *Interpretarentur*, not *famam* but the facts above mentioned, and the necessity A. was under of living as he did.—*Viso aspectoque.* *On seeing him and directing their attention particularly to him.*

XLI. *Crimen*=*public accusation.*—*Querela*=*private complaint.*—*Princeps, gloria, genus.* Supply, as a predicate, *causa periculi;* these were the causes that put A's life in jeopardy.

Militares viri=duces. So Corbulo is called, Ann. 15, 26.

Expugnati et capti. Defeated and taken captive, For. and Fac. Properly *expugnare* is said of a fortress or city. But ἐκ πολιορκεῖν in Greek is used in the same way, of persons. Compare *expugnatis praesidiis,* 16, note. The wars particularly referred to are those against Decebalus, leader of the Dacians, which lasted four years and in which Moesia also was invaded by the Dacians, and several Roman armies with their commanders were lost (Suet. Dom. 6.); and that of the Pannonian legions against the German tribes of the Marcomanni and the Quadi (Dion, 67, 7).

Hibernis–dubitatum, i. e. the enemy not only met them on the river banks, which formed the borders of the empire, but attacked the winter quarters of their troops, and threatened to take away the territory they had already acquired.

Funeribus, sc. militarium virorum. — *Cladibus,* sc. cohortium. Dr.

Amore et fide. Out of affection and fidelity (sc. to their imperial master).—*Malignitate et livore. Out of envy and hatred* (sc. towards A.).

Pronum deterioribus. Inclined to the worse measures, or it may be, to the *worse advisers.*

In ipsam–agebatur=invito gloria aucta, simulque pernicies accelerata. W.

XLII. *Asiae et Africae.* He drew lots, *which* he should have, *both* being put into the lot.—*Proconsulatum.* See H. 1, 49. note, on proconsul. A. had already been consul, 9.

Sortiretur. In which he would, or such that he must, obtain by lot, etc. Cf. H. 501, I.; Z. 558.

Occiso Civica. Cf. Suet. Dom. 10: complures senatores, et in his aliquot consulares, interemit, ex quibus *Civicam Cerealem in ipso Asiae proconsulatu.*

Nec Agricolae–exemplum. A warning was not wanting to A. (to avoid the dangerous post); *nor a precedent to Dom.* (for disposing of A. in the same way if he accepted the office).

Iturusne esset. Subj. cf. H. 525; Z. 552.—*Interrogarent.* H. 500; Z. 567.

In–excusatione. In urging his request (before Dom.) *to be excused.*

Paratus simulatione. Al. simulationi. *Furnished with deceit, armed,* as it were, *with hypocrisy.*

In arrogantiam compositus. Assuming a proud demeanor.

Beneficii invidia, lit. *the odium of such a kindness=so odious a favor.* The idea is, he did not blush to let A. return thanks for a signal injury, as if it were a real kindness. "A refinement of cruelty not unfrequently practised by the worst Roman Emperors." Ky. The only peculiarity in the case of Dom. was, the unblushing impudence with which he perpetrated the wrong, cf. 45. See a fine commentary on this passage in Sen. de Benef. 4, 17: Quis est, qui non beneficus *videri* velit? qui non inter scelera et injurias opinionem bonitatis affectet? velit quoque *iis videri beneficium dedisse, quos laesit? gratias itaque agi sibi ab his, quos afflixere, patiuntur.*

Salarium. Properly salt-money, i. e. a small allowance to the soldiers for the purchase of salt. Cf. *clavarium,* H. 3, 50, note. But after Augustus, official pay, *salary.*

Ne–emisse. That he might not appear to have purchased a compliance with his virtual prohibition (viz. of A.'s accepting the proconsulship).

Proprium humani, etc. Mark the sentiment.

Irrevocabilior. More implacable. Found in this sense only in T. Cf. Böt. Lex. Tac.

Illicita. Unlawful, i. e. forbidden by the powers that be. Explained by *contumacia* and *inani jactatione libertatis* above. T. is animadverting upon the conduct of certain stoics and republicans, who obtruded their opinions upon those in power, and coveted the glory of martyrdom.

Eo–excedere. Reach the same height of distinction. *Eo.* Old dat. cf. *eo inopiae* 28, note. *Excedere,* lit. come out to, *arrive at.* Cf. Val. Max. 5, 6, 4: *ad summum imperii fastigium excessit.*

Per abrupta. "Through abrupt and dangerous paths." Ky.

Ambitiosa morte, i. e. morte ultro adita captandae gloriae causa apud posteros. For. and Fac.

XLIII. *Luctuosus, afflictive,* is stronger than *tristis, sad.*

Vulgus. The lower classes, *the ignorant and indolent rabble.—Populus. The common people, tradesmen, mechanics,* and the like. Hence, *aliud agens,* which implies that they were too busy with something else of a private nature, to give much attention to public affairs or the concerns of their neighbors.—*Populus* and *vulgus* are brought together in a similar way, Dial. de Clar. Orat. 7: Vulgus quoque imperitum et tunicatus hic populus, etc.

Nobis-ausim. I should not dare to affirm that we (the friends of A.) *found any conclusive proof,* that he was poisoned.—*Ceterum. But.* This implies that the circumstantial evidence, which he goes on to specify, convinced the writer and his friends, as well as the public, that poison administered by direction of Dom., was really the means of hastening A. out of the world. Dion Cassius expressly affirms, that he was poisoned, 66, 20.

Principatus. The imperial government in general, i. e. former Emperors.

Momenta ipsa deficientis. Each successive stage of his decline. Ipsa is omitted in the common editions. But it rests on good authority and it adds to the significance of the clause: *the very moments,* as it were, were reported to Dom.

Per dispositos cursores. Dom. appears not to have been at Rome at this time, but in the Alban Villa (cf. 45), or somewhere else.

Constabat. That was an *admitted point,* about which there was entire *agreement* (*con* and *sto*).

Animo vultuque. Hendiadys: *he wore in his countenance an expression of heartfelt grief.*

Securus odii. Now, that A. was dead, Dom. had nothing to fear in regard to the *object of his hatred,* or the *gratification of his hate. Odii.* Gen. of the respect.—*Qui-dissimularet. Qui=talis, ut,* hence the subj. H. 501, I.; Z. 558.

Lecto testamento. When A.'s will was read.

Honore judicioque. As if a mark of honor and esteem. E. says= judicio honorifico.—*Piissimae,* devoted, affectionate.

Malum principem. It was customary for rich men at Rome, who were anxious to secure any of their property to their heirs, to bequeath a part of their estates to *bad emperors* in order to secure the remainder from their rapacity.

This and several preceding sections present a most graphic *outline* of the *life and times* of Dom., the more to be prized, because the full *picture,* which T. doubtless drew of him in the Histories, is lost. The Histories and the Annals are a vast portrait gallery full of such pictures drawn to the life.

XLIV. *Natus-excessit.* The dates assigned for A.'s birth and death, do not agree with the age ascribed to him. They may be harmonized in either of two ways, each of which has its advocates: by reading *primum* instead of *tertium*, or, which is perhaps a more probable amendment, since it only alters the relative position of the two characters, by reading LIV instead of LVI.

Quod si. And if, *now if.*—*Habitum.* *Personal appearance*, cf. G. 5.

Decentior quam sublimior. *Well proportioned, rather than tall.* R.

Nihil metus. *Nothing to inspire fear in his countenance.* Antith. to *gratia–supererat: kindness of expression rather prevailed.* So Gr. and R. For this sense of *metus*, see note G. 2: ob metum. Död. distinguishes between *vultus* and *oris*, making the former refer more to the *eyes* (as if from *volvo*, the rolling of the eye), to which it belongs to express anger and fierceness; the latter to the mouth, which is more expressive of kindness.

Medio–aetatis. We should hardly say so of a man dying at 56. But in Dial. de Clar. Orat., T. speaks of 120 years, as *unius hominis aetas.*

Et vera bona. T. has here in mind the distinction made by philosophers, particularly the Stoics, between the virtues, which they called the only *real good*, and the gifts of fortune, which they declared to be indifferent.—*Et–et*, *both–and*, marks the distinction more strongly.

Impleverat. *Had enjoyed to the full.*

Consulari. *Having attained to the rank of consul* (the summit of a Roman's ambition) *and having been honored with triumphal insignia.* Al. consularibus. But *consulari* has the better authority and makes the better sense.

Opibus–contigerant. *Great riches he did not desire; a respectable property it was his good fortune to possess*, cf. 5: medio rationis atque abundantiae. Al. non contigerant. But considerable property is implied in the circumstances attending his will, 43, also in his not asking the usual salary, 42. Dion Cass says, however, (66, 20.), that A. spent his last days in want, as well as in disgrace. For another explanation of *gaudebat*, cf. n. G. 5.

Quod–ominabatur. *Quod* is omitted in the common editions. But it is found in the MSS. And it may be explained on the principle of Zeugma, by supplying with *durare* and *videre* a verb implied in *grande solatium tulit* thus: *though* (*sicuti*) *it would have been a great gratification to A. to behold the dawn of this auspicious age and see Trajan Emperor, of which he expressed in my hearing a sort of prophetic anticipation and desire, yet* (*ita*), etc. Dion Cassius affirms (69, 12), that by auguries the elevation of Trajan to the throne was foretold, as early as A. U. C. 844, i. e. *two years before the death of A.* The reference to Trajan here, as in 3, marks clearly the date of the composition, cf. note, 3: augeatque Trajanus.

Spiramenta. Breathing-spells, i. e. intervals to recover and take breath in. The word is found only in poetry and post-Augustan prose, and, in the expressive sense in which it is here used, only in Ammian. Marc. 29, 1. See Or. and Freund.

Velut uno ictu. The commentators illustrate the force of this expression by reference to Caligula's wish (Vid. Sen. de Ira. 3, 19), that the Roman people had but one neck, ut scelera sua in *unum ictum* et unum diem cogeret.

XLV. *Non vidit.* Did not see, as he would have done, had he lived a few years longer. This passage resembles Cic. de Orat. 3, 2, 8, too closely to be mere coincidence. Imitator tamen, id quod uni Tacito contigit, auctore suo praestantior. Rit.

Consularium. Rhen. collects from Suet. the names of several victims of Dom.'s displeasure, *who had been consuls.*

Feminarum. Pliny has preserved the names of several of this list—Gratilla, wife of Rusticus, Arria, wife of Thrasea, Fannia, daughter of Thrasea and betrothed to Helvidius. Their husbands will be remembered as having been mentioned in 1 and 2.

Carus Metius. An infamous informer, cf. Plin. Epist. 7, 19; Juv. 1, 35; Mart. 12, 25, 5.

Censebatur. Was honored, ironice. *Censeri* est aestimari, sive existimationem consequi. Dr.

Una-victoria. He had occasioned the death of but one innocent victim.—*Adhuc.* Up to the death of A., cf. G. 38: adhuc, note.

Albanam arcem. A favorite retreat of Dom. (situated at the foot of the Alban Mount, about seventeen miles from Rome), where he sometimes convened the Senate, and held his court with its troop of informers, cf. note, 43: cursores. Rit. in loc. suggests, that by the use of *arcem* instead of *palatium*, T. means to represent Domitian as shutting himself up, like many tyrants, in a fortified castle, and thence sending forth the emissaries of his jealousy and cruelty.

Sententia. His voice, his sentiment expressed in council before Dom. — *Intra Albanam arcem,* i. e. *privately, not publicly,* as afterwards at Rome.

Messalini. Fuit inter principes adulatores et delatores. Dr. cf. Plin. Epist. 4, 22; Juv. 4, 113, seq.

Massa Bebius. Primus inter pares of Domitian's tools. He began his career under Vesp. cf. His. 4, 50. He was afterwards impeached and condemned at the instance of the Province of Baetica, Pliny and Senecio advocates for the impeachment, Plin. Epist. 7, 33; 3, 4; 6, 29.—*Jam tum. At that very time* on trial, not merely *already at that time.* Cf. Hand's Tursel. 3, 113.

Nostra, sc. of the Senate, of which T. was a member, though abroad at the time. Helvidius was arrested *in the senate house*, cf. Plin. Ep. 9, 13. This was Helvidius the *son*, who was put to death by Dom. (Suet. 10), as his father was by Vesp. (Suet. 15).

Visus. Al. divisus. *Visus*=species, adspectus, Wr.—*Perfudit.* Zeugma. Understand in the first clause *horrore perfudit* (Dr.) or probro affecit (R.): *the spectacle of Mauricus and Rusticus* (hurried away, the one to exile, the other to death), *filled us with horror; we were stained by the innocent blood of Senecio.* Of Rusticus and Senecio, see 2, note. Of Mauricus, see Plin. Ep. 4, 22: quo viro nihil firmius, nihil verius. Also Plin. Ep. 3, 11.

Videre, sc. Domitianum.—*Aspici*, sc. a Domitiano. For difference in the signification in these words, cf. 40: viso aspectoque, note.

Suspiria-subscriberentur. When our sighs (of sympathy with the condemned) *were registered against us* (by spies and informers, as a ground of accusation before the Emperor).

Rubor. Redness, referring to the complexion of Dom., which was such as to conceal a blush, cf. Suet. Dom. 18: vultu ruboris pleno.

Opportunitate mortis. An expression of Cic., in the similar passage above cited (de Orat. 3, 2, 8), touching the death of Crassus.

Pro virili portione, lit. for one man's share, referring primarily to pecuniary assessments. Here: *for thy part—so far as thou wast concerned.* A. died with a calmness which would scarcely admit of the supposition, that he felt himself to be a victim of poison and imperial jealousy.

Filiaque ejus. The apostrophe is here dropped to be resumed at *optime parentum.* So the MSS. For they read *ejus* here, and *amissus est* below. Rhenanus omitted *ejus*, and wrote *es* for *est;* and he has been followed in the common editions since.

Conditione. By the circumstance, or by virtue of our long absence. T. and his wife had parted with A. four years before his death, and had been absent from Rome ever since, where or why does not appear.

Superfuere. Cf. *superest,* G. 6, note.

XLVI. *Sapientibus.* Cf. *sapientiae professoribus,* 2, note.—*Te immortalibus laudibus.* I feel constrained to recur to the reading of Lipsius and Ritter, it is so much more spirited than *quam temporalibus. Potius* manifestly should refer back to *lugeri* and *plangi.* The comparison contained in the more common reading is uncalled for in the connection, and of little significance in itself. The MSS. read *temporalibus laudibus* without *quam* and this may be more easily resolved into *te immortalibus,* than *quam* can be supplied. — *Similitudine.* Al. aemulatione. For such a use of similitudo, cf. Cic. Tusc. Quaest. 1, 46, 110: quorum (sc. Curii, Fabricii, Scipionum, etc.), *similitudinem* aliquam qui arripuerit, etc.

Decoremus. Ennius (cited by Cic. Tusc. Q. 1, 49, 117, and de Senect. 20, 73), uses the same word in expressing the same sentiment: nemo me lacrumis *decoret* nec funera fletu faxit. Cf. also G. 26.

Formam. This makes the sense so much better (than *famam*), that E. Dr. Wr. R. and most others have adopted it against the authority of the MSS. cf. *forma mentis,* below, and Cic. passim.

Intercedendum. To be prohibited. Properly said of a *veto interposed* by the Tribunes; then of any prohibition.—*Non quia*=*not that,* is characteristic of late writers. It is followed by the subj. Z. 537, and note H. 1, 15.

Manet, mansurumque est. Cf. Vell. Paterc. 2, 66, 5: vivit, vivetque per omnem saeculorum memoriam. The periphrastic form (*mansurum est*) differs however from the future (*manebit*), as our *is to remain* from *will remain.* See Z. 498.

Oblivio obruet, sc. for want of a historian, carent quia *vate sacro,* cf. Hor. Od. 4, 9, 25, seq. By *multos veterum,* T. means many ancients of *real worth.* So *velut* implies. A. is to be immortalized through his biographer. This is implied in *narratus et traditus.* Ancient authors thought it not improper to express a calm consciousness of merit and a proud confidence of immortality. T. is very modest and delicate in the manner of intimating his expectations. But the sentiment of these last words is substantially the same with the line of Horace: Exegi monumentum aere perennius. The whole peroration of this Biography is one of singular beauty and moral elevation. Pathetic, yet calm, rich in noble sentiments and animated by the purest and loftiest spirit, it is a fit topstone to that monument, in respect to which T. felt so well founded an assurance, which still *manet mansurumque est in animis hominum, in aeternitate temporum, fama rerum.* There is scarcely an educated youth in Christendom who is not as familiar with the name of Agricola, as with that of Æneas and Ulysses. And the only reason why we know anything of these heroes, is the genius of their respective biographers. There had been other Agricolas before the age of Trajan, as there had been other heroes like Æneas, and other wandering sages like Ulysses, before the war of Troy. But they found no Tacitus, Virgil, and Homer to record their adventurous and virtuous deeds. It is the prerogative of eminent writers to confer immortality; and though Alexander would prefer to be Achilles rather than Homer, we should have known little of his achievements, had he not encouraged scholars as well as warriors, and rewarded genius no less than valor.

Arnold's Latin Course:

I. FIRST AND SECOND LATIN BOOK AND PRACTICAL GRAMMAR Revised and carefully Corrected, by J. A. SPENCER, D.D. 12mo, 359 pages.

II. PRACTICAL INTRODUCTION TO LATIN PROSE COMPOSITION. Revised and carefully Corrected, by J. A. SPENCER. D.D. 12mo, 356 pages.

III. CORNELIUS NEPOS. With Questions and Answers, and an Imitative Exercise on each Chapter. With Notes by E. A. JOHNSON, Professor of Latin in University of New York. New Edition, enlarged, with a Lexicon, Historical and Geographical Index, &c. 12mo, 350 pages.

Arnold's Classical Series has attained a circulation almost unparalleled, having been introduced into nearly all the leading educational institutions in the United States. The secret of this success is, that the author has hit upon the true system of teaching the ancient languages. He exhibits them not as dead, but as living tongues; and by imitation and repetition, the means which nature herself points out to the child learning his mother tongue, he familiarizes the student with the idioms employed by the elegant writers and speakers of antiquity.

The First and Second Latin Book should be put in the hands of the beginners, who will soon acquire from its pages a better idea of the language than could be gained by months of study according to the old system. The reason of this is, that every thing has a practical bearing, and a principle is no sooner learned than it is applied. The pupil is at once set to work on exercises.

The Prose Composition forms an excellent sequel to the above work, or may be used with any other course. It teaches the art of writing Latin more correctly and thoroughly, more easily and pleasantly, than any other work. In its pages Latin synonymes are carefully illustrated, differences of idioms noted, cautions as to common errors impressed on the mind, and every help afforded toward attaining a pure and flowing Latin style.

From N. WHEELER, *Principal of Worcester County High School.*

"In the skill with which he sets forth the *idiomatic peculiarities*, as well as in the directness and simplicity with which he states the facts of the ancient languages, Mr. Arnold has no superior. I know of no books so admirably adapted to awaken an *interest* in the study of the language, or so well fitted to lay the foundation of a correct scholarship and refined taste."

From A. B. RUSSELL, *Oakland High School.*

"The style in which the books are got up are not their only recommendation. With thorough instruction on the part of the teacher using these books as text-books, I a confident a much more ample return for the time and labor bestowed by our youth upon Latin must be secured. The time certainly has come when an advance must be made upon the old methods of instruction. I am glad to have a work that promises so many advantages as Arnold's First and Second Latin Book to beginners."

From C. M. BLAKE, *Classical Teacher, Philadelphia.*

"I am much pleased with Arnold's Latin Books. A class of my older boys have just finished the First and Second Book. They had studied Latin for a long time before, but never *understood* it, they say, as they do now."

Arnold's First Latin Book ;

Remodelled and Rewritten, and adapted to the Ollendorff Method of Instruction. By ALBERT HARKNESS, A.M. 12mo, 302 pages.

Under the labors of the present author, the work of Arnold has undergone radical changes. It has been adapted to the Ollendorff improved method of instruction, and is superior to the former work in its plan and all the details of instruction. While it proceeds in common with Arnold on the principle of imitation and repetition, it pursues much more exactly and with a surer step the progressive method, and aims to make the pupil master of every individual subject before he proceeds to a new one, and of each subject by itself before it is combined with others; so that he is brought gradually and surely to understand the most difficult combinations of the language. An important feature of this book is, that it carries along the Syntax *pari passu* with the Etymology, so that the student is not only all the while becoming familiar with the forms of the language, but is also learning to construct sentences and to understand the mutual relations of their component parts.

Special care has been taken in the exercises to present such idioms and expressions alone as are authorized by the best classic authors, so that the learner may acquire, by example as well as precept, a distinct idea of pure Latinity.

It has been a leading object with the author so to classify and arrange the various topics as to simplify the subject, and, as far as possible, to remove the disheartening difficulties too often encountered at the outset in the study of an ancient language.

From W. E. TOLMAN, *Instructor in Providence High School.*

"I have used Arnold's First Latin Book, remodelled and rewritten by Mr. Harkness, in my classes during the past year, and find it to be a work not so much remodelled and rewritten as one *entirely new*, both in its plan and in its adaptation to the wants of the beginner in Latin."

From WM. RUSSELL, *Editor of the First Series of the Boston Journal of Education.*

"The form which this work has taken under the skilful hand of Mr. H. is marked throughout by a method purely elementary, perfectly simple, gradually progressive, and rigorously exact. Pupils trained on such a manual cannot fail of becoming distinguished, in their subsequent progress, for precision and correctness of knowledge, and for rapid advancement in genuine scholarship."

From GEORGE CAPRON, *Principal of Worcester High School.*

"I have examined the work with care, and am happy to say that I find it superior to any similar work with which I am acquainted. I shall recommend it to my next class."

From J. R. BOISE, *Professor of Ancient Languages in Michigan University.*

"I have examined your First Book in Latin, and am exceedingly pleased both with the plan and execution. I shall not fail to use my influence toward introducing it into the classical schools of this State."

Second Latin Book;

Comprising an Historical Latin Reader, with Notes and Rules for Translating, and an Exercise Book, developing a Complete Analytical Syntax, in a series of Lessons and Exercises, involving the Construction, Analysis, and Reconstruction of Latin Sentences. By ALBERT HARKNESS, A.M., Senior Master in the Providence High School. 12mo, 362 pages.

This work is designed as a sequel to the author's "First Latin Book." It comprises a complete analytical syntax, exhibiting the essential structure of the Latin language, from its simplest to its most expanded and elaborate form.

The arrangement of the lessons is decidedly philosophical, gradually progressive, and in strict accordance with the law of development of the human mind. Every new principle is stated in simple, clear, and accurate language, and illustrated by examples carefully selected from the reading lessons, which the student is required to translate, analyze, and reconstruct. He is also exercised in forming new Latin sentences on given models. This, while it gives variety and interest to what would otherwise be in the highest degree monotonous, completely fixes in the mind the subject of the lesson, both by analysis and synthesis.

The careful study of this volume, on the plan recommended by the author, will greatly facilitate the pupil's progress in the higher departments of the language. Such is the testimony of the numerous institutions in which Harkness's improved edition of Arnold has been introduced.

From J. A. SPENCER, D.D., *late Professor of Latin in Burlington College, N. J.*

"The present volume appears to me to carry out excellently the system on which the late lamented Arnold based his educational works; and in the Selections for Reading, the Notes and Rules for Translating, the Exercises in Translating into Latin, the Analyses, &c., I think it admirably adapted to advance the diligent student, not only rapidly, but soundly, in an acquaintance with the Latin language."

From PROF. GAMMELL, *of Brown University.*

"The book seems to me, as I anticipated it would be, a valuable addition to the works now in use among teachers of Latin in the schools of the United States, and for many of them it will undoubtedly form an advantageous substitute."

From PROF. LINCOLN, *of Brown University.*

"It seems to me to carry on most successfully the method pursued in the First Book. Though brief, it is very comprehensive, and combines judicious and skilfully formed exercises with systematic instruction."

From J. J OWEN, D.D., *Professor of the Latin and Greek Languages and Literature in the Free Academy, New York.*

"This Second Latin Book gives abundant evidence of the author's learning and tact to arrange, simplify, and make accessible to the youthful mind the great and fundamental principles of the Latin language. The book is worthy of a place in every classical school, and I trust will have an extensive sale."

From PROF. ANDERSON, *of Lewisburg University, Pennsylvania.*

"A faithful use of the work would diminish the drudgery of the student's earlier studies, and facilitate his progress in his subsequent course. I wish the work a wide circulation."

A Latin Grammar for Schools and Colleges.

By A. HARKNESS, PH.D., Professor in Brown University.

To explain the general plan of the work, the Publishers ask the attention of teachers to the following extracts from the Preface:

1. This volume is designed to present a systematic arrangement of the great facts and laws of the Latin language; to exhibit not only grammatical forms and constructions, but also those *vital principles* which underlie, control, and explain them.

2. Designed at once as a text-book for the class-room, and a book of reference in study, it aims to introduce the beginner easily and pleasantly to the first principles of the language, and yet to make adequate provision for the wants of the more advanced student.

3. By brevity and conciseness in the choice of phraseology and compactness in the arrangement of forms and topics, the author has endeavored to compress within the limits of a convenient manual an amount of carefully-selected grammatical facts, which would otherwise fill a much larger volume.

4. He has, moreover, endeavored to present the whole subject in the light of modern scholarship. Without encumbering hi spages with any unnecessary discussions, he has aimed to enrich them with the *practical results* of the recent labors in the field of philology.

5. Syntax has received in every part special attention. An attempt has been made to exhibit, as clearly as possible, that beautiful system of laws which the genius of the language—that highest of all grammatical authority—has created for itself.

6. Topics which require extended illustration are first presented in their completeness in general outline, before the separate points are discussed in detail. Thus a single page often foreshadows all the leading features of an extended discussion, imparting a completeness and vividness to the impression of the learner, impossible under any other treatment.

7 Special care has been taken to explain and illustrate with the requisite fulness all difficult and intricate subjects. The Subjunctive Mood—that severest trial of the teacher's patience—has been presented, it is hoped, in a form at once simple and comprehensive.

Harkness's Latin Grammar.

From Rev. Prof. J. J. Owen, D.D., *New York Free Academy.*

"I have carefully examined Harkness's Latin Grammar, and am so well pleased with its plan, arrangement, and execution, that I shall take the earliest opportunity of introducing it as a text-book in the Free Academy."

From Mr. John D. Philbrick, *Superintendent of Public Schools, Boston, Mass.*

"This work is evidently no hasty performance, nor the compilation of a mere book maker, but the well-ripened fruit of mature and accurate scholarship. It is eminently practical, because it is truly philosophical."

From Mr. G. N. Bigelow, *Principal of State Normal School, Framingham, Mass.*

"Harkness's Latin Grammar is the most satisfactory text-book I have ever used."

From Rev. Daniel Leach, *Superintendent Public Schools, Providence, R. I.*

"I am quite confident that it is superior to any Latin Grammar before the public. It has recently been introduced into the High School, and all are much pleased with it."

From Dr. J. B. Chapin, *State Commissioner of Public Instruction in Rhode Island.*

"The vital principles of the language are clearly and beautifully exhibited. The work needs no one's commendation."

From Mr. Abner J. Phipps, *Superintendent of Public Schools, Lowell, Mass.*

"The aim of the author seems to be fully realized in making this 'a *useful* Book, and as such I can cheerfully commend it. The clear and admirable manner in which the intricacies of the Subjunctive Mood are unfolded, is one of its marked features.

"The evidence of ripe scholarship and of familiarity with the latest works of German and English philologists is manifest throughout the book."

From Dr. J. T. Champlin, *President of Waterville College.*

"I like both the plan and the execution of the work very much. Its matter and manner are both admirable. I shall be greatly disappointed if it does not at once win the public favor."

From Prof. A. S. Packard, *Bowdoin College, Brunswick, Maine.*

"Harkness's Latin Grammar exhibits throughout the results of thorough scholarship. I shall recommend it in our next catalogue."

From Prof. J. J. Stanton, *Bates College.*

"We have introduced Harkness's Grammar into this Institution. It is much more logical and concise than any of its rivals."

From Mr. Wm. J. Rolfe, *Principal Cambridge High School.*

"Notwithstanding all the inconveniences that must attend a change of Latin Grammars in a large school like mine, I shall endeavor to secure the adoption of Harkness's Grammar in place of our present text-book as soon as possible."

From Mr. L. R. Williston, *Principal Ladies' Seminary, Cambridge, Mass.*

"I think this work a decided advance upon the Grammar now in use."

From Mr D. B. Hager, *Princ. Eliot High School, Jamaica Plain, Mass.*

"This is, in my opinion, *by far the best Latin Grammar ever published.* It is admirably adapted to the use of learners, being remarkably concise, clear, comprehensive and philosophical. It will henceforth be used as a text-book in this school."

Harkness's Latin Grammar.

From Prof. C. S. HARRINGTON *and* Prof. J. C. VAN BENSCHOTEN, *of the Wesleyan University.*

"This work is clear, accurate, and happy in its statement of principles, is simple yet scholarly, and embraces the latest researches in this department of philological science. It will appear in our catalogue."

From Mr. ELBRIDGE SMITH, *Principal Free Academy, Norwich, Ct.*

"This is not only the best Latin Grammar, but one of the most thoroughly prepared school-books that I have ever seen. I have introduced the book into the Free Academy, and am much pleased with the results of a month's experience in the class-room."

From Mr. H. A. PRATT, *Principal High School, Hartford, Ct.*

"I can heartily recommend Harkness's new work to both teachers and scholars. It is, in my judgment, the best Latin Grammar ever offered to our schools."

From Mr. I. F. CADY, *Principal High School, Warren, R. I.*

"The longer I use Harkness's Grammar the more fully am I convinced of its superior excellence. Its merits must secure its adoption wherever it becomes known."

From Messrs. S. THURBER *and* T. B. STOCKWELL, *Public High School, Providence.*

"An experience of several weeks with Harkness's Latin Grammar, enables us to say with confidence, that it is an improvement on our former text-book."

From Mr. C. B. GOFF, *Principal Boys' Classical High School, Providence, R. I*

"The practical working of Harkness's Grammar is gratifying even beyond my expectations."

From Rev. Prof. M. H. BUCKHAM, *University of Vermont.*

"Harkness's Latin Grammar seems to me to supply the desideratum. It is philosophical in its method, and yet simple and clear in its statements; and this, in my judgment, is the highest encomium which can be bestowed on a text-book."

From Mr. E. T. QUIMBY, *Appleton Academy, New Ipswich, N. H.*

"I think the book much superior to any other I have seen. I should be glad to introduce it at once."

From Mr. H. ORCUTT, *Glenwood Ladies' Seminary, W. Brattleboro', Vt.*

"I am pleased with Harkness's Latin Grammar, and have already introduced it into this seminary."

From Mr. CHARLES JEWETT, *Principal of Franklin Academy.*

"I deem it an admirable work, and think it will supersede all others now in use. In the division and arrangement of topics, and in its mechanical execution, it is superior to any Latin Grammar extant."

From Mr. C. C. CHASE, *Principal of Lowell High School.*

"Prof. Harkness's Grammar is, in my opinion, admirably adapted to make the study of the Latin language agreeable and interesting."

From Mr. J. KIMBALL, *High School, Dorchester, Mass.*

"It meets my ideal of what is desirable in every grammar, to wit: compression of general principles in terse definitions and statements, for ready use; and fulness of detail, well arranged for reference."

The Works of Horace.

With English Notes, for the use of Schools and Colleges. By J. L. LINCOLN, Professor of the Latin Language and Literature in Brown University. 12mo, 575 pages.

The text of this edition is mainly that of Orelli, the most important readings of other critics being given in foot-notes. The volume is introduced with a biographical sketch of Horace and a critique on his writings, which enable the student to enter intelligently on his work. Peculiar grammatical constructions, as well as geographical and historical allusions, are explained in notes, which are just full enough to aid the pupil, to excite him to gain a thorough understanding of the author, and awaken in him a taste for philological studies, without taking all labor off his hands. While the chief aim has been to impart a clear idea of Latin Syntax as exhibited in the text, it has also been a cherished object to take advantage of the means so variously and richly furnished by Horace for promoting the poetical taste and literary culture of the student.

From an article by PROF. BAHR, *of the University of Heidelberg, in the Heidelberg Annals of Literature.*

"There are already several American editions of Horace, intended for the use of schools; of one of these, which has passed through many editions, and has also been widely circulated in England, mention has been formerly made in this journal; but that one we may not put upon an equality with the one now before us, inasmuch as this has taken a different stand-point, which may serve as a sign of progress in this department of study. The editor has, it is true, also intended his work for the use of schools, and has sought to adapt it, in all its parts, to such a use; but still, without losing sight of this purpose, he has proceeded throughout with more independence. In the preparation of the Notes, the editor has faithfully observed the principles (laid down in his preface); the explanations of the poet's words commend themselves by a compressed brevity which limits itself to what is most essential, and by a sharp precision of expression; and references to other passages of the poet, and also to grammars, dictionaries, &c., are not wanting."

Sallust's Jugurtha and Catiline.

With Notes and a Vocabulary. By NOBLE BUTLER and MINARD STURGUS. 12mo, 397 pages.

The editors have spent a vast amount of time and labor in correcting the text, by a comparison of the most improved German and English editions. It is believed that this will be found superior to any edition hitherto published in this country. In accordance with their chronological order, the "Jugurtha" precedes the "Catiline." The Notes are copious and tersely expressed; they display not only fine scholarship, but (what is quite as necessary in such a book) a practical knowledge of the difficulties which the student encounters in reading this author, and the aids that he requires. The Vocabulary was prepared by the late WILLIAM H. G. BUTLER. It will be found an able and faithful performance.

Virgil's Æneid.

With Explanatory Notes. By HENRY S. FRIEZE, Professor of Latin in the State University of Michigan. Illustrated. 12mo, 598 pages.

The appearance of this edition of Virgil's Æneid will, it is believed, be hailed with delight by all classical teachers. Neither expense nor pains have been spared to clothe the great Latin epic in a fitting dress. The type is unusually large and distinct, and errors in the text, so annoying to the learner, have been carefully avoided. The work contains eighty-five engravings, which delineate the usages, costumes, weapons, arts, and mythology of the ancients with a vividnesss that can be attained only by pictorial illustrations. The great feature of this edition is the scholarly and judicious commentary furnished in the appended Notes. The author has here endeavored not to show his learning, but to supply such practical aid as will enable the pupil to understand and appreciate what he reads. The notes are just full enough, thoroughly explaining the most difficult passages, while they are not so extended as to take all labor off the pupil's hands. Properly used, they cannot fail to impart an intelligent acquaintance with the syntax of the language. In a word, this work is commended to teachers as the most elegant, accurate, interesting, and practically useful edition of the Æneid that has yet been published.

From JOHN H. BRUNNER, *President of Hiwasee College.*

"The typography, paper, and binding of Virgil's Æneid, by Prof. Frieze, are all that need be desired; while the learned and judicious notes appended, are very valuable indeed."

From Principal of Piedmont (Va.) Academy.

"I have to thank you for a copy of Prof. Frieze's edition of the Æneid. I have been exceedingly pleased in my examination of it. The size of the type from which the text is printed, and the faultless execution, leave nothing to be desired in these respects The adherence to a standard text throughout, increases the value of this edition."

From D. G. MOORE, *Principal U. High School, Rutland.*

"The copy of Frieze's 'Virgil' forwarded to me was duly received. It is so evidently superior to any of the other editions, that I shall unhesitatingly adopt it in my classes"

www.ingramcontent.com/pod-product-compliance
Lightning Source LLC
LaVergne TN
LVHW011210110826
845150LV00006B/1386

9781425517793